Second Joint SIGHUM Workshop on Computational Linguistics for Cultural Heritage, Social Sciences, Humanities and Literature (LaTeCH-CLfL-2018)

Santa Fe, New Mexico, USA
25 August 2018

ISBN: 978-1-5108-6910-3

Printed by Curran Associates, Inc. (2018)

For permission requests, please contact the Association for Computational Linguistics
at the address below.

Association for Computational Linguistics
209 N. Eighth Street
Stroudsburg, Pennsylvania 18360

Phone: 1-570-476-8006
Fax: 1-570-476-0860

acl@aclweb.org

Additional copies of this publication are available from:

Curran Associates, Inc.
57 Morehouse Lane
Red Hook, NY 12571 USA
Phone: 845-758-0400
Fax: 845-758-2633
Email: curran@proceedings.com
Web: www.proceedings.com

COLING 2018

**The 27th International Conference
on Computational Linguistics**

**Proceedings of the
Second Joint SIGHUM Workshop
on Computational Linguistics for Cultural Heritage,
Social Sciences, Humanities and Literature
(LaTeCH-CLfL-2018)**

August 25, 2018
Santa Fe, New Mexico, USA

Introduction

Welcome to the 2nd Joint SIGHUM Workshop on Computational Linguistics for Cultural Heritage, Social Sciences, Humanities and Literature. After a great joint event last year, we are happy to present another lineup of high-quality papers at this year's workshop. Everything you want to know about it has been placed on-line (https://sighum.wordpress.com/events/latech-clfl-2018/). We accepted 64.3% of submitted papers. You can appreciate the thematic variety in what follows.

We thank all submitters, congratulate those whose work appears here, and express our debt of gratitude to the members of the program committee. We wish to single out one participant: Ted Underwood, who has graciously accepted our invitation to be the workshop's guest speaker.

Enjoy!

Beatrice, Stefania, Anna, Anna, Nils, Stan

Invited Talk

Ted Underwood is a Professor of Information Science and English at the University of Illinois, Urbana-Champaign. He has published widely on quantitative approaches to literary history, with articles in New Literary History, Cultural Analytics, Representations, and Modern Language Quarterly. His research currently focuses on questions about literary character, and ways of using machine learning to compare situated historical perspectives. In 2019, the University of Chicago Press will publish his next book, Distant Horizons: Digital Evidence and Literary Change.

Measurement and Human Perspective

Researchers who use quantitative methods to study culture may find themselves torn between two approaches to knowledge. Quantitative disciplines often value generalizable methods that make different frames of reference comparable. But humanists have long insisted that knowledge about culture is irreducibly perspectival, relative to a particular vantage point. Of course, the tension between these two approaches is not exactly a contradiction. Contemporary quantitative methods are sometimes flexible enough to incorporate varied human perspectives as elements of a model. This talk will describe a few recent projects that have attempted perspectival modeling, and reflect on opportunities for further research.

Invited Speaker

Ted Underwood, University of Illinois, United States

Organizers

Beatrice Alex, School of Informatics, University of Edinburgh
Stefania Degaetano-Ortlieb, Dept. of Language Science & Technology, Universität des Saarlandes
Anna Feldman, Dept. of Linguistics & Dept. of Computer Science, Montclair State University
Anna Kazantseva, National Research Council of Canada
Nils Reiter, Institute for Natural Language Processing (IMS), Stuttgart University
Stan Szpakowicz, School of Electrical Engineering and Computer Science, University of Ottawa

Program Committee

Cecilia Ovesdotter Alm, Rochester Institute of Technology, USA
JinYeong Bak, KAIST, Republic of Korea
Gosse Bouma, University of Groningen, The Netherlands
Paul Buitelaar, National University of Ireland, Galway, Ireland
Thierry Declerck, Deutsche Forschungszentrum für Künstliche Intelligenz GmbH, Germany
Stefanie Dipper, Ruhr-University, Bochum, Germany
Jacob Eisenstein, Georgia Institute of Technology, United States
Micha Elsner, Ohio State University, United States
Mark Finlayson, Florida International University, United States
Serge Heiden, École normale supérieure de Lyon, France
Iris Hendrickx, Radboud University, Nijmegen, The Netherlands
Gerhard Heyer, University of Leipzig, Germany
Graeme Hirst, University of Toronto, Canada
Amy Isard, University of Edinburgh, United Kingdom
Adam Jatowt, Kyoto University, Japan
Mike Kestemont, University of Antwerp, Belgium
Dimitrios Kokkinakis, University of Gothenburg, Sweden
Stasinos Konstantopoulos, National Centre of Scientific Research "Demokritos", Greece
John Lee, City University of Hong Kong, Hong Kong
Chaya Liebeskind, Jerusalem College of Technology, Israel
Barbara McGillivray, Alan Turing Institute/University of Cambridge, United Kingdom
Gerard de Melo, Tsinghua University, China
Rada Mihalcea, University of Michigan, United States
Borja Navarro Colorado, University of Alicante, Spain
John Nerbonne, University of Freiburg, Germany
Pierre Nugues, Lund University, Sweden
Mick O'Donnel, Universidad Autónoma de Madrid, Spain
Petya Osenova, Sofia University and IICT-BAS, Bulgaria
Michael Piotrowski, University of Lausanne, Switzerland
Georg Rehm, DFKI, Germany
Martin Reynaert, Tilburg University, Radboud University Nijmegen, The Netherlands
Marijn Schraagen, Utrecht University, The Netherlands
Sarah Schulz, University of Stuttgart, Germany

Eszter Simon, Research Institute for Linguistics, Hungarian Academy of Sciences, Hungary
Caroline Sporleder, Göttingen University, Germany
Elke Teich, Saarland University, Germany
Sara Tonelli, FBK, Trento, Italy
Thorsten Trippel, University of Tübingen, Germany
Menno van Zaanen, Tilburg University, The Netherlands
Kalliopi Zervanou, Utrecht University, The Netherlands
Heike Zinsmeister, University of Hamburg, Germany

Table of Contents

Conference Program

13:50–14:50   **Invited Talk**

Measurement and Human Perspective
Ted Underwood

14:50–15:50   **Poster Teasers and Poster Session**

One Size Fits All? A simple LSTM for non-literal token and construction-level classification
Erik-Lân Do Dinh, Steffen Eger and Iryna Gurevych

Supervised Rhyme Detection with Siamese Recurrent Networks
Thomas Haider and Jonas Kuhn

Normalizing Early English Letters to Present-day English Spelling
Mika Hämäläinen, Tanja Säily, Jack Rueter, Jörg Tiedemann and Eetu Mäkelä

Power Networks: A Novel Neural Architecture to Predict Power Relations
Michelle Lam, Catherina Xu and Vinodkumar Prabhakaran

Automated Acquisition of Patterns for Coding Political Event Data: Two Case Studies
Peter Makarov

A Method for Human-Interpretable Paraphrasticality Prediction
Maria Moritz, Johannes Hellrich and Sven Büchel

Exploring word embeddings and phonological similarity for the unsupervised correction of language learner errors
Ildikó Pilán and Elena Volodina

Towards Coreference for Literary Text: Analyzing Domain-Specific Phenomena
Ina Roesiger, Sarah Schulz and Nils Reiter

An Evaluation of Lexicon-based Sentiment Analysis Techniques for the Plays of Gotthold Ephrain Lessing
Thomas Schmidt and Manuel Burghardt

16:20–17:20   Session 3

Automatic identification of unknown names with specific roles
Samia Touileb, Truls Pedersen and Helle Sjøvaag

Induction of a Large-Scale Knowledge Graph from the Regesta Imperii
Juri Opitz, Leo Born and Vivi Nastase

Learning Diachronic Analogies to Analyze Concept Change

Matthias Orlikowski
Digital Humanities
Paderborn University
morlikow@mail.upb.de

Matthias Hartung
CITEC
Bielefeld University
mhartung@cit-ec.uni-bielefeld.de

Philipp Cimiano
CITEC
Bielefeld University
cimiano@cit-ec.uni-bielefeld.de

Abstract

We propose to study the evolution of concepts by learning to complete diachronic analogies between lists of terms which relate to the same concept at different points in time. We present a number of models based on operations on word embedddings that correspond to different assumptions about the characteristics of diachronic analogies and change in concept vocabularies. These are tested in a quantitative evaluation for nine different concepts on a corpus of Dutch newspapers from the 1950s and 1980s. We show that a model which treats the concept terms as analogous and learns weights to compensate for diachronic changes (weighted linear combination) is able to more accurately predict the missing term than a learned transformation and two baselines for most of the evaluated concepts. We also find that all models tend to be coherent in relation to the represented concept, but less discriminative in regard to other concepts. Additionally, we evaluate the effect of aligning the time-specific embedding spaces using orthogonal Procrustes, finding varying effects on performance, depending on the model, concept and evaluation metric. For the weighted linear combination, however, results improve with alignment in a majority of cases. All related code is released publicly.

1 Introduction

Research on the evolution of concepts is a long-standing topic within philosophy, history and linguistics. However, recent work on the computational analysis of semantic change based on word embeddings has surprisingly little to offer in this regard. Most work focuses on the meaning of individual words. In comparison, there are only few contributions which analyze concepts and the changing vocabularies which are used to express them (Kenter et al., 2015; Recchia et al., 2016).

The goal of this paper is to provide insights into how distributional semantics (Harris, 1954; Firth, 1957), in particular word embeddings (Mikolov et al., 2013a; Levy et al., 2015), can be used to analyze concept change. We propose to model concept change in terms of analogies between concept vocabularies at different points in time. This extends well-established synchronic models of analogy based on word embeddings (Mikolov et al., 2013b) to the diachronic case. We build on the underlying *parallelogram model* of analogy (Rumelhart and Abrahamson (1973), cf. Chen et al. (2017)), assuming that analogies of the type of "a is to b as c is to d" can be described by linear relationships between distributional representations of the four words. While parallelogram relationships can be found in other vector representations as well (Levy and Goldberg, 2014), embeddings derived with skip-gram can be considered a robust baseline for analogy tasks (Levy et al., 2015).

We detail our approach (Section 3) and propose a number of simple models to learn diachronic analogies (Section 4) which are evaluated quantitatively (Section 6) on a corpus of historical Dutch newspapers (Section 5). We report on two related experiments which are motivated by the intuition that diachronic analogies should be *coherent* in regard to the represented concept and *discriminative* in regard to the vocabulary of other concepts. All related code is released publicly[1].

[1]https://gitlab.com/morlikowski/diachronic-analogies-code

Proceedings of Workshop on Computational Linguistics for Cultural Heritage, Social Sciences, Humanities and Literature, pages 1–11
Santa Fe, New Mexico, USA, August 25, 2018.

2 Related work: Distributional approaches to semantic change

Word-level semantic change. There is a great body of work which uses word vector representations to study changes in word semantics. Examples include Gulordava and Baroni (2011) or Radinsky et al. (2011), while Kim et al. (2014) are among the first to use neural word embeddings to analyze changes in word meanings. Kulkarni et al. (2015) use a similar approach, but automatically identify points of meaning changes based on shifts in the mean of the respective time series. Hamilton et al. (2016) and Dubossarsky et al. (2017) present methods to more precisely quantify trends in changes of word meaning and address a central problem in using word embeddings for diachronic analyses: They align the axes of the vector spaces from neighboring time periods using a mapping derived with orthogonal Procrustes (Hamilton et al., 2016). This method will be presented in more detail in Section 4.3.

Concept-level semantic change. There are a number of approaches to studying lexical semantic change above the level of individual words. These include simple co-occurrence statistics or topic modeling (Blei and Lafferty, 2006) which are only loosely related to our work based on word embeddings. For example, Tan et al. (2017) present a topic modeling approach to study relations between ideas that helps to detect gradual substitution and prevalence, or mutual fostering and coexistence.

Kenter et al. (2015) is a central reference point for our work, because they explicitly attempt to model changes in concept meaning, use word embeddings and also adress their method at use cases from the (digital) humanities. Most importantly, Kenter et al. (2015) also published a ground truth dataset for quantitative evaluation. The authors present a method to trace concept vocabularies through a time-stamped corpus based on a set of seed terms (few words, typically one or two) which is tailored towards ad-hoc use over broad time periods. This method is also at the heart of the related systems presented in Martinez-Ortiz et al. (2016b), Martinez-Ortiz et al. (2016a) and Wevers et al. (2015). The authors create vector space models for overlapping periods of the corpus. They then use a number of graph-based unsupervised algorithms that they combine in different ways to generate the final vocabularies. In their evaluation, all their methods beat a baseline that outputs the n most related terms per queried time period using a vector space trained on that period.

Recchia et al. (2016) present a variation of this method, but do not give evaluation results as they report on work in progress of constructing more extensive ground truth data. Their method selects a fully connected graph of k nodes that must contain all words in the previous time period (or seed terms for the first time slice) and have the highest possible minimum edge weight.

3 Concept change as diachronic analogies

Following Kenter et al. (2015), we denote concepts as a set of terms, the *concept vocabulary*. Each term in the concept vocabulary is represented using time-period-specific word embeddings which are derived from training on slices of a time-stamped corpus. We distinguish concept terms which make up the conceptual core (*core concept terms*) from the rest of the vocabulary (*characterizing concept terms*), carrying forward Kenter et al.'s distinction of the core and the margin of concepts. For example, for the concept of ECONOMIC EFFICIENCY, core terms might be *efficiency* and *efficient*, while characterizing terms might be *robotization*, *automatization* or *labor productivity*. In our notion of *diachronic concept change*, the characterizing terms are expected to change over time, while the surface forms of the core terms are assumed to stay the same.

In previous approaches (Kenter et al., 2015; Recchia et al., 2016), the role of the time-specific vector spaces is limited to providing a similarity metric that is used in constructing a weighted semantic graph. Taking the concept vocabulary of the previous time period as input, similar terms are added to the graph which is subsequently pruned based on a centrality measure to generate the new concept vocabulary. In contrast, we are interested in utilizing the features of the time-specific vector spaces directly when predicting concept change to allow for more detailed analyses and comparisons, using models which are based on vector operations.

We reduce the problem of concept change to the problem of predicting valid characterizing terms for a core concept term given a respective characterizing term at an earlier point in time. More formally, given the embedding of a core concept term $\vec{a}_{t_0}$ for a time period t_0, the embedding for the *same* core concept term $\vec{a}_{t_1}$ for a later time period t_1 and the embedding of a characterizing term for the earlier period $\vec{b}_{t_0}$, our goal is to predict the embedding for the missing characterizing term $\vec{b}_{t_1}$ with some function f:

$$\vec{b}_{t_1} = f(\vec{a}_{t_0}, \vec{b}_{t_0}, \vec{a}_{t_1}) \tag{1}$$

In the following section, we will present and discuss a number of possible instantiations of f, which are motivated by an inductive learning perspective on analogy (Cornuéjols and Ales-Bianchetti, 1998) and methods of analogy recovery used in connection with word embeddings (Mikolov et al., 2013b). Consequently, we view a 4-tuple $(\vec{a}_{t_0}, \vec{b}_{t_0}, \vec{a}_{t_1}, \vec{b}_{t_1})$ as constituting a loose diachronic analogy between concept terms, for ECONOMIC EFFICIENCY e.g. "*efficiency* is to *robotization* at one point in time as *efficiency* was to *mechanization* at an earlier point in time".

Analogies between two word pairs are based on highly similar semantic relations among the words in each pair (Turney, 2006). In our adaptation of analogies between concept terms, relational similarity is implied by the assumption that both term pairs relate to the same concept. Note that the type of semantic relation underlying our notion of diachronic concept analogies is rather generic, as it only describes *membership* of a characterizing term in a concept.

4 Learning diachronic analogies

4.1 Baselines and models

This section describes two baselines and two preliminary models to learn to complete diachronic analogies. Each model is based on different intuitions and assumptions about the characteristics of diachronic analogies which will be detailed and subsequently tested in the quantitative evaluation.

No transfer baseline. As a naive baseline we set $\vec{b}_{t_1} = \vec{a}_{t_1}$, which predicts the embedding of the core concept term at t_1 by effectively ignoring the previous time period. We refer to this model as the NO baseline. It is intended to provide a minimal benchmark for model performance.

Linear combination baseline. The baseline described in equation (2) performs a linear combination of the known term vectors to recover the fourth, unknown vector. This corresponds to the analogy recovery method used by Mikolov et al. (2013b) without a search for the closest word vector in the vocabulary. We refer to this model as the ADD baseline. It assumes a direct linear relationship between the analogy vectors, even though the source and target vectors belong to vector spaces computed from two distinct subsets of the corpus.

$$\vec{b}_{t_1} = \vec{b}_{t_0} - \vec{a}_{t_0} + \vec{a}_{t_1} \tag{2}$$

Transformation. This model amounts to explicitly encoding the relation between the source terms as a function and reapplying it to the target. The model encodes the assumption that the two vector spaces are structurally similar, so that the same (geometric) relation holds in both instances. In the following, it is referred to as TRANS. The model learns a transformation between the concept term vectors at t_0 and applies the same function to the core concept term at t_1 to approximate the unknown term vector. This means that we learn

$$\vec{b}_{t_0} = \mathbf{A}_{t_0} \cdot \vec{a}_{t_0} \tag{3}$$

and then predict by reusing $\mathbf{A}_{t_0}$ on t_1 as

$$\vec{b}_{t_1} = \mathbf{A}_{t_0} \cdot \vec{a}_{t_1} \tag{4}$$

Weighted linear combination. The weighted linear combination model (equation 5) is equivalent to the ADD baseline with weights attached to each word vector before combining them. We refer to this system as the WEIGHTS model. In contrast to ADD, this model is based on the intuition that for diachronic analogies the model has to compensate for the displacement of vectors due to semantic change when trying to complete the analogy based on the parallelogram assumption.

$$\vec{b}_{t_1} = \mathbf{B}_{t_0} \cdot \vec{b}_{t_0} - \mathbf{A}_{t_0} \cdot \vec{a}_{t_0} + \mathbf{A}_{t_1} \cdot \vec{a}_{t_1} \tag{5}$$

4.2 Training method

We view the equations in Section 4.1 as describing shallow neural networks which we implemented using the framework PyTorch.[2] The models are trained for 10 iterations over the training data using the Adam optimization method (Kingma and Ba, 2014). The model's error is measured using the cosine distance between the predicted vector and a gold vector. Weights are initialized with an identity matrix, which makes the output of the untrained TRANS model equal to the NO baseline and the untrained WEIGHTS model equal to the ADD baseline. Other initialization strategies were tested (in particular random weights and an identity matrix combined with small random values), but were not found to improve results.

4.3 Vector space alignment

For low-dimensional vector representations, specifically derived with skip-gram as used in the reported experiments, vectors for the same word from different spaces can be arbitrary orthogonal transformations (Hamilton et al., 2016). To counteract this problem, the authors frame the alignment of two matrices of word embeddings as an orthogonal Procrustes problem and solve it using the closed form solution from Schönemann (1966). As Bamler and Mandt (2017) point out, this method conceptualizes the differences of diachronic word vectors as the result of a global rotation (introduced by the rotation-invariant cost functions used in deriving the embeddings) and some semantic drift that becomes available for analysis after alignment.

Note that aligned embeddings can only be computed for the intersection of the vocabularies of the two time periods, discarding all words that occur only in one of the time periods. Thus, while the reasoning of Hamilton et al. (2016) is convincing, we will empirically assess the effects of alignment in our task.

5 Data

In our experiments we use a dataset of Dutch newspaper articles digitized by the National Library of the Netherlands with related ground truth data published by Kenter et al. (2015). In the following, we will describe the data in more detail and will outline the performed data collection and preprocessing.

5.1 Ground truth data

Kenter et al. (2015) provide evaluation data for predictions of diachronic changes in concept vocabularies, which we adapt slightly to generate diachronic analogies between concept terms. In their dataset, for every 5-year interval, two domain experts (historians of contemporary history) rate the relevance of a number of words in relation to a given set of concept terms (*seed terms*). This is done for 21 sets of seed terms in total, each corresponding to a distinct concept. The rating scale goes in integer steps from -1 (not related) up to 2 (perfect match).

For each concept, we first choose a time interval t_0 for the analogy source and an interval t_1 for the analogy target. We treat the seed terms as core concept terms and use them to derive the vectors $\vec{a}_{t_0}$ and $\vec{a}_{t_1}$. The vectors $\vec{a}_{t_0}$ and $\vec{a}_{t_1}$ are derived from any term in the concept vocabulary with an average score greater than a threshold τ.

For the ground truth dataset used in the reported experiments, we chose $\tau = 0$, $t_0 = (1955, 1959)$ and $t_1 = (1985, 1989)$. Note that an example can only be used in training and evaluation if there are representations for every term in the analogy in the respective vector space. To be able to use as much of the validation data as possible, we tried to obtain a corpus for training the embeddings as similar to the one used by Kenter et al. (2015) as possible (see Section 5.2). Table 1 gives an overview of the concepts that were used in the experiments after taking into account the effective number of analogies for each and filtering out concepts with only few examples. In the following, we will mostly refer to individual concepts by the last word of the concept core words, e.g. to the DUTCH CITIES concept by *utrecht*.

Besides presumably changing concepts, the evaluation set also includes concepts which are expected to have stayed semantically stable over the evaluation period. These concepts are used to evaluate whether the models are able to predict both semantic change and semantic constancy. In detail, concepts with a tendency towards stability are *utrecht*, *violen*, *boekje*, *beethoven* and *koeien*. While diachronic analogies

---

[2]PyTorch 0.2.0, https://github.com/pytorch/pytorch/tree/v0.2.0

Concept core words	Description	N	N_{emb}
amsterdam, rotterdam, utrecht	Dutch cities	7350	5940
neger, negers, negerin, kleurling	(Discriminating) terms for black people	312	160
efficiency, efficiëntie	Economic efficiency	1008	684
viool, violen	Musical instruments	1682	1512
boek, boeken, boekje	Writings and books	5472	4773
mozart, brahms, beethoven	Famous composers	720	720
waterstofbom, waterstofbommen, atoombom, atoombommen	Nuclear weapons	1440	540
koe, koeien	Cattle farming	1380	900
jodenvervolging, deportatie, deportaties	Persecution of jews	264	150

Table 1: Overview of all conceptual diachronic analogies in the dataset for 1955–1959 and 1985–1989 with concept core words and number of examples with untrimmed (N) and embedding vocabulary (N_{emb})

between concept term embeddings seem to be primarily suitable to describe semantic change in the strict sense, constancy can be expressed equally well in terms of smaller differences between vectors. In the edge case of identical semantic spaces for two time periods, the assumed parallelogram between analogy vectors becomes a line.

Note that while the number of examples is reduced by the embeddings' vocabulary as influenced by hyperparameters (cf. N_{emb} in Table 1), the number of examples already varies notably per concept on the basis of the untrimmed corpus-specific vocabulary (N). Also, in the original dataset the number of annotated words differs between the concepts. However, no systematic relation could be established between the number of original annotations and the number of examples in the generated analogies, so that the influence of the (effective) vocabulary seems to be decisive.

5.2 Koninklijke Bibliotheek Historical Newspaper Corpus

Kenter et al. (2015) train their embeddings on a subset (1950–1994) of the historical collection of digitized Dutch newspapers which are archived by the Koninklijke Bibliotheek (KB), the National Library of the Netherlands. Unfortunately, the exact corpus used by the authors is not available as there is no self-contained dataset available for the KB historical newspapers corpus. The individual articles have to be crawled using a set of related APIs which are only available after signing a contract with the KB due to copyright restrictions of the newspapers' content.

First, the complete set of article identifiers for a time period was crawled. Then a 10% sample was drawn for full-text retrieval, resulting in about 500.000 articles for both selected periods. Tokenization, sentence detection and normalization (lowercasing, stop word and punctuation removal) were applied using the spaCy library[3] with a pretrained[4] Dutch model. No lemmatization or stemming was applied, following Kenter et al. (2015). Note that the resulting dataset is nevertheless different from Kenter et al. (2015), as the collection changed in the meantime and also was not sampled in their work. Our final corpus for $t_0 = (1955, 1959)$ contains 8.527.393 sentences with 63.556.890 tokens in total. The corpus for $t_1 = (1985, 1989)$ contains 15.025.711 sentences with 113.813.461 tokens in total. Note that for the later period the number of tokens is almost twice as much. Exemplary analysis showed that articles in the 1980s tend to be longer, so that the number of sentences and tokens is higher.

For each period, word embeddings were trained using the implementations by the Gensim library[5]. In correspondence with Kenter et al. (2015), we used the skip-gram architecture to train embeddings with 300 dimensions. We use a slightly different configuration, however, in particular negative sampling, a subsampling threshold of 10^{-5}, a context width of 4 and a minimum word count of 10.

---

[3] https://github.com/explosion/spaCy/tree/v2.0.5

[4] Dutch multi-task CNN trained on the Universal Dependencies and WikiNER corpus, version 2.0.0, https://github.com/explosion/spacy-models/releases/tag/nl_core_news_sm-2.0.0

[5] Gensim 3.2.0, https://github.com/RaRe-Technologies/gensim/tree/3.2.0

To align the coordinate axes of two word embeddings spaces as proposed by Hamilton et al. (2016), we use a port of their code by Ryan Heuser that provides an interface to the Gensim library[6].

6 Experiments and results

Despite relying on their data, we cannot compare our results directly to Kenter et al. (2015), due to the differences in approach and evaluation period. Therefore, we evaluate the models presented in Section 4 intrinsically in two separate experiments: The first experiment tests how well the different systems predict the missing vector $\vec{b}_{t_1}$. Subsequently, we report on an experiment that evaluates how well these vectors can be mapped back onto the vocabulary to receive human-readable lists of terms. These experiments are designed to assess as to what extent the diachronic transformations applied result in *semantically coherent* as well as *discriminative* concepts at t_1.

Results will be discussed and compared with and without alignment (cf. Section 4.3). Note that drawing conclusions from this comparison is difficult, because the alignment inevitably changes the vocabulary and thereby the composition of the dataset, so that we effectively compare across two different datasets. However, given the decisive stance of Hamilton et al. (2016) on alignment for diachronic embedding spaces, it seems important to evaluate its effects on the task.

We train and evaluate all four models separately for each concept listed in Table 1. As some concepts only have few examples, all experiments are run in a k-fold cross-validation setting. We use $k = 5$ and report scores averaged over all folds along with their standard deviation (in plots indicated by error bars).

6.1 Experiment 1: Predicting the missing analogy vector

To evaluate the prediction of the missing concept term, we use the cosine similarity between the predicted and the label vector and average over all examples. For a set of analogies A, the predicted vector $\vec{b}_{t_1_i}$ and the label vector $\vec{b}_{t_1_i}^*$ for the i-th analogy, the average cosine similarity (COS) score is defined as

$$COS = \frac{1}{|A|} \sum_{i=1}^{|A|} \frac{\vec{b}_{t_1_i} \cdot \vec{b}_{t_1_i}^*}{\|\vec{b}_{t_1_i}\|_2 \|\vec{b}_{t_1_i}^*\|_2} \tag{6}$$

Hence, this experiment addresses the *coherence* aspect in evaluating the diachronic transformations in the sense that higher COS values indicate smaller distances between predicted and expected terms, thus resulting in more coherent concept representations at t_1.

Figure 1 shows the average cosine similarity scores of a 5-fold cross-validation for both aligned and non-aligned vector spaces per concept for each of the models and baselines for the 1955–1959 and 1985–1989 time intervals on the subset of the KB historical newspapers corpus described in Section 5.2.

For all concepts and models as well as irrespective of alignment, the standard deviation is very low, indicating stable performance across folds.

The ADD baseline generally has a lower score than the NO baseline except for *koeien* and *boekje* with alignment. Apparently a naive search in the neighborhood of the core concept term for the later period is better than assuming a simple linear relationship between the terms across time periods. Alignment improves the scores for the ADD baseline, but we see hardly any differences for NO. As the NO baseline ignores the aligned space t_0, the small differences in performance might be caused by the differences in the dataset due to the altered vocabulary.

The results for TRANS are strongly influenced by alignment. With non-aligned spaces, the model is worse than the NO baseline for all concepts. With aligned spaces, the score of the TRANS model is dramatically higher than without, sometimes more than twice as high (*boekje, utrecht*), and consistently beats both baselines. Apparently it is only beneficial to assume that the same transformation is applicable to both vector spaces across time when their dimensions are aligned, so that the transformation will have a similar effect.

WEIGHTS is the best performing model, sometimes with a notable margin. When using alignment, we see hardly any improvements for WEIGHTS. Probably, in the non-aligned case the weights manage

<hr>

[6]https://gist.github.com/quadrismegistus/ 09a93e219a6ffc4f216fb85235535faf

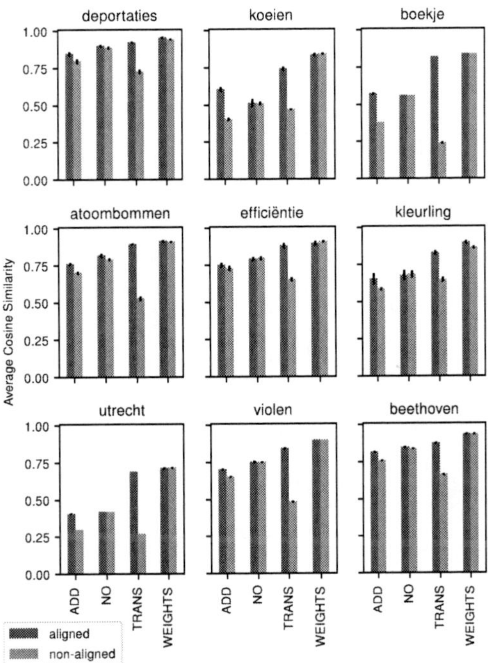

Figure 1: Averaged (5-fold cross-validation) cosine similarities between predicted and label vector per model and concept for aligned and non-aligned vector spaces

to compensate for the missing alignment to a high degree, so that the alignment does not add much. Comparing these results to ADD, it seems to be beneficial to include the t_0 embeddings for predicting the missing vector at t_1 only if weights are learned to account for the differences between the two vector spaces. Comparing to the simple TRANS model, the performance without alignment is clearly superior, but with alignment WEIGHTS is only slightly better.

6.2 Experiment 2: Using predicted vectors for vocabulary retrieval

In the following, we will report on experiments that evaluate how well the predicted vectors can be used to retrieve meaningful word lists that help to study concept change. To perform the mapping from an embedding to a term, the system takes a predicted vector and performs an n-nearest neighbor search over all word embeddings of the t_1 vector space using cosine similarity as proximity metric. In the reported experiments, $n = 10$ is used. Note that this evaluation setting is comparatively hard for the proposed models, as the vocabulary retrieval performance is not only determined by the quality of the prediction, but also by the other vectors in the t_1 space outside the set of vectors that are part of the ground truth dataset. As these vectors were not seen by the model during training, performance inevitably is influenced to an arbitrary degree by the specific concepts and embedding spaces used.

We evaluate the vocabulary retrieval performance in terms of the mean reciprocal rank (MRR) (Voorhees, 1999) of the label terms in the ranked lists of vocabulary terms. For a set of analogies A and the rank of the label term in the list of vocabulary terms for the i-th analogy $rank_i$, the MRR is defined as

$$MRR = \frac{1}{|A|} \sum_{i=1}^{|A|} \frac{1}{rank_i} \tag{7}$$

When for any analogy the label term is not in the list of returned vocabulary terms (i.e., $rank_i$ is not defined), the reciprocal rank $\frac{1}{rank_i}$ is set to 0. Hence, this experiment aims at assessing whether the diachronic transformations applied yield a semantic space at t_1 that effectively *discriminates* between

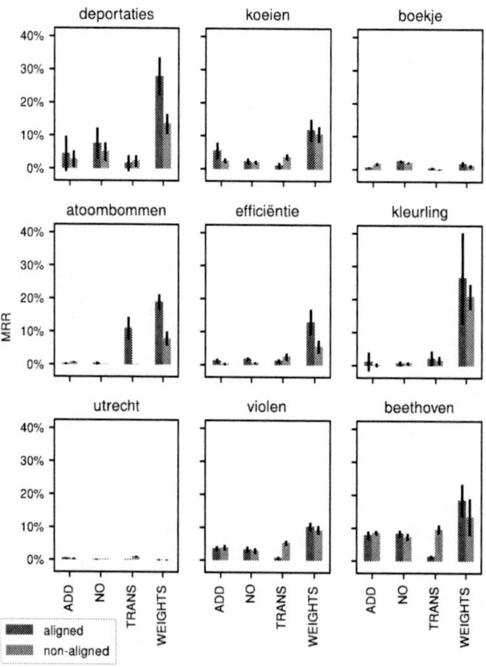

Figure 2: Averaged (5-fold cross-validation) mean reciprocal rank scores (in percent) per model and concept for aligned and non-aligned vector spaces

different concepts such that terms included in the vocabulary of a concept should be consistently ranked higher than confounders from the vocabulary of other concepts, thus resulting in higher MRR scores.

Figure 2 shows MRR results per concept for each of the models and baselines using aligned and non-aligned vector spaces computed for the same dataset and 5-fold cross-validation setting as in Section 6.1. Overall, compared to Experiment 1, the results are much less uniform and stable. The ADD baseline performs worse or comparable to the NO baseline. An exception is *koeien* with alignment. These overall results for ADD are expected, since NO has higher COS scores than ADD for almost all concepts, independent of alignment. Alignment has no clear effect on MRR scores for ADD. For some concepts (e.g., *boekje*) the baseline performs worse than non-aligned, for others (e.g., *koeien*) it performs better.

Surprisingly, without alignment TRANS often yields more relevant predictions than the two baselines, even though its COS scores are mostly lower (cf. Figure 1). With aligned embedding spaces, the MRR performance of TRANS shows very variable behavior. For some concepts, we see small improvements with alignment, in the case of *atoombommen* it is even very large. For other concepts, we see a drop in performance, sometimes very sharp as for *beethoven* or *violen*. This is a puzzling result, since we see notable improvements in the cosine similarity score for TRANS when the vector spaces are aligned.

For most concepts, WEIGHTS performs best and often does so with a large margin – with or without alignment. Exceptions are *utrecht* and *boekje* with a score below the baselines. Interestingly, while applying rotational alignment only leads to negligible improvements in COS for WEIGHTS, the MRR score is always higher with alignment than without, although for some concepts (e.g., *kleurling*) the standard deviation increases exceptionally.

7 Discussion

Taken together, the vector transformations applied in our experiments in order to solve diachronic analogies tend to produce robust and promising results with regard to local conceptual coherence (cf. Experiment 1); however, the resulting conceptual spaces barely exhibit the property of discriminability between concepts (cf. Experiment 2).

Comparing the individual models' performance, it is notable that while the differences between TRANS and WEIGHTS in terms of COS are small with aligned axes, WEIGHTS has much higher MRR scores for both aligned and non-aligned embeddings. This result is consistent for all concepts, so that the WEIGHTS model is the best- performing system overall.

Due to its comparable performance with non-aligned embeddings, when training WEIGHTS, differences between the vocabularies of the two time periods could be included in the data (see section 4.3). Because of this, WEIGHTS can also be applied to cases of concept change where words disappear from the concept vocabulary or new ones are added. On the other hand, the TRANS model requires less complex training data which only needs to contain conceptual word pairs for one time period. This allows for more exploratory use cases where expert knowledge about concepts only exists for t_0. Taking into account the often negative effect of alignment on MRR for TRANS, the embeddings should be non-aligned. While we admittedly would expect less relevant term lists when using this model instead of WEIGHTS, it should, according to the evaluation, nevertheless give better results than the baseline approaches.

As discussed in Section 5.1, our evaluation data contains concepts that exhibit semantic change as well as ones that tend towards semantic stability. The results observed in Experiment 1 are largely unaffected by this difference, which may suggest that the models are applicable to cases of diachronic change and stability as well. This hypothesis is only partially corroborated in Experiment 2, though. From our current analyses, we conjecture that the variance in performance across concepts is mostly explained by concept size (cf. Table 1) rather than the difference between changing vs. stable concepts. A more detailed investigation of these effects is left to future work.

8   Conclusions and outlook

We have introduced the task of completing diachronic analogies to analyze concept change. We have presented two learned models to recover diachronic analogies and tested them in a quantitative evaluation. The experiments showed that, for most of the evaluated concepts, a model based on a weighted linear combination of the analogous words' embeddings is able to more accurately predict the missing vector which also corresponds to more relevant terms than a learned transformation and two related baselines. More specifically, we have evaluated the effect of a rotational alignment of the time-period-specific embedding spaces, finding varying effects on performance, depending on the model, concept and evaluation metric. For the weighted linear combination, however, results improve with alignment in the majority of cases. In sum, it is beneficial for prediction of diachronic changes in concept vocabularies to treat the concept terms as analogous when weights are learnt to compensate for diachronic drift. However, while all models tend to be coherent in relation to the represented concept, they are only to some degree discriminative in regard to the vocabulary of other concepts.

Future work should carry out more in-depth evaluations, annotating task-specific ground truth data and exploring evaluation settings like zero-shot learning which has been show to obtain promising results in related problems (cf. Hartung et al. (2017)). We also expect benefits from training with an objective function which includes negative examples and relates more closely to MRR. Beyond this, we are interested in designing more complex and task-specific models. Not last, we plan to explore use cases based on cooperation with scholars from the humanities. For example, we see potential in analysing how an author's use of specific concepts changes across works using a combination of both interpretative and automatic methods of diachronic analogy recovery.

Acknowledgments

We thank Steven Claeyssens, Curator of Digital Collections at the Koninklijke Bibliotheek, for providing access to the data as well as further documentation and support. This work was supported by the Cluster of Excellence Cognitive Interaction Technology 'CITEC' (EXC 277) at Bielefeld University, which is funded by the German Research Foundation (DFG).

References

Robert Bamler and Stephan Mandt. 2017. Dynamic Word Embeddings. In *PMLR*, pages 380–389, July.

David M. Blei and John D. Lafferty. 2006. Dynamic Topic Models. In *Proceedings of the 23rd International Conference on Machine Learning*, ICML '06, pages 113–120, New York, NY, USA. ACM.

Dawn Chen, Joshua C. Peterson, and Thomas L. Griffiths. 2017. Evaluating vector-space models of analogy. *arXiv:1705.04416 [cs]*, May. arXiv: 1705.04416.

Antoine Cornuéjols and Jacques Ales-Bianchetti. 1998. Analogy and Induction: Which (missing) link? In *Proceedings of Workshop on Analogy*, Sofia, Bulgaria, July.

Haim Dubossarsky, Daphna Weinshall, and Eitan Grossman. 2017. Outta Control: Laws of Semantic Change and Inherent Biases in Word Representation Models. In *Proceedings of the 2017 Conference on Empirical Methods in Natural Language Processing*, pages 1147–1156, Copenhagen, Denmark. Association for Computational Linguistics.

John Rupert Firth. 1957. A synopsis of linguistic theory 1930-1955. In *Studies in Linguistic Analysis*, pages 1–31. Blackwell, Oxford.

Kristina Gulordava and Marco Baroni. 2011. A Distributional Similarity Approach to the Detection of Semantic Change in the Google Books Ngram Corpus. In *Proceedings of the GEMS 2011 Workshop on GEometrical Models of Natural Language Semantics*, GEMS '11, pages 67–71, Stroudsburg, PA, USA. Association for Computational Linguistics.

William L. Hamilton, Jure Leskovec, and Dan Jurafsky. 2016. Diachronic word embeddings reveal statistical laws of semantic change. In *Proceedings of the 54th Annual Meeting of the Association for Computational Linguistics (Volume 1: Long Papers)*, pages 1489–1501, Berlin, Germany, August. Association for Computational Linguistics.

Zellig S. Harris. 1954. Distributional Structure. *Word*, 10(2-3):146–162, August.

Matthias Hartung, Fabian Kaupmann, Soufian Jebbara, and Philipp Cimiano. 2017. Learning compositionality functions on word embeddings for modelling attribute meaning in adjective-noun phrases. In *Proceedings of the 15th Conference of the European Chapter of the Association for Computational Linguistics: Volume 1, Long Papers*, pages 54–64, Valencia, Spain, April. Association for Computational Linguistics.

Tom Kenter, Melvin Wevers, Pim Huijnen, and Maarten de Rijke. 2015. Ad Hoc Monitoring of Vocabulary Shifts over Time. In *Proceedings of the 24th ACM InternationalConference on Information and Knowledge Management (CIKM'15)*.

Yoon Kim, Yi-I Chiu, Kentaro Hanaki, Darshan Hegde, and Slav Petrov. 2014. Temporal Analysis of Language through Neural Language Models. In *Proceedings of the ACL 2014 Workshop on Language Technologies and Computational Social Science*, pages 61–65, Baltimore, MD, USA. Association for Computational Linguistics.

Diederik P. Kingma and Jimmy Ba. 2014. Adam: A Method for Stochastic Optimization. *arXiv:1412.6980 [cs]*, December. arXiv: 1412.6980.

Vivek Kulkarni, Rami Al-Rfou, Bryan Perozzi, and Steven Skiena. 2015. Statistically Significant Detection of Linguistic Change. In *Proceedings of the 24th International Conference on World Wide Web*, WWW '15, pages 625–635, Republic and Canton of Geneva, Switzerland. International World Wide Web Conferences Steering Committee.

Omer Levy and Yoav Goldberg. 2014. Linguistic Regularities in Sparse and Explicit Word Representations. In *Proceedings of the 18th Conference on Computational Language Learning (CoNLL)*, pages 171–180. Association for Computational Linguistics.

Omer Levy, Yoav Goldberg, and Ido Dagan. 2015. Improving Distributional Similarity with Lessons Learned from Word Embeddings. *Transactions of the Association for Computational Linguistics*, 3(0):211–225, May.

Carlos Martinez-Ortiz, Tom Kenter, Melvin Wevers, Pim Huijnen, Jaap Verheul, and Joris van Eijnatten. 2016a. Design and implementation of ShiCo: Visualising shifting concepts over time. In *Proceedings of the 3rd International Workshop on Computational History (HistoInformatics 2016)*.

Carlos Martinez-Ortiz, Tom Kenter, Melvin Wevers, Pim Huijnen, Jaap Verheul, and Joris van Eijnatten. 2016b. ShiCo: A Visualization Tool for Shifting Concepts Through Time. In *Proceedings of the 3rd DH Benelux Conference (DH Benelux 2016)*.

Tomas Mikolov, Kai Chen, Greg Corrado, and Jeffrey Dean. 2013a. Efficient Estimation of Word Representations in Vector Space. *arXiv:1301.3781 [cs]*, January. arXiv: 1301.3781.

Tomas Mikolov, Wen-tau Yih, and Geoffrey Zweig. 2013b. Linguistic Regularities in Continuous Space Word Representations. In *Proceedings of the 2013 Conference of the North American Chapter of the Association for Computational Linguistics: Human Language Technologies*, pages 746–751, Atlanta, Georgia. Association for Computational Linguistics.

Kira Radinsky, Eugene Agichtein, Evgeniy Gabrilovich, and Shaul Markovitch. 2011. A Word at a Time: Computing Word Relatedness using Temporal Semantic Analysis. In *Proceedings of the 20th International World Wide Web Conference*, pages 337–346, Hyderabad, India, March.

Gabriel Recchia, Ewan Jones, Paul Nulty, John Regan, and Peter de Bolla. 2016. Tracing Shifting Conceptual Vocabularies Through Time. In *Knowledge Engineering and Knowledge Management*, Lecture Notes in Computer Science, pages 19–28. Springer, Cham, November.

David E Rumelhart and Adele A Abrahamson. 1973. A model for analogical reasoning. *Cognitive Psychology*, 5(1):1–28, July.

Peter H. Schönemann. 1966. A generalized solution of the orthogonal Procrustes problem. *Psychometrika*, 31(1):1–10, March.

Chenhao Tan, Dallas Card, and Noah A. Smith. 2017. Friendships, Rivalries, and Trysts: Characterizing Relations between Ideas in Texts. In *Proceedings of the 55th Annual Meeting of the Association for Computational Linguistics (Volume 1: Long Papers)*, pages 773–783, Vancouver, Canada. Association for Computational Linguistics.

Peter D. Turney. 2006. Similarity of Semantic Relations. *Computational Linguistics*, 32(3):379–416, August.

Ellen M. Voorhees. 1999. The TREC-8 Question Answering Track Report. In *Proceedings of TREC-8*, pages 77–82.

Melvin Wevers, Tom Kenter, and Pim Huijnen. 2015. Concepts Through Time: Tracing Concepts in Dutch Newspaper Discourse (1890-1990) using Word Embeddings. *Digital Humanities 2015 (DH2015)*.

A Linked Coptic Dictionary Online

Frank Feder
Akademie der Wissenschaften
zu Göttingen
`frank.feder@`
`mail.uni-goettingen.de`

Maxim Kupreyev
Berlin-Brandenburgische
Akademie der Wissenschaften
`maxim.kupreyev@`
`bbaw.de`

Emma Manning
Department of Linguistics
Georgetown University
`esm76@`
`georgetown.edu`

Caroline T. Schroeder
Department of Religious Studies
University of the Pacific
`carrie@carrieschroeder.com`

Amir Zeldes
Department of Linguistics
Georgetown University
`amir.zeldes@georgetown.edu`

Abstract

We describe a new project publishing a freely available online dictionary for Coptic. The dictionary encompasses comprehensive cross-referencing mechanisms, including linking entries to an online scanned edition of Crum's Coptic Dictionary, internal cross-references and etymological information, translated searchable definitions in English, French and German, and linked corpus data which provides frequencies and corpus look-up for headwords and multiword expressions. Headwords are available for linking in external projects using a REST API. We describe the challenges in encoding our dictionary using TEI XML and implementing linking mechanisms to construct a Web interface querying frequency information, which draw on NLP tools to recognize inflected forms in context. We evaluate our dictionary's coverage using digital corpora of Coptic available online.

1 Introduction

Coptic is the final stage of the indigenous language of Egypt, spoken in Egypt in the first millennium and used as a liturgical language of Christian Copts in Egypt and the Coptic diaspora today. Together with Ancient Egyptian, the language of the hieroglyphs, it forms part of the longest continuously attested language documentation of any language on Earth. Unlike Ancient Egyptian, Coptic is written with a script derived from the Greek alphabet, with several letters added from the earlier Demotic script for native sounds not found in Greek.

Although the Coptic corpus, attested in six main dialects, is vast, it is very much under-studied compared with materials from contemporaneous Greek and Latin sources. The amount of freely available data for Coptic online is still small (see Schroeder and Zeldes 2016), and published book editions of Coptic texts are mostly limited to the main important literary works, covering only a fraction of the data preserved in the language, including literary, documentary and epigraphic material. The situation for Coptic lexicography on paper, by contrast, is more comprehensive, with Crum (2000 [1939]) and subsequent dictionaries offering excellent coverage of native Coptic words. More recently, progress has been made in the lexicography of the abundant inventory of Greek and other loan words in Coptic (Almond et al., 2013), and work is in progress in matching existing Egyptological resources, such as the Thesaurus Linguae Aegyptiae (Seidlmayer and Hafemann, 2011) with equivalent Coptic entries (Feder, 2016).

At the same time, there has been a substantial gap in providing an openly available electronic dictionary of Coptic linked with digital corpora to provide easy look-up functionality and frequency information. The present paper describes a new project, the 'Coptic Dictionary Online' (CDO), which is freely available and fully linked with the growing digital resources and NLP tools which are becoming available for Coptic. We discuss issues in TEI XML (`http://www.tei-c.org`) representations for Coptic data, unique issues arising from Coptic morphology, as well as linked open data standards, such as REST API connectivity. We evaluate the coverage of our lexicon based on currently available corpus data.

Proceedings of Workshop on Computational Linguistics for Cultural Heritage, Social Sciences, Humanities and Literature, pages 12–21
Santa Fe, New Mexico, USA, August 25, 2018.

2   Related work

The dataset of the Coptic Dictionary Online is based on a part of the 'Thesaurus Linguae Aegyptiae' (TLA), provided by the Berlin-Brandenburg Academy of Sciences (BBAW). TLA is a digital offspring of the long-term research project 'Wörterbuch der Ägyptischen Sprache' (Dictionary of the Egyptian Language), started in 1897 at the Prussian Acedemy of Sciences (now BBAW). Following the paper publication of the five volume Egyptian lexicon, the TLA began work on the digital edition of the dictionary, which went online in 2004, with extensions including Demotic Egyptian and Coptic lemmas, but not yet broadly covering the Coptic vocabulary targeted in this paper.

A second project, 'Database and Dictionary of Greek Loanwords in Coptic' (DDGLC), originally based in Leipzig and since 2015 at the Freie Universität Berlin, has indexed Greek words in the attested Coptic corpus. DDGLC data is organized around Greek lemmas and currently contains 4,971 Greek source lemmas, 8,406 resulting Coptic lemmas and 100,106 'attestations' of the latter. CDO plans to integrate these to overcome a major drawback of current Coptic lexicographical projects, which disregard non-Egyptian vocabulary (see Section 5).

The other most extensive lexicographical project is the lexicon by the Marcion project,[1] which contains 11,437 head words indexing 87,169 items, and closely follows the printed edition of Crum's dictionary. This resource is not linked to corpora and NLP tools and does not offer a REST API or multilingual definitions, but does include links to the scanned online version of Crum's work, much like the CDO.

Finally, the situation for lexically tagged corpora is more limited: the currently largest open collection of lemmatized and grammatically analyzed Coptic data is provided by the project Coptic Scriptorium,[2] based at Georgetown University and the University of the Pacific, and open for querying via the ANNIS web interface (Krause and Zeldes, 2016). The corpora encompass approximately 500,000 running tokens of Coptic text, just under 20% of which has been manually checked (this data will be used for the evaluation in Section 5). Scriptorium data is described in more detail further below, and is the source of both linked frequency data and example look-up in the CDO project.

3   Lexical data representation

3.1   Coptic grammar

Coptic is an agglutinative Afro-Asiatic language, descended from the earlier highly inflected system of Ancient Egyptian, which was more similar to Semitic languages. Originally, Coptic was written in manuscripts in *scriptio continua*, without spaces between words, as shown in Figure 1. However, like other languages of the Middle East, such as Arabic and Hebrew, modern conventions spell Coptic with spaces between stressed word groups, known as bound groups (see Layton 2011 in detail). Bound groups most often include only one content lexeme, usually either a noun or a verb, along with accompanying clitic articles, auxiliaries, prepositions and object or possessor pronouns, and therefore do not receive individual lexicon entries.

Figure 1: Excerpt from a manuscript of Shenoute's Canon 5 in Three Folios at the National Library in Vienna showing text in *scriptio continua*. Image: Österreichische Nationalbibliothek, http://data.onb.ac.at/rec/RZ00002466.

However, analyzing what constitutes a content item for dictionary entries is non-trivial, since within each bound group, Coptic nominal compounds are uninterrupted and spelled together (unlike Arabic or

[1] http://marcion.sourceforge.net/dictionary/coptic.html
[2] http://copticscriptorium.org

Hebrew), and verbal incorporation (see Grossman 2014) can often create complex lexical items containing multiple content morphemes (cf. English complex verbs such as 'breastfeed'), which are often listed in dictionaries as a complex item if they are frequent or have opaque senses. Both incorporation and cliticization also lead to changes to verb and noun stems, as shown in the following examples.[3] Example (1) shows a bound group with a preposition, article and the noun 'name', while (2) shows a reduced form of the same noun with a possessive 2nd person masculine singular clitic.

(1)   ϩⲙ-ⲡ-ⲣⲁⲛ   hm-p-ran   'in-the-name'

(2)   ⲣⲛⲧ=ⲕ   rnt=k   'name-your (SG.M)'

The noun's form in (1) is referred to as 'absolute' (*status absolutus*), while in (2) it is in a bound-pronoun state (also called *status pronominalis*; forms fused to a subsequent noun, rather than pronoun, take a third possible form called *status nominalis*). Examples (3)-(5) show a verbal bound group, with stem reduction via incorporation in (4), and nominalization of a complex verb in (5).

(3)   ⲁ-ϥ-ϩⲱⲧⲃ   (4)   ϩⲉⲧⲃ-ⲯⲧⲭⲏ   (5)   ⲙⲛⲧ-ⲣⲉϥ-ϩⲉⲧⲃ-ⲯⲧⲭⲏ
     a-f-hōtb   hetb-psychē   mnt-ref-hetb-psychē
     PST-he-kill   kill-soul   ness-er-kill-soul
     'he killed'   '(to) soul-kill'   'soul-killing'
                       (incorporated)   (lit. 'soul-kill-er-ness')

The last example shows that incorporated verbs behave like normal verbs in allowing subsequent derivations. Representing these forms consistently is challenging, as we discuss in the sections below.

3.2 Properties of lexicon composition

The coverage of the dataset used in the Coptic Dictionary Online is based on W. Crum's 'Coptic Dictionary' (2000 [1939]) and currently contains 8,042 words ("entries") and 18,150 word forms. The Coptic data follows the design of the combined Egyptian-Demotic-Coptic lexicon in the TLA, with the aim of integrating the Coptic dataset to form a collection of all lexical items from 4,500 years of the language's recorded history. With regards to the coverage of the Coptic lexicon, CDO has two types of restrictions. A lexeme may be absent:

- because it is absent in Crum's dictionary (notably Greek and Arabic loan words)

- due to data model design despite being in Crum (bound forms of verbs and plural nouns; see below)

Here we outline the major principles behind the lexicon data composition and encoding, and provide details on the ongoing extension of the project.

The backbone of entries from Crum in the CDO is extended with cross-references to the later Coptic dictionaries of Westendorf (2008 [1965-1977]), Černý (1976), Vycichl (1983) and Cherix (2014). What all these have in common is the absence of loanwords – a tradition in Coptic lexicography, going back to the 18th century. Beginning from the *Lexicon Aegyptiaco-Latinum* of the Huguenot polymath Maturin Veyssière de La Croze of 1721, lexicographers were interested primarily in 'autochthonous' Egyptian vocabulary, and disregarded Greek and Arabic as 'too familiar' (Richter, 2017). Recent research has challenged traditional conceptualizations of "loan words" as a classification of vocabulary separate or distinct from "autochthonous" words, particularly in the multilingual context of Roman Egypt (Grossman 2013, Papaconstantinou 2010). The lack of loan words is one of the issues which CDO is currently working on (see Section 5 on the impact of their absence, and Section 6 on future plans). Apart from loan words, word forms available in Crum but missing in CDO include orthographic forms in Coptic dialects other than Sahidic, the classical dialect supplying the reference forms in the dictionary, and bound forms of Coptic words when used as clitics. Entries only attested in other dialects are included.[4]

---

[3] We follow the convention in Coptic studies of joining clitic lexical items in bound groups with hyphens, and clitic pronouns with the '=' sign.

[4] A pilot including all entries from Crum and all dialect forms for the letters *alpha* and *beta* has also been carried out, but due to time constraints has not been extended to further letters.

incorporated		multi-word expression	
ti-meeue	*give-thought, think*	ti-m-p-meeue	*give-of-the-thought, suggest*
ti-erxot	*give-wound, to wound*	ti-n-ou-erxot	*give-of-a-wound, inflict a wound*
k^{y}i-bekhe	*get-wage, get-paid*	či-m-p-beke	*receive payment*

Table 1: Incorporated complex verbs and unincorporated multi-word expressions.

Bound forms are exceptionally recorded only if the absolute (non-clitic) form is not available, as is the case with inalienable possessed nouns, e.g. ⲣⲁⲧ꞊ *rat-* 'foot (of)'. Inflected forms are also not included, but are findable using automatic lemmatization (see Section 4.4). This means the small class of morphological plurals is not listed (pluralization is usually indicated by the article), and the same applies to stative verb forms (also called 'qualitative', distinct forms denoting a *state* resulting from the action, rather than the action itself). Statives are entered if they are the only form of a verb attested in Coptic.

Verbal clitic status also determines spelling of verbal compounds in CDO: verbs in bound state followed by incorporated objects are treated as morphemes, forming one lexical unit with the following word, and are thus written together, though purely compositional productive formations are only included if they have entries in Crum's dictionary. Verbs in absolute state are treated as separate lexical units and are written separately. Compounds in which absolute and bound state are indistinguishable are treated as bound forms if they are not followed by prepositions.

Determining whether a complex verb form is considered a single entry depends on whether a bare noun is incorporated without determiners in a generic reading (cf. 'breastfeed') vs. using a full nominal bound group, e.g. with determiners, possessives or prepositions (cf. 'feed with her breast'). Table 1 contrasts similar items: incorporated single verbs, and multi-word expressions. Although the latter entries contain information on object nouns, verb valency information is otherwise not included in the dictionary.

The guidelines for handling complex verbs correspond to the word segmentation practices in current corpora available from the project Coptic Scriptorium (see Section 2), and therefore facilitate compatibility with corpus look-up and frequency data (see Section 4.3), as well as interoperability with existing NLP tools for Coptic (Zeldes and Schroeder, 2016). However there are a number of cases in which bound forms are accompanied by explicitly or implicitly specific nouns that are represented as entries in Crum's dictionary, but are segmented apart by NLP tools and corpora based on their outputs:

- Verbs with possessed nouns: k^{y}n-rat= 'search (lit. find one's foot)', meh-hēt= 'fill one's belly'

- Fixed verb + article + noun: r-p-ke 'do another (thing)', r-t-k^{y}ot 'be like, lit. do the likeness (of)'

- Verbs bound with compound prepositions (preposition + possessed noun + suffix): r-ha-čō= 'go towards (do to head of)', r-hi-čn- 'be over (do on head of)'

We expose the lexical units in such compounds using XML encoding in the element oRef, described in the next section. Summing up, the current limitations of the lexicon are:

- no loan words, and dialect forms usually included only if not attested in Sahidic

- bound forms only if unattested in absolute form, and stative only if verb is unattested in infinitive

- no inflected forms of nouns (but see Section 4.4 on auto-redirecting from most inflected forms)

3.3 Properties of lexicon encoding

CDO is encoded in XML, managed using the Python libraries ElementTree and LXML, as well as Xpath queries. Data integrity is validated by an XSD Schema, developed as a subset of the TEI's Dictionary module.[5] The basic element is `<entry>`, defined by standard spelling, part of speech and

---

[5] See http://www.tei-c.org/release/doc/tei-p5-doc/en/html/DI.html. TEI's dictionary module is also viewed by Romary (2015) as a standard serialization of the Lexical Mark-up Framework (ISO, 2008). For the CDO's latest schema, see https://github.com/KELLIA/dictionary/blob/master/xml/Coptic_Lemma_Schema.xsd, which represents our underlying conceptual UML model, cf. Routledge et al. (2002).

gender information, and senses: only one `<form type="lemma">`, `<pos>` and `<gen>` element (gender) is allowed per entry (meaning feminine derivations receive separate entries) and at least one `<sense>` element is required. At the same time, multiple orthographical variants (`<form>`) and meanings (`<sense>`) are possible in one entry. Entries belong to the superordinate entity `<superentry>`, which corresponds to Crum's dictionary entry, uniting lemmas derived from the same root in Coptic. The schema is outlined in Figure 2.[6]

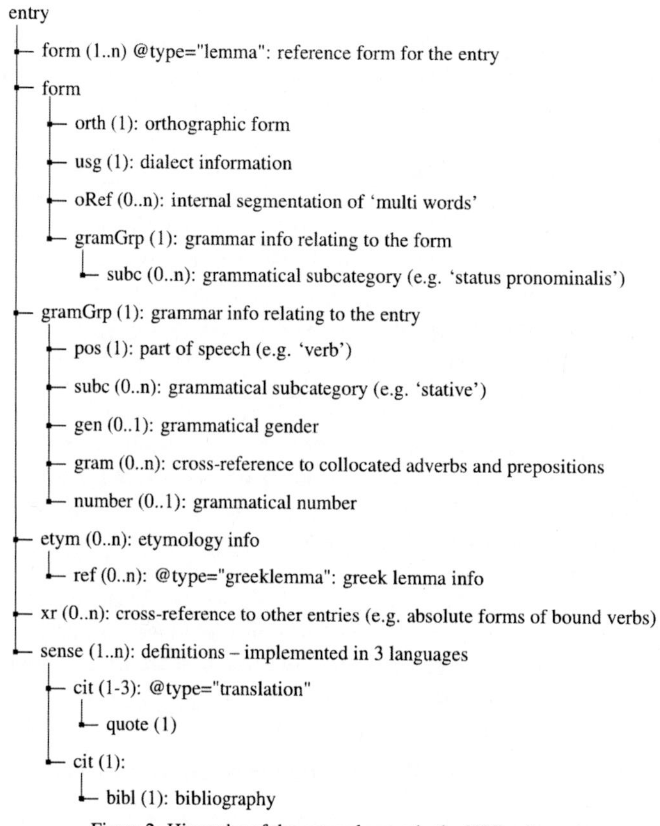

Figure 2: Hierarchy of the entry element in the XSD schema

Grammatical information can be set on both the 'entry' and on the 'form' level. The boundedness status information is encoded within form, e.g. `<subc>`Status nominalis`</subc>`, while information pertaining to inflected forms belongs to the entry level, e.g. for stative forms: `<pos>`Vb.`</pos>` with the subcategory `<subc>`Qualitativ`</subc>`. The `<gram>` tag provides information about prepositions and adverbs collocated with a given verb. The values available in elements such as `<pos>`, `<subc>` and `<usg>` (dialects) are controlled by the vocabulary set in the XSD Schema.

Each entry and each form have unique IDs. The `<xr>` tag is currently used for cross-referencing the absolute form of lexical verbs appearing as bound in complex entries. However, multi-word expressions also encode all of their constituents (including function words): the multi-word expression is listed spelled together inside `<orth>`, but separated in the element `<oRef>`, as in (6) for the expression he-p-ouō 'inquire, lit. find-the-news':

---

[6]We follow the mapping in Romary (2015) between LMF concepts and corresponding TEI elements as follows:

LMF component	TEI representation	LMF component	TEI representation
LexicalEntry	`<entry/>`	writtenForm	`<orth/>`
Lemma	`<form type="lemma"/>`	partOfSpeech	`<pos/>`
Word Form	`<form type="inflected"/>`	grammaticalNumber	`<number/>`

(6)   <orth>ϩⲉⲡⲟⲩⲱ</orth> <oRef>ϩⲉ ⲡ ⲟⲩⲱ</oRef>

This segmentation information will be used below to search for multi-word entries in corpus data.

4   Web interface

4.1   User interface design

To facilitate efficient search, the lexicon's XML files are compiled into a SQL database providing records for each entry, with multiple orthographic forms grouped into super-entries, which correspond to Crum's entries.[7] Each record contains the dictionary information such as orthographic forms, morphological information, definitions in English, French and German, and etymological and bibliographic information. A record also contains both a unique entry number and a super-entry number used to link it to related entries based on Crum's groupings. We then designed an online interface to search this database and view entries. From the search page, users may search any combination of:

- Coptic word form/regular expression (with a virtual keyboard option to enter Coptic characters)

- Dialect (using Crum's dialect sigla, subject to the restrictions mentioned above)

- Part-of-Speech tag (using Scriptorium NLP tags, mapped onto the TLA's model; see below)

- Definition, with options to search for the exact sequence entered or for definitions containing all words entered in any order, as well as an option to search a specific one of the three definition languages, or any language. Regular expressions are also allowed.

To reconcile the different part of speech tags used by the TLA's data model and Coptic Scriptorium's model, we have collapsed tags for some of the more fine grained tag distinctions. This is necessary, among other things, for the benefit of NLP-tool based look-up (see Section 4.4). Currently, users can limit searches to the following options:

- **A** - any auxiliary (merges Scriptorium/TLA)

- **ART** - articles

- **C** - any of the so called 'converters', a morphological class of Coptic conjunctions

- **CONJ** - all other, independent conjunctions

- **N** - nouns, collapses common and proper nouns

- **NEG** - negations

- **NUM** - numerals

- **pronouns** - demonstrative (PDEM), interrogative (PINT), personal (PPER), possessive (PPOS)

- **PREP** - prepositions

- **PTC** - particles

- **V** - collapses all verbal tags, including finite, non-finite, imperative and 'verboids'

The original grammar info encoded in XML (using German terms) is displayed along with the Coptic Scriptorium part of speech tags. In addition to the main search page, shown in Figure 3a, a Quick Search is available in the navigation bar at the top of any page. Users can enter any combination of Coptic words and English, French and German words to search the word form and definitions, respectively. These, too, support regular expressions, and space-delimited search words are automatically classified as either Coptic (for search in the entries themselves) or not (for search in the definitions).[8]

---

[7]An anonymous reviewer has inquired about the possibility of encoding the database version of the lexicon in RDF format – this is certainly possible and the adoption of a SQL database is in no way a principled decision, but rather one of convenience. We regard the XML representation as the primary serialization of the lexicon's data model and use the tabular SQL schema only internally as an index for the search interface.

[8]We do not currently classify non Coptic words as English, French or German, but rather match non-Coptic script words in all definition languages.

When a search uniquely identifies an entry, it takes the user directly to the entry page, which displays the word's form or forms, each with morphological information, dialect if available, and ANNIS frequency information (see Section 4.3). Each entry page also contains Scriptorium part of speech tags, the definitions in all three languages for each sense, as well as any etymological and bibliographic information, including cross-reference links. If there are other entries in the same super-entry, they are linked in a 'See Also' section at the bottom of the entry page. When a search has more than one result, users are taken to a page which lists up to 100 matches, displaying Coptic forms and English definitions for each. Users can click on any of these Coptic words to go to the associated entry page.

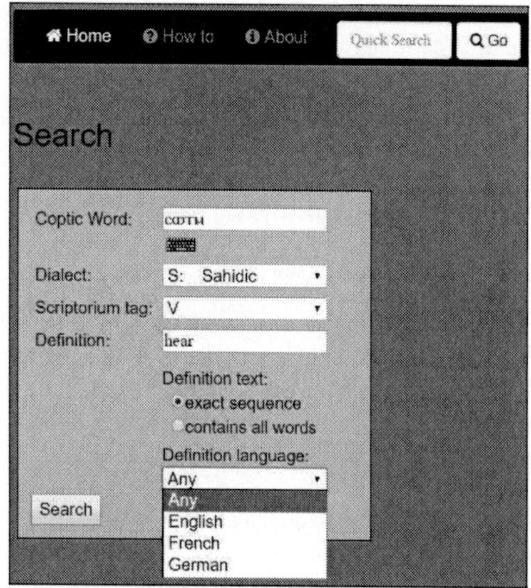

(a) Main search form

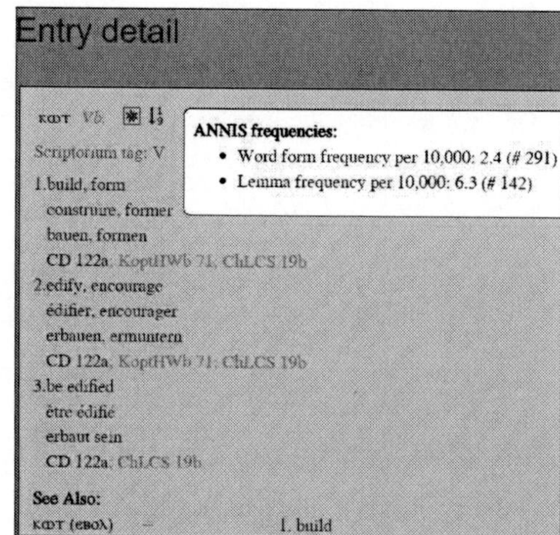

(b) Entry with frequency information for ⲕⲱⲧ *kōt* 'build'.

Figure 3: CDO web interface.

4.2 Corpus query link up

The dictionary is linked to freely available corpora provided by the Coptic Scriptorium project (`http://copticscriptorium.org`), which currently include over 500,000 tokens from 16 corpora containing over 700 Coptic documents. Each entry page provides a link to a lemma search in all corpora for each form specified by an `<orth>` element (i.e. a single entry page will have multiple search links if there are multiple variant forms). Conversely, Scriptorium corpora offer links to the CDO for all lemmas, which connect to the relevant entry pages whenever available (see Section 6 for some limitations).

One challenge in implementing the linking capacity is dealing with differences in segmentation for lemma definitions in the dictionary, and existing segmentation standards used in the corpora based on current NLP tools for Coptic. Several types of mismatch are possible – an entry may: 1. specify a variant not considered a lemma in the corpora due to normalization; 2. be a multiword expression, with more than one lemma in the corpora; or 3. contain added words not included in the head word proper, e.g. collocated prepositions.

To overcome the first difficulty, we automatically harvest the list of available lemmas in the current version of the corpora using the REST API provided by Coptic Scriptorium's ANNIS web interface. Single word dictionary items not attested in the corpora as lemmas can then fall back to searching on the word form level instead of the lemma level, which may include the desired form.[9]

The second problem is more complex, but can be addressed using the `<oRef>` tags in the dictionary XML files. The contents of these tags indicate a space-delimited segmentation for multiword entries,

---

[9]A further option of using fuzzy search to find unknown inflected forms is not currently supported, but remains a possibility for future development.

which are then searched for as a sequence of (possibly inflected) word forms. Since a multiword expression often contains inflected forms, the linked search uses the word form level of the corpora, rather than a sequence of lemmas. A reverse look-up for multiword expressions in the corpora is not yet implemented: the corpora are currently lemmatized with the Coptic NLP pipeline (Zeldes and Schroeder, 2016), which always assigns token-wise lemmas; however, we are considering how 'secondary lemmas' may be introduced whenever corpora contain sequences of words which are attested as dictionary entries.

Finally, for the third problem above, we currently suppress collocated elements in search queries. For example, for the entry ⲕⲱⲧ (ⲉⲃⲟⲗ) 'build (out)', we omit the optional adverb given in brackets, and simply search for the verb 'build' by itself. This approach produces more search results than might be intended, and a better solution for these cases in the future would be desirable (see Section 6).

4.3 Corpus frequency information

Using the same corpora and REST API above, we collect frequency information for all dictionary <orth> elements in their capacity as both word forms and lemmas. We then rank words by frequency and offer users, for each word form, the frequencies and ranks of the item being viewed, as shown in Figure 3b. Tied ranks are shared across items, i.e. there can be multiple entries with lemma rank 100, if multiple items are tied for this position. A limitation of using corpus frequencies is that the corpora are not truly aligned in an intelligent way to dictionary entries, and are not sense disambiguated, i.e. homonyms all contribute to one frequency pool for each orthographic string. This is unlike cross-reference links to Crum's dictionary, which point to page numbers based on actual senses.

Notwithstanding this limitation, frequencies can be useful to users and used to decide how likely it is that an unclear passage contains a possible word, or to prioritize learning high frequency items when studying the language. While frequency information cannot be used for searches yet, we plan to expose it to searches as well as building frequency visualizations to make the data more interactive and accessible.

4.4 NLP and lemma look-up

Since inflected forms are not included in the dictionary, users searching for them will not find any results. Although this is generally not an issue for users coming in from linked corpora (since links point to lemmatized forms), users who manually enter inflected forms will run into this problem.

To circumvent this issue, we use all possible outputs of the same lemmatizer used by the NLP pipeline from Zeldes and Schroeder (2016), without context information. Since morphologically inflected items in Coptic are largely closed-class, and productive stem-altering inflection is rare, the possible responses from the lemmatizer virtually always contain the correct analysis. This means that users can find singular entries for nouns with morphological plurals, or infinitive forms in searches for stative verbs, etc.

Linking from the corpora to the dictionary also depends on correct lemmatization, which, unlike the 'multiple options' look-up strategy, is deterministic (the corpora contain a single 'gold' lemma). This lemma is generally correct in manually annotated corpora, but also very likely to be correct for automatically annotated corpora, if automatic segmentation of word forms was correct. The lemmatization accuracy of the NLP pipeline on correctly segmented text is 97.23% (see Zeldes and Schroeder 2016), though automatic segmentation accuracy is currently lower, at about 94.5%.

5 Evaluation

In order to evaluate the coverage of our dictionary, we use the publicly available corpora from the Coptic Scriptorium project (http://copticscriptorium.org/). We restrict the evaluation to the manually annotated corpora of literary Coptic and remove items overlapping lacunae from damaged manuscripts, and items not in Coptic script, as well as punctuation. The remaining data covers over 74,000 gold segmented running lexical items in Coptic, of which about 6,500 are foreign loanwords, not currently part of the target language covered by the dictionary, and 775 of which are proper names, which are mostly not covered. Table 2 gives the rate of coverage for tokens and types, as well as the numbers when loan words and proper names are not penalized.

	tokens			types		
	covered	total	%	covered	total	%
all lemmas	65,347	74,744	87.43	1,079	2,602	41.47
names ok	66,273	74,744	88.67	1,264	2,602	48.58
foreign ok	71,763	74,744	96.01	1,976	2,602	75.94
both ok	72,689	74,744	97.25	1,991	2,602	76.52

Table 2: Lexicon coverage on 80K lexical items from Coptic Scriptorium corpora.

The table shows that, for proficient users who can identify the need to look up foreign words in a Greek dictionary, and the presence of proper names, coverage at the token level is very good, with less than 3% of tokens in the corpora that might need to be in the dictionary (native common nouns) not being found. The situation is considerably worse for beginners, who may not be able to distinguish Greek words, and we are therefore planning to integrate loan words into the lexicon soon (see Section 6).

Looking at the type coverage, the situation is more partial: about 23.5% of native types are not covered. Given the high token coverage of the native vocabulary, it is clear that the remaining types without coverage are a large number of rare items. This is due to the 'long tail' of productive formations, created via incorporation, derivation and compounding processes, as shown in Section 3.1. We are therefore considering linking the morphologically analyzed sub-parts of words, which are outputted by the Coptic NLP pipeline's morphological analyzer, which are currently not linked. An evaluation of coverage using this strategy remains outstanding.

6 Conclusion and outlook

This paper has presented the Coptic Dictionary Online, a freely available, linked lexical resource for Coptic with definitions in English, French and German, cross-references to the main paper Coptic dictionary by W. Crum as well as other dictionaries, and frequency information connected to corpus search in a collection of open access digitized texts. The coverage of the lexicon for lexicalized native items is high, corresponding to all entries in Crum's dictionary, and if foreign words and names are ignored, covering over 97% of non-punctuation tokens in running text.

At the same time, integration of loan word definitions is a high priority for future work. A total of 8,406 Coptic lemmas of Greek loanwords, recorded by the DDGLC project (Almond et al., 2013), has just been integrated into our data set in May, and is currently being prepared for release after conversion to the TLA's entry semantics (checking spelling, grammatical information, and recording the source Greek lemmas). We also intend to integrate non-Sahidic vocabulary, compiled by W. P. Funk but as yet unpublished online, in the near future.

A further goal is integrating links for multi-word entries from corpora, and linking units smaller than words for productive derivations and incorporation. This development will require separate evaluation and is expected to increase our coverage of the remaining lexical types from the native Coptic vocabulary.

Acknowledgments

This work was supported by joint funding from the National Endowment for the Humanities Office of Digital Humanities and a bilateral NEH (HG-229371)/ DFG project (273503199). We also thank the Berlin-Brandenburg Academy of Sciences (BBAW), the Göttingen Academy of Sciences and Humanities, and in particular the Digital Edition of the Coptic Old Testament Project, as well as the DDGLC project at Leipzig and Freie Universität in Berlin for their contributions to the lexicon. We thank Sonja Dahlgren, Julien Delhez, Lena Krastel, Tonio Sebastian Richter and Anne Sörgel who contributed to compiling the lexical data and Mitchell Abrams for contributions to the Web interface.

References

Mathew Almond, Joost Hagen, Katrin John, Tonio Sebastian Richter, and Vincent Walter. 2013. Kontaktinduzierter Sprachwandel des Ägyptisch-Koptischen: Lehnwort-Lexikographie im Projekt Database and Dictionary of Greek Loanwords in Coptic (DDGLC). In Ingelore Hafemann, editor, *Perspektiven einer corpusbasierten historischen Linguistik und Philologie*, pages 283–315, Berlin. BBAW.

Pierre Cherix. 2014. *Lexique copte dialecte sahidique*. Pierre Cherix, Geneva.

Walter E. Crum. 2000 [1939]. *A Coptic Dictionary*. Clarendon Press, Oxford.

Frank Feder. 2016. The integration of a Coptic lexicon and text corpus into the Thesaurus Linguae Aegyptiae. In Paola Buzi, Alberto Camplani, and Federico Contardi, editors, *Coptic Society, Literature and Religion from Late Antiquity to Modern Times. Proceedings of the Tenth International Congress of Coptic Studies, Rome, September 17th-22nd, 2012, and Plenary Reports of the Ninth International Congress of Coptic Studies, Cairo, September 15th-19th, 2008*, Orientalia Lovaniensia Analecta 247, pages 1375–1382.

Eitan Grossman. 2013. Greek loanwords in Coptic. In Georgios K. Giannakis, editor, *Encyclopedia of Ancient Greek Language and Linguistics*.

Eitan Grossman. 2014. Transitivity and valency in contact: The case of Coptic. In *47th Annual Meeting of the Societas Linguistica Europaea*, Poznań, Poland.

ISO. 2008. ISO24613:2008: Language resource management - lexical markup framework (LMF).

Thomas Krause and Amir Zeldes. 2016. ANNIS3: A new architecture for generic corpus query and visualization. *Digital Scholarship in the Humanities*, 31(1):118–139.

Bentley Layton. 2011. *A Coptic Grammar*. Porta linguarum orientalium 20. Harrassowitz, Wiesbaden, third edition, revised and expanded edition.

Arietta Papaconstantinou, editor. 2010. *The Multilingual Experience in Egypt, from the Ptolemies to the Abbasids*. Ashgate Publishing, Farnham, Surrey and Burlington, Vermont.

Tonio Sebastian Richter. 2017. Whatever in the Coptic language is not Greek, can wholly be considered Ancient Egyptian: Recent approaches toward an integrated view of the Egyptian-Coptic lexicon. *Journal of the Canadian Society for Coptic Studies*, 9.

Laurent Romary. 2015. TEI and LMF crosswalks. *Journal for Language Technology and Computational Linguistics*, 30:47–70.

Nicholas Routledge, Linda Bird, and Andrew Goodchild. 2002. UML and XML schema. In *Proceedings of the 13th Australasian database conference*, pages 157–166, Melbourne.

Caroline T. Schroeder and Amir Zeldes. 2016. Raiders of the lost corpus. *Digital Humanities Quarterly*, 10(2).

Stephan J. Seidlmayer and Ingelore Hafemann. 2011. *Handbuch zur Benutzung des Thesaurus Linguae Aegyptiae (TLA). Auf der Grundlage der Hilfetexte des Thesaurus Linguae Aegyptiae (TLA)*. BBAW, Berlin.

Jaroslav Černý. 1976. *Coptic Etymological Dictionary*. Cambridge University Press, Cambridge.

Werner Vycichl. 1983. *Dictionnaire étymologique de la langue copte*. Peeters, Leuven.

Wolfhart Westendorf. 2008 [1965–1977]. *Koptisches Handwörterbuch*. Carl Winter, Heidelberg.

Amir Zeldes and Caroline T. Schroeder. 2016. An NLP pipeline for Coptic. In *Proceedings of the 10th ACL SIGHUM Workshop on Language Technology for Cultural Heritage, Social Sciences, and Humanities (LaTeCH2016)*, pages 146–155, Berlin.

Using relative entropy for detection and analysis of periods of diachronic linguistic change

Stefania Degaetano-Ortlieb
Language Science and Technology
Universität des Saarlandes
Saarbrücken, Germany
s.degaetano@mx.uni-saarland.de

Elke Teich
Language Science and Technology
Universität des Saarlandes
Saarbrücken, Germany
e.teich@mx.uni-saarland.de

Abstract

We present a data-driven approach to detect periods of linguistic change and the lexical and grammatical features contributing to change. We focus on the development of scientific English in the late modern period. Our approach is based on relative entropy (Kullback-Leibler Divergence) comparing temporally adjacent periods and sliding over the time line from past to present. Using a diachronic corpus of scientific publications of the Royal Society of London, we show how periods of change reflect the interplay between lexis and grammar, where periods of lexical expansion are typically followed by periods of grammatical consolidation resulting in a balance between expressivity and communicative efficiency. Our method is generic and can be applied to other data sets, languages and time ranges.

1 Introduction

The awareness of the necessity and possibilities of large scale analysis of the temporal dynamics of cultural phenomena has risen considerably in the last two decades or so in a number of scientific disciplines, including literary studies, musicology, biology and marketing research. One common challenge is to determine the periods of change. For example, to detect periods of stylistic change in popular music Mauch et al. (2015) use data-driven methods from bioinformatics based on a set of predefined audio features; or for periodization of prose texts van Hulle and Kestemont (2016) use stylometric methods with selected function words.

Here, we come from the perspective of language and linguistics. Specifically, we are interested in the formation of discourse types and registers. Focusing on scientific writing in the period of late Modern English (1700-1900) — the period in which scientific writing evolved as a distinctive discourse type (Atkinson, 1999; Bazerman, 1988) — we want to test the hypothesis that scientific writing became increasingly specialized, expert-oriented and geared towards communicative efficiency (Halliday, 1988). Linguistic reflexes are expected in vocabulary expansion, notably in the area of terminology, and consolidation in grammatical usage. Therefore, we consider both the lexical and the grammatical level as well as their interplay.

While there is a long tradition in diachronic, corpus-based analysis (see Nevalainen (2006) for an overview), time periods and linguistic features considered are typically predefined, thus introducing possible biases. To avoid this, we have designed a data-driven approach based on the information-theoretic measure of relative entropy by which we can both detect features involved in diachronic linguistic change and discern the time periods change(s) occur(s). Our approach is generic and can be applied to any diachronic data set with any type of linguistic feature.

Following a more detailed presentation of related work (Section 2), we describe our approach in Section 3. In Section 4, we report our results capturing important aspects of change in language use in the scientific domain. Section 5 provides a brief summary of our main results and an outlook on follow-up studies.

Proceedings of Workshop on Computational Linguistics for Cultural Heritage, Social Sciences, Humanities and Literature, pages 22–33
Santa Fe, New Mexico, USA, August 25, 2018.

2 Related work

The traditional linguistic method of describing temporal change in language use is to start with a set of preselected linguistic features and inspect their frequency distributions across predefined time spans (cf. Nevalainen (2006) for an overview in the area of corpus linguistics). While clearly providing interesting and relevant descriptive insights on changing language use, this kind of approach is biased in two regards. First, features are selected on the basis of the human analyst's educated guesses about which linguistic features are subject to change with a view to high-frequency features (e.g. Atkinson (1999), Banks (2008), Biber and Finegan (1989), Biber and Gray (2016), Degaetano-Ortlieb et al. (2014), Fanego (1996), Michel et al. (2011), Moskowich and Crespo (2012), Rissanen et al. (1997), Teich et al. (2016)). Other frequency bands, while potentially relevant, are not considered. Second, the time spans are typically predefined, too. For example, for a period of two to three hundred years under consideration, typically 20 or 50-year periods are selected. This approach may obscure trends present in the data and prevent the exact periodization of a given change or set of changes.

To remedy these drawbacks, more exploratory, data-driven approaches have been argued for. In corpus-linguistics, Gries and Hilpert (2008) propose a specific clustering approach which they apply to the historical development of English. In van Hulle and Kestemont (2016) stylometry methods are applied to the periodization of literary works of Samuel Beckett. Popescu and Strapparava (2013) use a statistical approach for the characterization of epochs. Within the field of computational sociolinguistics, various techniques (such as topic modeling, correlations, regression) are tested for applicability to sociological questions and interpretability of the features involved in variation (see e.g., McFarland et al. (2013), O'Connor et al. (2011), Eisenstein (2018)). A recent strand of data-driven approaches for the analysis of diachronic change applies information-theoretic divergence measures. In particular, the use of relative entropy, implemented as Kullback-Leibler Divergence (KLD) or its symmetrical variant Jensen-Shannon Divergence (JSD) (Kullback and Leibler, 1951), as a measure of changes in the probability distribution over linguistic features has proven effective. For example, Hughes et al. (2012) measure stylistic influence in the evolution of literature and Klingenstein et al. (2014) analyze to what extent the ways of talking in criminal trials differed between violent and nonviolent offenses over time. Or Bochkarev et al. (2014) use KLD to compare change in the frequency distribution of words within one language and a symmetric version to compare changes across languages in the Google Books Corpus. Also working on the Google Books data set, Pechenick et al. (2015) use JSD to assess the corpus' validity for analysis of cultural and linguistic evolution. Furthermore, Fankhauser et al. (2014) demonstrate the applicability of KLD for corpus comparison at large, showing KLD on various corpora (including the Brown corpora), and provide an interactive visualization for exploratory inspection of (degrees of) divergence between corpora as well as the items (here: words) contributing to the divergence. In our own previous work, besides other applications such as intra-textual variation across sections of research articles from biology (Degaetano-Ortlieb and Teich, 2017), we have used KLD to analyze the linguistic development of scientific writing over time considering pre-defined time periods (50 years) and comparison to general English to discern change specific to scientific writing (Degaetano-Ortlieb and Teich, 2016; Degaetano-Ortlieb et al., 2018; Degaetano-Ortlieb and Strötgen, 2018). In particular, we found major changes going on around the period of 1750-1800.

We build on this work and extend the existing approaches by capturing periods of change, i.e. determining when a change occurs rather than a priori setting *specific* periods. Most similar to our approach is the recent study of Barron et al. (2018) on debates held in the French Revolution's first parliament using KLD between sequential speeches considering the notions of novelty (abrupt change), transience (novelty of the past), and resonance (novelty minus transience). While they only employ the aggregated KL divergence, we consider the contribution of individual linguistic features to KL divergence. On this basis, we are able to determine which features are involved in change at different linguistic levels and to inspect how different linguistic levels interact to allow for a balanced information density in (scientific) communication. Thus, our approach addresses the above mentioned drawbacks — predefined periods and preselected features — and provides a generic, exploratory method for periodization combining feature detection and period determination on the basis of one mechanism.

3   Method

3.1   Royal Society Corpus

The data set we use is the Royal Society Corpus (RSC) (Kermes et al., 2016), consisting of the journal publications of the Transactions and Proceedings of the Royal Society of London – the first and longest-running English periodical of scientific writing. The RSC has approx. 32 million running tokens and around 10.000 documents, spanning from 1665 (first publication) to 1869. It is encoded for text type (article, abstract), author, title, date of publication, and time periods (decades, fifty years). Linguistic annotation is provided at the levels of tokens (with normalized and original forms), lemmas, and parts of speech using TreeTagger (Schmid, 1995), achieving 95.1% on normalized word forms (normalization is based on VARD; see Baron and Rayson (2008)). The corpus is hosted by a CLARIN-D repository[1], which provides a free download as a vertical text format (vrt). The RSC provides a well-suited test bed for periodization, as it spans approx. two centuries and there are a number of linguistic studies on some parts of this material (e.g. Biber and Finegan (1997), Atkinson (1999), Banks (2008)). As we detected major changes around the period of 1750-1800 in previous studies (Degaetano-Ortlieb and Teich, 2016; Degaetano-Ortlieb et al., 2018), we select texts from 1700 to 1850 for periodization with a cut off of five occurrences per document to exclude (especially for the older documents) OCR errors and other possible biases. Table 1 lists by decade the number of lemmas and part-of-speech (POS) trigrams used to approximate the lexical and grammatical level, respectively, as well as the number of types of lemmas and POS trigrams.

decade	lemmas	POS trigrams
1700	407,801	2,905
1710	261,143	2,605
1720	283,123	2,578
1730	307,049	2,114
1740	538,567	4,494
1750	626,685	8,725
1760	507,820	9,828
1770	855,618	20,751
1780	827,720	18,562
1790	809,482	23,966
1800	971,271	18,550
1810	808,536	15,766
1820	809,682	17,388
1830	1,567,919	43,794
1840	1,237,025	36,633
types	15,611	1,154

Table 1: Number of lemmas and POS trigrams in the RSC per decade and number of types for each.

3.2   Method of periodization at different linguistic levels

We exemplify our proposed method for periodization with Kullback-Leibler Divergence (KLD) considering two linguistic levels – lexical and grammatical – without preselecting single linguistic features. For the lexical level we use all lemmas (unigrams) occurring at least five times in a document. The grammatical level is captured by sequences of three parts of speech (POS trigrams, e.g. noun-preposition-noun) again with a minimum of five occurrences per document. Trigrams were chosen as shorter sequences tend to not reflect grammatical structures, longer sequences lead to quite sparse data. To further avoid possible POS tagging errors, in the extraction procedure nouns were restricted to a size of >2 characters. Furthermore, we exclude POS trigrams consisting of characters constituting sentence markers (e.g. fullstops, colons), brackets, symbols (e.g. equal signs), and words tagged as foreign words. By looking at lemmas, we capture vocabulary changes and by looking at POS trigrams we capture changes in grammatical use. Note however that any kind of linguistic unit could be used (phoneme, morpheme, word, etc).

---

[1] `https://fedora.clarin-d.uni-saarland.de/rsc`

Relative entropy or Kullback-Leibler Divergence (KLD; Kullback and Leibler (1951)) is a method of comparing probability distributions measuring the number of additional bits needed to encode a given data set A when a (non-optimal) model based on a data set B is used (cf. Equation (1)).

$$D(A||B) = \sum_i p(feature_i|A)log_2\frac{p(feature_i|A)}{p(feature_i|B)} \tag{1}$$

Applied to the comparison of language corpora, KLD gives us an indication of the degree of difference between corpora measured in bits as well as the features that are primarily associated with a difference, i.e. those features that need (relatively) high amounts of additional bits for encoding[2]. In the models we employ, difference in vocabulary size is controlled for by representing the data sets by ngram language models smoothed with Jelinek-Mercer smoothing and lambda 0.05 (cf. Zhai and Lafferty (2004) and Fankhauser et al. (2014)).

To detect periods of change using KLD, we slide over the time line of the corpus to find relative peaks or troughs in relative entropy which are taken to indicate a change. For this we select a starting year (e.g. 1720) and a sliding window (e.g. 2 years). We then use KLD to compare preceding (*pre* period) and subsequent years (*post* period) from the sliding window. Defining the size of the sliding window depends on the data set used. In our case, as publications do not appear yearly in the Proceedings of the Royal Society, we use a minimum of a 2-year sliding window. For other text types, such as news texts, for example, the sliding window could be based on months or even days. The bigger the sliding window based on a particular data set the less fine-grained the observed changes will be. A further parameter to be set is the time range of comparison for *pre* and *post* periods, which again has to be set according to the data set used and the aimed periodization. In our case, we use a period range of 20 and 10 years in which we assume changes to occur. Note that KLD is asymmetric and we are only interested in the direction from *post* to *pre* as we aim to determine periodization from past to present in the development of scientific writing. Thus, we measure divergence only between *post* (after sliding window) and *pre* (before sliding window) as shown in Equation (2).

$$D(post||pre) = \sum_i p(unit_i|post)log_2\frac{p(unit_i|post)}{p(unit_i|pre)} \tag{2}$$

Based on this, we build KLD models for lemmas and POS trigrams to observe divergences at lexical and grammatical levels, respectively. For both linguistic levels, we use all lemmas/POS trigrams for modeling that occur at least five times in a document. For each window, KLD models are created comparing *post* with *pre* periods. For the analysis we use 2-, 5-, and 10-year windows inspecting 10- and 20-year ranges.

Moreover, the individual contribution (discriminative power) of a feature to relative entropy allows us to observe which features are involved in change. The higher the KLD value of a feature (here: lemma or POS trigram), the more discriminative the feature is for the *post* period (see Equation (3)).

$$D_{feature}(post||pre) = p(feature|post)log_2\frac{p(feature|post)}{p(feature|pre)} \tag{3}$$

We then also test if there is a significant difference between the relative frequencies of a feature in the *pre* and *post* periods by an unpaired Welch's t-test (see equation (3) with *var* denoting the variance and n the number of documents in a corpus).

$$t = \frac{mean_{pre} - mean_{post}}{\sqrt{(\frac{var_{pre}}{n_{pre}} + \frac{var_{post}}{n_{post}})}} \tag{4}$$

Thus, for each *post* with *pre* period comparison, we obtain a list of those features that contribute most to the distinction of a *post* period (high KLD value) and which pass the significance test (p-value<0.05).

---

[2]Note that KLD is an asymmetric measure, i.e. there may be a significant difference between a data set A and B when B is used as a basis for encoding but not necessarily when A is used as a basis. Also, the features responsible for a difference may be different ones.

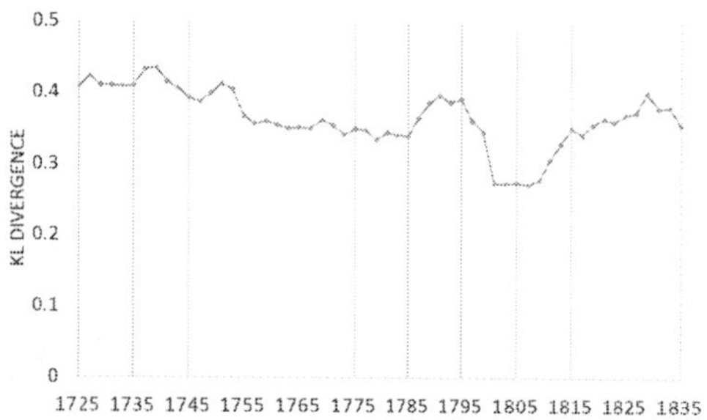
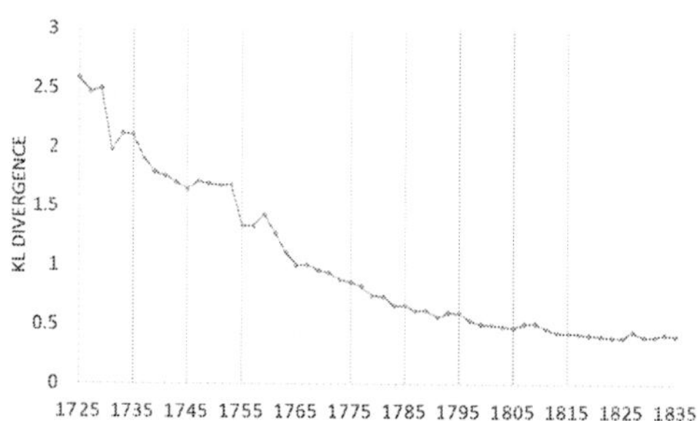

Figure 1: Relative entropy based on KLD for *post* vs. *pre* periods for lemmas (with parameters set at a 2-year window and 20-year period).

Figure 2: Relative entropy based on KLD for *post* vs. *pre* periods for POS trigrams (with parameters set at a 2-year window and 20-year period).

In addition, at the lexical level to select from these lists those lemmas that show the greatest variation in terms of their contribution over time, we calculate the standard deviation of the KLD value of each lemma across all comparisons. At the grammatical level, as the set of possible options is more confined, we consider all discriminative and significant POS trigrams but still rank them by the standard deviation over time.

Given a data set of the features' occurrences across time (e.g. by years, months, days), the periodization procedure is operationalized with the software environment R (R Development Core Team, 2010) with a script allowing to select the window and period range and run the process automatically. The R code will be released upon publication through Github via a link on https://stefaniadegaetano.com/.

4 Change of language use in scientific writing (18th and 19th century)

We present the results of application of the described method on the time period of 1700-1850 of the Royal Society Corpus at the lexical and grammatical levels. The focus is on comparison of *post* periods with *pre* periods, tracing the development of scientific writing over time. For this, we inspect different parameters as described in Section 3.2. For both analyses, we consider (1) overall diachronic trends, (2) when possible changes occur, and (3) which features contribute to changes.

4.1 Overall diachronic trends at the lexical and grammatical level

First, we want to investigate which diachronic trends we can observe over time in scientific writing across different linguistic levels.

At the lexical level, Figure 1 shows KLD values plotted on the time line based on lemmas (with a 2-year window and 20-year slices of *pre* and *post* periods). The general tendency shows peaks and troughs in KLD, i.e. periods of lexical expansion (where a *post* period shows higher KL divergence from a *pre* period) are followed by periods of lexical consolidation (where a *post* period shows lower KL divergence from a *pre* period). We can observe that there are smaller peaks around the 1740s, 1750s, and a major peak around the end of the 18th century followed by a trough in KLD and again an increase in the early 19th century. For example, considering the year 1795 (here: 2-year window (1795-1796)), KL divergence between the 20 years following (*post*) and the 20 years preceding (*pre*) the window is 0.39 bits, while considering 1805 it drops to 0.27 bits. Thus, around 1795 we have a period of lexical expansion, while around 1805 we have a period of consolidation.

Let us now consider the grammatical level approximated by POS trigrams. In Figure 2, we clearly see a declining tendency of KLD at the grammatical level, i.e. over time grammatical usage consolidates in comparison to a more varied usage in the past. Comparing Figure 1 with 2, while at the lexical level we have waves of expansion and consolidation, at the grammatical level there is a strong tendency of consolidation. This tendency becomes even more pronounced from the mid 18th century onwards. The formation of the scientific register and processes of professionalization (Ure, 1982; Biber and Gray, 2011; Halliday, 1988) are presumably reflected here. In fact, from 1751 onwards the Proceedings of the

Royal Society started to have a reviewing process.

In summary, we can deduce that the lexical and grammatical levels play different roles in the development of scientific writing in the RSC. The consolidation of the grammatical level might be a counterbalance to the phases of expansion at the lexical level. In the next sections, we present a detailed account on which lemmas and grammatical structures contribute to periods of change occurring at both levels.

4.2 Lexical contributions to periods of change

In a second step, we investigate which lemmas contribute most to the observed differences by selecting lemmas based on their discriminative power as described in Section 3.2. To consider how different time windows and ranges might impact the results, we will consider windows of 2, 5, and 10 years with 20 and 10 years of *pre* and *post* periods.

Figure 3 shows lemmas contributing to periods of change over time across window sizes (years between a *pre* and *post* period) and ranges (of *pre* and *post* periods compared by KLD)[3]. Across the window sizes, the general trend remains relatively stable, with specific lemmas contributing to periods of change. From around 1725 to 1745 lemmas related to the field of electricity are distinct (light blue: *electricity, electrify, wire*). From the mid 18th century to the beginning of the 19th century a whole field arises that marks the discovery of oxygen (orange) with *air, nitrious, dephlogisticated, gas* marking the beginning of this research field driven by experiments and *oxide, oxygen, hydrogen* marking the terminology building process around the new field. In fact, a landmark paper on the discovery of oxygen by Joseph Priestley in 1774 entitled *Observations on different kinds of air* brought about a series of publications in the Royal Society dedicated to this new strand of research. Towards the mid 19th century biology terms arise (*cell, corpuscule*).

Tuning the period range allows us to inspect the data further (compare Figure 3 (c) and (d), 20-year range vs. 10-year range, respectively). For example, a period of change related to the solar system (purple: *sun, venus, limb, parallax*) is better captured with a smaller range (10 years, Figure 3 (d)). Thus, while some periods of change are more persistent (e.g. the discovery of oxygen) and can thus be captured by using wider ranges (e.g. 20 years), others (such as new observations on the solar system) are more transient and therefore can be better detected by more narrow comparisons of ranges (e.g. 10 years). Also detectable at the 10-year window (see Figure 3 (d)) are variants of use: *oxygen* vs. *oxygene*, where the latter was distinctively used but only for a small period of time (from 1790-1820), while *oxygen* was increasingly used over time and became the standard variant. Thus, this allows us to observe competing forms or lexemes.

A further major change takes place around the end of the 18th century, where besides words related to terminology as discussed so far, the function words *the* and *of*, reflecting the use of nominal phrases, drastically increase their discriminative power for the *post* period as well as the verb *be*, which might reflect here a relational use (such as e.g. X *is* Y).

These diachronic tendencies across the inspected time frame show how at the lexical level, specific terms become typical of a time period marking strands of terminological evolution which can be attributed to groundbreaking events in the world (such as the discovery of oxygen). The rise and fall in discriminative power of function words seems to indicate changes in the use of grammatical structures. To observe whether this is really the case and which grammatical structures are involved in change, we inspect changes at the grammatical level by approximating grammatical structures with POS trigrams.

4.3 Grammatical structures contributing to periods of change

To inspect which POS trigrams have significantly contributed to changes over time, we again plot the individual KLD value of each discriminative POS trigram on the time line (see Figure 4 showing the 5-year window). A major change in the use of discriminative POS trigrams takes place between the 1740s and 1760s. Here, nominal phrase patterns with prepositions (DT NN IN, NN TO DT), coordinating conjunctions (NN CC NN) and possessives (IN NP POS) are discriminative. Both nominal phrase patterns reflect a conventionalized usage of general nouns combined with the prepositions *of* and *to* (e.g. *the end*

---

[3]Selection of 100 distinctive lemmas ranked by standard deviation across time are displayed (see Section 3.2).

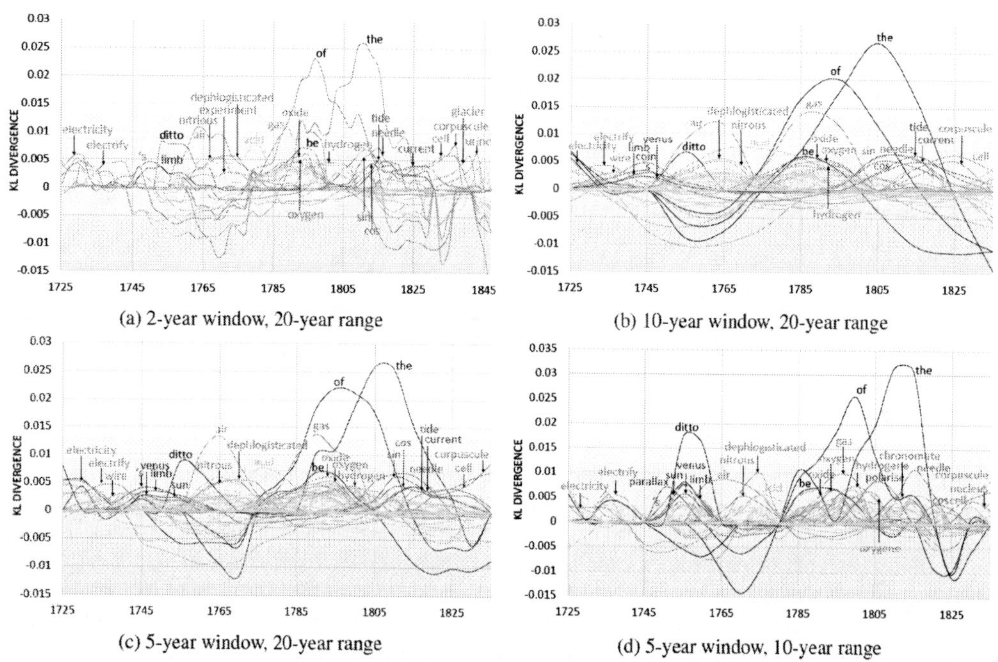

(a) 2-year window, 20-year range   (b) 10-year window, 20-year range

(c) 5-year window, 20-year range   (d) 5-year window, 10-year range

Figure 3: Lemmas contributing to periods of change for different window sizes and period ranges. The higher the KLD value the higher the pattern's contribution to the overall KL divergence. The KLD values are based on comparison between a *post* vs. *pre* period ($D(post||pre)$) to inspect change from past to present. Positive values reflect distinctness for *post*, negative values distinctness for *pre*. Selection of 100 distinctive lemmas ranked by standard deviation across time are displayed.

of, a letter from, the time of for the DT NN IN pattern; *with regard/respect to* for the IN NN TO pattern). The possessive pattern reflects the peaks shown at the lexical level where the *'s* and the lemmas related to the solar system mark a period of change.

After this major period of change, from the 1750s onwards individual patterns become typical that can be related to specific grammatical structures. First, a nominal compound pattern followed by a preposition (NN NN IN) becomes typical around the 1750s (e.g. *zenith distance of, logarithm sine of*), which appears again as distinct after 1810 (e.g. *knife edge of the pendulum*) with a greater variation of use (around 10 vs. 30 instances of at least 5 occurrences). Around the 1760s a comparative pattern arises (VBZ JJR IN; with realizations such as *is greater than, is less than, is more than*).

At the same time a particularly interesting pattern reflecting relational or passive clauses (JJ NN VBZ) is discriminative, used to define specific types of materials such as air, acid, fluid etc. (e.g. *inflammable air is pure phlogiston, dephlogisticated air is only water deprived of phlogiston*) or to explain what these materials are used for (e.g. *nitrous air is mixed with, alkaline air is saturated by*). This pattern is closely related to the beginnings of early modern chemistry marked by the discovery of oxygen as shown at the lexical level. A constant increase of KLD value of this relational pattern might also indicate an increasing need for specification in this new research field (i.e. defining what it is exactly that has been discovered). As the field around oxygen became established, one may think that also the need for this specification pattern may no longer exist. However, in terms of frequency (see Figure 5) it rises steeply from 1760 to 1780, has a period of stagnation between 1780 and 1830, rising again afterwards. Thus, it rises considerably in frequency due to the need to elaborate on the findings of this new research field around chemistry (rising period). This pattern then becomes established in scientific writing (stagnation period). The decline in KLD confirms this tendency: the pattern is no longer discriminative for a *post* vs. *pre* by 1790s, as it is similarly used in both *pre* and *post* slices.

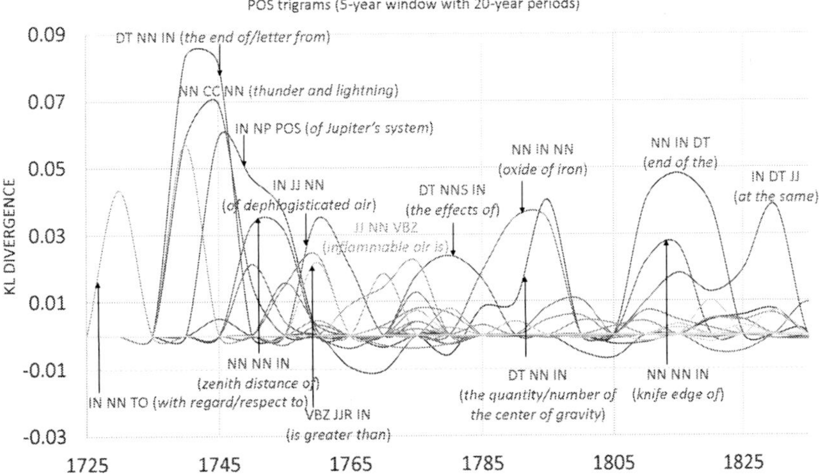

Figure 4: Grammatical structures (approximated by POS trigrams) contributing to periods of change. The higher the KLD value the higher the pattern's contribution to the overall KL divergence. The KLD values are based on comparison between a *post* vs. *pre* period ($D(post\|pre)$) to inspect change from past to present. Positive values reflect distinctness for *post*, negative values distinctness for *pre*. Selection of 100 distinctive lemmas ranked by standard deviation across time are displayed.

Starting around the 1780s longer noun phrases with a plural head (DT NNS IN) become discriminative (such as *the effects/observations/results of*) pointing to scientific outcomes. Around the 1790s and 1800s the terminological pattern 'noun of noun' (NN IN NN) is typical (with realizations such as *centre of gravity, carbonate of lime, phosphate of lime, oxide of iron, sulphate of iron*). If we compare this again with the lexical level (see Figure 3), we can see how after specific terms were established, grammatical structures arise around these terms. This terminological pattern is also reflected in the discriminative power of the preposition *of* at the lexical level (see Figure 3). By considering the level of grammar (approximated here with POS trigrams), we have a clearer picture of the changes that have occurred in terms of grammatical structures.

Starting from the late 1780s, the discriminative power of the nominal pattern DT NN IN rises again, this time not only marking conventionalized usage by particular expressions (such as *the quantity of* or *the number of*) but also terminological usage by terms establishing themselves in that period (such as *the center of gravity, the bulb of the thermometer, the temperature of the air*).

At the beginning of the 19th century, there is again a rise of specific nominal patterns with prepositions (NN IN DT, NN NN IN, IN DT JJ). The first two patterns (NN IN DT and NN NN IN) both reflect longer nominal phrases related to terminology (e.g. *length of the second pendulum, part of the nervous system, knife edge of the pendulum*). The IN DT JJ pattern instead marks a rise of functional expressions pointing to contrast/comparison (e.g. *at the same time, on the other hand*) and elaboration (e.g. *in the same way, in the same manner*).

Comparing our findings to previous accounts on the Proceedings and Transactions of the Royal Society (PTRS), we are clearly in line a.o. with Halliday (1988) and Atkinson (1999), who showed a shift from an involved to an informational style of writing between the 17th and 19th century based on a manual and a multi-dimensional analysis, respectively, reflected in higher nominal style in the later productions. In Degaetano-Ortlieb et al. (2018) we confirm this finding using a data-driven approach. In this paper, we were able to show when particular nominal patterns reflecting informational style become distinctive in comparison to earlier periods and how their use is intertwined with changes occurring at the lexical level. In summary, the diachronic tendencies at the grammatical level, first, show a major period of change around the 1750s marked by a strong contribution of patterns related to conventionalized style of writing

Figure 5: Frequency distribution of the JJ NN VBZ trigram

(*of* and *to* prepositional phrases, conjunctive and possessive phrases). Second, this period is followed by rise of individual lexico-grammatical patterns over time due to needs driven by expansions at the lexical level, on the one hand, and further lexical conventionalization of the patterns, on the other hand. Thus, in comparison to previous work, we are able to detect when and possibly why particular patterns become distinctive showing not only reflections of specialization in the formation of terminology but also of conventionalization in particular lexically confined grammatical patterns.

5   Summary and outlook

We have presented a generic, data-driven approach based on Kullback-Leibler Divergence (KLD) for detecting features involved in diachronic linguistic change and discerning periods of change without pre-selection of features and periods. Our method is illustrated on the Royal Society Corpus, showing which features are involved in change and observing periods of change in scientific writing. The features detected indicate two types of change, *lexical expansion* and *grammatical consolidation*. Note here that while the first type of change relates to low-frequency instances, it is a highly distinctive feature over time — a fact that a traditional frequency-based approach would have missed.

What we can also see from our sample analysis is that changes proceed in waves — a wave of lexical expansion is typically followed or partially paralleled by reduction in grammatical variation, thus indicating the continuous effort to balance expressivity and communicative efficiency. In this way, rational language users make sure that, while language use changes, communication remains successful. Lexis and grammar thus show a nice symbiosis in enhancing expressivity and maintaining communicative efficiency.

In a wider perspective, our research is a contribution to information-theoretic accounts of language use with rational communication as an explanatory framework, adding to it a diachronic perspective (cf. Hume and Mailhot (2013) for related work in phonology). In future work, we plan to look at register-mixed language as a reflection of 'general' language and longer time ranges using the proposed method, going over attested periods of evolution of the English language, starting from Early Modern English to Late Modern English and contemporary English, in order to observe long-term, more persistent grammatical changes. For lexical development, we are currently exploring measures of vocabulary expansion from a paradigmatic perspective on the basis of word embeddings, both for scientific as well as 'general' language (cf. Hamilton et al. (2016), Fankhauser and Kupietz (2017a), and Fankhauser and Kupietz (2017b) for related work).

Acknowledgments

This research is funded by the German Research Foundation (Deutsche Forschungsgemeinschaft) under grants SFB1102: Information Density and Linguistic Encoding (www.sfb1102.uni-saarland.de) and EXC 284: Multimodal Computing and Interaction (www.mmci.uni-saarland.de). We are also indebted to

Stefan Fischer and Jörg Knappen for their contributions to corpus processing and Peter Fankhauser (IdS Mannheim) for support in questions of data analysis and code sharing. Also, we thank the anonymous reviewers for their constructive and valuable comments.

References

Dwight Atkinson. 1999. *Scientific Discourse in Sociohistorical Context: The Philosophical Transactions of the Royal Society of London, 1675-1975*. Erlbaum, New York.

David Banks. 2008. *The Development of Scientific Writing: Linguistic Features and Historical Context*. Equinox, London/Oakville.

Alistair Baron and Paul Rayson. 2008. VARD 2: A Tool for Dealing with Spelling Variation in Historical Corpora. In *Proceedings of the Postgraduate Conference in Corpus Linguistics*, Birmingham, UK.

Alexander T. J. Barron, Jenny Huang, Rebecca L. Spang, and Simon DeDeo. 2018. Individuals, Institutions, and Innovation in the Debates of the French Revolution. *Proceedings of the National Academy of Sciences*, 115(18):4607–4612.

Charles Bazerman. 1988. *Shaping Written Knowledge: The Genre and Activity of the Experimental Article in Science*. University of Wisconsin Press, Wisconsin.

Douglas Biber and Edward Finegan. 1989. Drift and the Evolution of English Style: A History of Three Genres. *Language*, 65(3):487–517.

Douglas Biber and Edward Finegan. 1997. Diachronic Relations among Speech-based and Written Registers in English. In Terttu Nevalainen and Leena Kahlas-Tarkka, editors, *To Explain the Present: Studies in the Changing English Language in Honour of Matti Rissanen*, pages 253–276. Société Néophilologique, Helsinki.

Douglas Biber and Bethany Gray. 2011. The Historical Shift of Scientific Academic Prose in English towards Less Explicit Styles of Expression: Writing without Verbs. In Vijay Bathia, Purificación Sánchez, and Pascual Pérez-Paredes, editors, *Researching Specialized Languages*, pages 11–24. John Benjamins, Amsterdam.

Douglas Biber and Bethany Gray. 2016. *Grammatical Complexity in Academic English: Linguistic Change in Writing*. Studies in English Language. Cambridge University Press, Cambridge, UK.

Vladimir Bochkarev, Valery D. Solovyev, and Soren Wichmann. 2014. Universals versus Historical Contingencies in Lexical Evolution. *Journal of The Royal Society Interface*, 11(101).

Stefania Degaetano-Ortlieb and Jannik Strötgen. 2018. Diachronic variation of temporal expressions in scientific writing through the lens of relative entropy. In Georg Rehm and Thierry Declerck, editors, *Language Technologies for the Challenges of the Digital Age: 27th International Conference, GSCL 2017, Berlin, Germany, September 13-14, 2017, Proceedings*, volume 10713 of *Lecture Notes in Computer Science*, pages 259–275. Springer International Publishing.

Stefania Degaetano-Ortlieb and Elke Teich. 2016. Information-based Modeling of Diachronic Linguistic Change: From Typicality to Productivity. In *Proceedings of the 10th LaTeCH Workshop*, pages 165–173, Berlin. ACL.

Stefania Degaetano-Ortlieb and Elke Teich. 2017. Modeling Intra-textual Variation with Entropy and Surprisal: Topical vs. Stylistic Patterns. In *Proceedings of the Joint LaTeCH and CLfL Workshop*, pages 68–77, Vancouver, Canada. ACL.

Stefania Degaetano-Ortlieb, Peter Fankhauser, Hannah Kermes, Ekaterina Lapshinova-Koltunski, Noam Ordan, and Elke Teich. 2014. Data Mining with Shallow vs. Linguistic Features to Study Diversification of Scientific Registers. In *Proceedings of the 9th edition of the Language Resources and Evaluation Conference (LREC 2014)*, Reykjavik, Iceland. ELRA.

Stefania Degaetano-Ortlieb, Hannah Kermes, Ashraf Khamis, and Elke Teich. 2018. An Information-Theoretic Approach to Modeling Diachronic Change in Scientific English. In Carla Suhr, Terttu Nevalainen, and Irma Taavitsainen, editors, *From Data to Evidence in English Language Research*, Language and Computers. Brill, Leiden.

Jacob Eisenstein, 2018. *The Handbook of Dialectology*, chapter Identifying Regional Dialects in On-Line Social Media, pages 368–383. Number 21. Wiley-Blackwell.

Teresa Fanego. 1996. The Gerund in Early Modern English: Evidence from the Helsinki Corpus. *Folia Linguistica Historica*, 17:97–152.

Peter Fankhauser and Marc Kupietz. 2017a. Visual Correlation for Detecting Patterns in Language Change. In *Visualisierungsprozesse in den Humanities. Linguistische Perspektiven auf Prägungen, Praktiken, Positionen (VisuHu 2017)*, Zürich.

Peter Fankhauser and Marc Kupietz. 2017b. Visualizing Language Change in a Corpus of Contemporary German. In *Proceedings of the Corpus Linguistics International Conference*, Birmingham, UK.

Peter Fankhauser, Jörg Knappen, and Elke Teich. 2014. Exploring and Visualizing Variation in Language Resources. In *Proceedings of the 9th LREC*, pages 4125–4128, Reykjavik, Iceland. ELRA.

Stefan Th. Gries and Martin Hilpert. 2008. The Identification of Stages in Diachronic Data: Variability-based Neighbor Clustering. *Corpora*, 3(1):59–81.

M.A.K. Halliday. 1988. On the Language of Physical Science. In Mohsen Ghadessy, editor, *Registers of Written English: Situational Factors and Linguistic Features*, pages 162–177. Pinter, London.

William L. Hamilton, Jure Leskovec, and Dan Jurafsky. 2016. Cultural Shift or Linguistic Drift? Comparing Two Computational Models of Semantic Change. In *Proceedings of the EMNLP*, Austin, Texas.

James M. Hughes, Nicholas J. Foti, David C. Krakauer, and Daniel N. Rockmore. 2012. Quantitative Patterns of Stylistic Influence in the Evolution of Literature. *Proceedings of the National Academy of Sciences*, 109(20):7682–7686.

Elizabeth Hume and Frédéric Mailhot. 2013. The Role of Entropy and Surprisal in Phonologization and Language Change. In Alan C. L. Yu, editor, *Origins of Sound Change: Approaches to Phonologization*, pages 29–47. Oxford University Press, Oxford.

Hannah Kermes, Stefania Degaetano-Ortlieb, Ashraf Khamis, Jörg Knappen, and Elke Teich. 2016. The Royal Society Corpus: From Uncharted Data to Corpus. In *Proceedings of the 10th LREC*, Portorož, Slovenia. ELRA.

Sara Klingenstein, Tim Hitchcock, and Simon DeDeo. 2014. The Civilizing Process in London's Old Bailey. *Proceedings of the National Academy of Sciences*, 111(26):9419–9424.

Solomon Kullback and Richard A. Leibler. 1951. On Information and Sufficiency. *The Annals of Mathematical Statistics*, 22(1):79–86.

Matthias Mauch, Robert M. MacCallum, Mark Levy, and Armand M. Leroi. 2015. The Evolution of Popular Music: USA 1960–2010. *Royal Society Open Science*, 2(5).

Daniel A. McFarland, Daniel Ramage, Jason Chuang, Jeffrey Heer, Christopher D. Manning, and Daniel Jurafsky. 2013. Differentiating Language Usage through Topic Models. *Poetics - Topic Models and the Cultural Sciences*, 41(6):607–625.

Jean-Baptiste Michel, Yuan Kui Shen, Aviva Presser Aiden, Adrian Veres, Matthew K. Gray, , Joseph P. Pickett, Dale Hoiberg, Dan Clancy, Peter Norvig, Jon Orwant, Steven Pinker, Martin A. Nowak, and Erez Lieberman Aiden. 2011. Quantitative Analysis of Culture Using Millions of Digitized Books. *Science*, 331(6014):176–182.

Isabel Moskowich and Begona Crespo, editors. 2012. *Astronomy Playne and Simple: The Writing of Science between 1700 and 1900*. John Benjamins, Amsterdam/Philadelphia.

Terttu Nevalainen, 2006. *Handbook of the History of English*, chapter Historical Sociolinguistics and Language Change, pages 558–588. Wiley-Blackwell.

Brendan O'Connor, David Bamman, and Noah A. Smith. 2011. Computational Text Analysis for Social Science: Model Assumptions and Complexity. *Proceedings of the Second Workshop on Computational Social Science and Wisdom of the Crowds (NIPS 2011)*.

Eitan Adam Pechenick, Christopher M. Danforth, and Peter Sheridan Dodds. 2015. Characterizing the Google Books Corpus: Strong Limits to Inferences of Socio-Cultural and Linguistic Evolution. *PLOS ONE*, 10(10):1–24, 10.

Octavian Popescu and Carlo Strapparava. 2013. Behind the times: Detecting epoch changes using large corpora. In *International Joint Conference on Natural Language Processing*, pages 347–355, Nagoya, Japan. ACL.

R Development Core Team, 2010. *R: A Language and Environment for Statistical Computing*. R Foundation for Statistical Computing, Vienna, Austria.

Matti Rissanen, Merja Kytö, and Kirsi Heikkonen, editors. 1997. *English in Transition: Corpus-based Studies in Linguistic Variation and Genre Analysis*. Mouton de Gruyter, Berlin.

Helmut Schmid. 1995. Improvements in Part-of-Speech Tagging with an Application to German. In *Proceedings of the ACL SIGDAT-Workshop*, Kyoto, Japan.

Elke Teich, Stefania Degaetano-Ortlieb, Peter Fankhauser, Hannah Kermes, and Ekaterina Lapshinova-Koltunski. 2016. The Linguistic Construal of Disciplinarity: A Data Mining Approach Using Register Features. *Journal of the Association for Information Science and Technology (JASIST)*, 67(7):1668–1678.

Jean Ure. 1982. Introduction: Approaches to the Study of Register Genre. *International Journal of the Sociology of Language*, (35):5–23.

Dirk van Hulle and Mike Kestemont. 2016. Periodizing Samuel Beckett's Works: A Stylochronometric Approach. *Style*, 50(2):172–202.

Chengxiang Zhai and John Lafferty. 2004. A Study of Smoothing Methods for Language Models Applied to Information Retrieval. *ACM Transactions on Information Systems*, 22(2):179–214.

Cliché Expressions in Literary and Genre Novels

Andreas van Cranenburgh
Heinrich Heine University of Düsseldorf
Universitätsstraße 1, 40225 Düsseldorf, Germany
cranenburgh@phil.hhu.de

Abstract

Should writers "avoid clichés like the plague"? Clichés are said to be a prominent characteristic of "low brow" literature, and conversely, a negative marker of "high brow" literature. Clichés may concern the storyline, the characters, or the style of writing. We focus on cliché expressions, ready-made stock phrases which can be taken as a sign of uncreative writing. We present a corpus study in which we examine to what extent cliché expressions can be attested in a corpus of various kinds of contemporary fiction, based on a large, curated lexicon of cliché expressions. The results show to what extent the negative view on clichés is supported by data: we find a significant negative correlation of -0.48 between cliché density and literary ratings of texts. We also investigate interactions with genre and characterize the language of clichés with several basic textual features. Code used for this paper is available at https://github.com/andreasvc/litcliches/

1 Introduction

What makes certain novels *literary*? Insofar as this is ascribed to the text itself, the text is said to exhibit the phenomenon of *literariness*: the hypothesized linguistic and formal properties that distinguish literary language from other language (Baldick, 2008). Others point to the prestige that publishers and critics confer (Bourdieu, 1996). Empirical support for literariness as a textual property is presented by van Cranenburgh and Bod (2017), who present machine learning experiments predicting literary ratings based on a wide range of textual features. This paper zooms in on the contribution of one particular feature, clichéd language.

A direct way to investigate literariness would be to define a way to measure its particular properties such as creative, original use of language. This is the aim of the Formalist tradition, which holds that poetic language distinguishes itself from standard language by the phenomena of foregrounding and defamiliarization (Mukarovsky, 1964). However, these phenomena seem difficult to operationalize computationally, at least without the collection of detailed human judgments. Text analysis can demonstrate how well a large number of textual features (such as bag of word models and syntactic features) predicts literariness, but due to the large number of features, the resulting model is hard to interpret (van Cranenburgh and Bod, 2017). By contrast, unoriginal language use can be readily detected, since it is by definition commonly attested in data. Therefore we opt to investigate clichés as a negative marker of literariness.

Clichés in literature can manifest themselves at various levels such as narrative, style, and characters. We focus on cliché expressions at the sentence level since they are the most amenable to automatic analysis using textual search.

2 Definitions & datasets

We define cliché expressions as follows:

DEFINITION. A *cliché expression* is a fixed, conventionalized multi-word expression which has become overused to the point of losing its original meaning or effect.

Proceedings of Workshop on Computational Linguistics for Cultural Heritage, Social Sciences, Humanities and Literature, pages 34–43
Santa Fe, New Mexico, USA, August 25, 2018.

Let's unpack the main terms in this definition:

FIXED: the expression in the form that is recognized cannot be changed, or only to a limited degree by filling in specified open slots.

CONVENTIONALIZED: i.e., the phrase is recognized by many speakers as a unit, instead of being put together word for word.

OVERUSED: this aspect is crucial but subjective and therefore harder to pin down. Many other multi-word expressions are accepted as a normal part of the lexicon, while cliché expressions are marked as formulaic, tired, unoriginal, etc.

Cook and Hirst (2013) state that "a cliché is a kind of ersatz novelty or creativity that is, *ipso facto*, unwelcome or deprecated by the reader." The term 'overused' might suggest that there is some range of acceptable frequency for expressions, but this limit seems hard to determine; the cliché-hood of an expression rests on a tacit, cultural judgment.

The cliché expressions we focus on are semantically compositional and syntactically regular, without non-literal meaning. However, since they are conventionalized, their use provides evidence that the author did not construct the expression word for word, but took a shortcut by employing a ready-made stock phrase. The occurrence of such expressions may therefore be taken as a negative marker for creativity and originality.

To operationalize the question of cliché-hood we use a cliché lexicon with 6,641 Dutch cliché expressions provided to us. This dataset is the source for a published collection of clichés (van Wingerden and Hendriks, 2015). In collecting this set of expressions, the focus was not on expressions that are established sayings or figures of speech, but rather formulaic commonplaces for mundane situations—language that does not necessarily stand out by itself but is recognizable as clichéd by how typical it is for a particular social situation.

We determine the frequencies of the clichés in a corpus of contemporary novels and relate them to the results of a survey investigating literary evaluations of the novels among the general public. The aim is to see whether the prevalence of cliché expressions offers insights into literary evaluations. For example, to what extent the intuition that less literary texts contain more clichés holds up.

The dataset of novels was the subject of a large online reader survey (about 14k participants), to obtain judgments of literary and general quality. This survey was conducted as part of the project The Riddle of Literary Quality,[1], investigating the textual characteristics of contemporary literature. The 401 recent Dutch novels (as well as works translated into Dutch) were the best selling and most lent books in 2007–2012. The corpus contains literary novels as well as genre novels such as thrillers and romantic novels. The participants were presented with the author and title of each novel, and for novels they had read were asked to provide ratings on a 7-point Likert scale from *definitely not* to *highly* literary. 96 % of the novels have 50 or more ratings. In the following, we use the mean of a novel's ratings as its literary evaluation.

As reference corpora we will also look at Lassy Small and CGN. Lassy Small (Van Noord, 2009) consists of written text (e.g., newswire and and Wikipedia text). CGN (van der Wouden et al., 2002) is a corpus of spoken language.

3 Matching cliché expressions

The process of searching through a corpus for a predefined lexicon of expressions is an instance of Multi-Word Expression (MWE) identification (Kulkarni and Finlayson, 2011; Constant et al., 2017).

We tokenize both the clichés and the novels to obtain a format of one cliché/sentence per line with space-separated tokens. Not all clichés consist of a fixed sequence of words; an informal notation is used allowing for optional and variable elements. In order to work with this notation, we formalize it into regular expressions. The following shows examples of the notation and its translation into regular expressions:

---

[1] Cf. `http://literaryquality.huygens.knaw.nl`

(1) a. Optional phrases: (. . .)
     (Kijk,) dat bedoel ik nou.
     (Look,) that's what I mean.
     `(Kijk , )?dat bedoel ik nou`
  b. Open slots: [. . .]
     Geen [bier] meer voor jou!
     No more [beer] for you!
     `Geen ([-\w+]* ){1,3}meer voor jou`
  c. Variables: X, Y
     Y, zoals X dan zou zeggen.
     Y, as X would say.
     `\w+ , zoals \w+ dan zou zeggen`
  d. Alternatives: A/B
     Daar zit een boek/artikel in!
     That's material for a book/paper!
     `Daar zit een (boek|artikel) in`

The vast majority of cliché expressions in this dataset consist of full sentences (indicated by capitalization and sentence-ending punctuation). To avoid spurious partial matches, expressions with an initial capital either have to occur at the start of a sentence, or at the start of quoted speech: (ˆ|'). Similarly, expressions with sentence-ending punctuation have to end with a form of sentence- or quote-ending punctuation: [.?!'"].[2] To increase recall, leading and trailing interjections are made optional. Accented characters (which can be used for emphasis) are also accepted in unaccented form. Where different forms of pronouns are possible, all alternatives are allowed (e.g., the possessive first personal pronoun *mijn* and its contraction *m'n*).

Some aspects cannot be translated precisely. When the alternatives span multiple words, the scope is not specified, so these have been edited manually. For lack of more specific criteria, and to ensure the regular expressions can be matched efficiently, we allow sequences of 1 to 3 words in open slots. Lastly, some clichés involve mini-dialogues; since we match on a per-sentence basis in the novels, these clichés will never be found.

After translating the clichés to regular expressions we remove duplicates. A handful of expressions are removed because they are too generic and generate too many matches (in these cases their cliché-hood depends on intonation or other contextual factors that cannot be automatically detected with textual matching). The resulting list of 5,771 patterns are counted across the whole corpus. We use Google's RE2 library to match the patterns efficiently using Deterministic Finite-State Automata.

4 Counting clichés in novels

Counting clichés in a corpus of texts results in a document-pattern matrix of occurrence counts. See Table 1 for the most frequent cliché expressions and expressions without any matches.

In order to get a picture of the overall rate of clichés, we sum the counts for all clichés in each novel, and normalize them for a fixed length (10,000 sentences) to get the cliché density of a text. This value is used to compute the correlation with the target value. See Figure 1 for the results. For both the literary ratings and quality there is a significant correlation (see the following section for how the strength of this correlation compares to other textual features). The plots show that most novels with a high number of clichés are non-literary. The highly literary novel *De Buurman* (the neighbor) by Voskuil is the strongest exception to this. This novel contains an exceptionally large proportion of dialogue, and the author is noted for his realistic depiction of arguments. In this case the use of clichés could well be a conscious stylistic choice (contrasting with the characterization of clichés as typically signalling ersatz creativity). On the other hand, novels with few clichés may or may not be literary. In other words, clichés are a

---

[2]A reviewer pointed out that these restrictions may bias the results toward specific authors or genres. In order to rule this out, we ran the experiments without these constraints, such that expressions only have to start and end at word boundaries. This did not have a substantial effect on the rates of clichés for any of the genres.

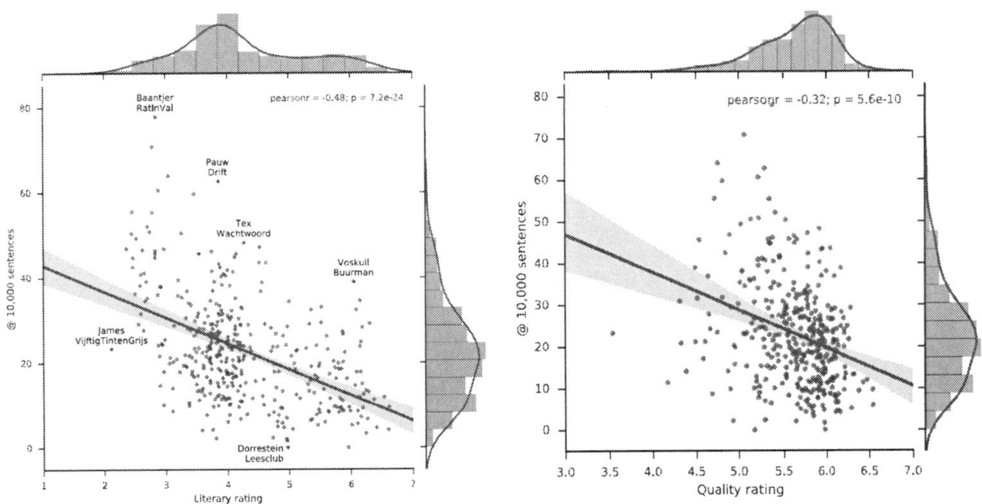

Figure 1: A simple regression of the number of clichés with literary ratings (left) and general quality ratings (right).

(2) a. Weet je het zeker ? (307)
    Are you sure?
  b. Is dat zo ? (245)
    Is that so?
  c. Waar heb je het over ? (231)
    What are you talking about?
  d. Laat maar . (140)
    Forget it.
  e. Is dat alles ? (139)
    Is that all?
  f. Dat meen je niet . (101)
    You can't be serious.
  g. Dat dacht ik al . (101)
    I thought so.

(3) a. Je moet wel kunnen zien dat je op vakantie geweest bent.
    It has to be clearly visible that you went on vacation.
  b. Zit ik in de weg?
    Am I in your way?
  c. Er staat nergens dat het niet mag.
    It doesn't say anywhere that it's not allowed.
  d. Ik voel de bui al hangen.
    I feel the storm is coming.

Table 1: Left: The cliché expressions with highest frequency.
Right: Examples of clichés without matches in any of the novels.

negative marker of literariness. For example, *50 shades of grey*, the least literary novel, has relatively few cliché expressions for novels with a similar rating, and falls below the regression line.

To compare the rate of clichés across genres and domains, Table 2 shows an overview aggregated across the main genres in the corpus and two reference corpora. The genres are derived from publisher-assigned categorizations of the novels. 'Fiction' are novels marketed as literary fiction. 'Other' is a mix of genres that did not fit in the other three and does not form a coherent category. We will therefore focus on analyzing Fiction, Suspense, and Romantic.

Especially the Romantic genre contains a larger number of clichés: twice as much as the Fiction genre. It also has more repetition of clichés than would be expected from the total number: the number of clichés that occur more than once is more than twice that of the Fiction genre. This is also confirmed by the lower type-token ratio—a ratio of 1 indicates that each type of cliché expression occurs only once; i.e., the lower the ratio, the more repetition. The violin plot in Figure 2 illustrates the genre differences and the variation within each genre. Fiction and Suspense, while having a different mean, show a similar distribution, with

	texts	sentences	clichés per 10,000 sents.	clichés per 10,000 sents., freq > 1	cliché type-token ratio
Novels	401	9,658.77	22.49	4.9	0.91
- Fiction	161	7,768.16	18.42	2.95	0.95
- Suspense	185	10,288.5	23.22	5.39	0.89
- Romantic	40	11,047.5	36.09	8.94	0.86
- Other	15	11,607.4	24.93	6.89	0.86
Reference					
- Written	1	52,157	0.38	0	1
- Spoken	1	70,277	9.25	4.41	0.63

Table 2: Overview of cliché occurrences. The rows with novels show the mean.

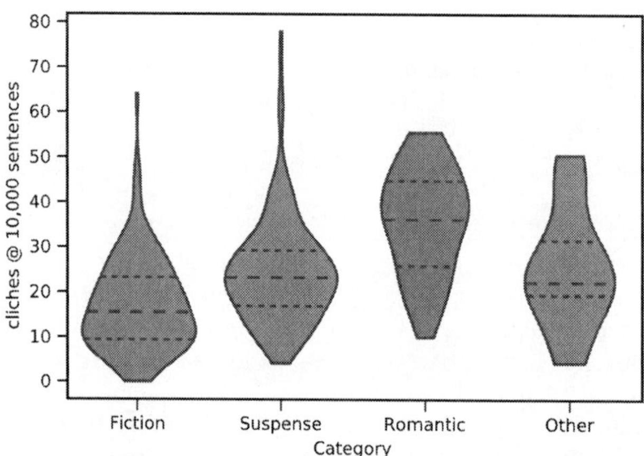

Figure 2: A violin plot of the number of clichés by genre.

outliers of novels that have more clichés (up to 65 and 80, respectively). The Romantic genre has a mean that is skewed closer to its maximum.

The reference corpora contain a much lower rate of clichés, which is probably attributable to their domain and either lack of informal dialogue (Lassy Small), or transcription of disfluencies and punctuation preventing matches (CGN).

5   Baselines features

We now consider simple baseline features, to characterize the language of cliché expressions and to see how clichés compare and relate to simpler features when predicting literary ratings. By simple we mean features that can be extracted from surface features without a trained model, as would be required for e.g., POS tagging, parsing, or named entity resolution. We consider the following four features:

MEAN SENTENCE LENGTH (number of tokens)
COMMON VOCABULARY the percentage of tokens part of the 3000 most common words in a large reference corpus. We use word counts from Sonar 500, a 500 million word corpus part of Lassy Large.
DIRECT SPEECH the percentage of sentences with direct speech punctuation.
COMPRESSION RATIO the number of bytes when the text is compressed divided by the uncompressed size. We use `bzip2` compression with the highest compression setting.

	% direct speech	Comp. ratio	% Common vocab.	mean sent. len.
Cliches	58.4	0.259	96.7	4.29
Novels	34.0	0.314	83.3	12.1
- Fiction	27.7	0.318	82.4	13.4
- Suspense	36.7	0.311	83.7	11.3
- Romantic	42.8	0.311	84.5	11.5
- Other	35.7	0.307	84.0	12.2
Reference				
- Written	14.3	0.373	73.4	9.96
- Spoken	(0.00)*	0.335	81.1	7.62

Table 3: Simple textual features compared across the clichés, novels, and reference corpora. The rows with novels show the mean. *The speech corpus does not transcribe direct speech with quotation marks.

The first two features represent a coarse measure of sentence and word complexity, respectively, similar to traditional readability measures (e.g., Flesch, 1948). If literary novels would be more difficult to read, we would expect a large correlation with these. Direct speech is relevant since most cliché expressions occur in dialogue, which is therefore a potential confounding factor. Compression ratio, by operationalizing repetitiveness, may also act as a proxy for cliché density, similar to the n-gram method we will look at in the next section (although it does not exploit an external reference corpus).

Table 3 compares the textual features for the clichés found in the novels, the novels themselves, and reference corpora. For each type of feature, clichés stand out as having simpler language: they consist almost exclusively of common words, are more repetitive (a lower compression ratio indicates more repetitiveness), and contain shorter sentences. The high percentage of direct speech for clichés indicates that the majority of matched clichés occurred as part of direct speech in the novels where they were found. Compared to the differences between genres, the contrast with clichés is much more dramatic.

These features can also be compared as predictors for the survey ratings; see Table 4. The degree to which a novel is seen as literary is better correlated with the textual features than general quality, as was observed before using clichés. This indicates that this difference between the predictability of literary and quality ratings is not specific to clichés. The simplest feature, sentence length, has the highest correlation, although cliché expressions have a still higher absolute correlation (-0.48 vs. 0.40).

	Ratings		Cliché
	Literary	Quality	density
Cliché density	-0.48*	-0.32*	1
Mean sentence length	0.40*	0.25*	-0.46*
Common vocabulary	-0.31*	-0.17*	-0.48*
Direct speech	-0.38*	-0.03	0.45*
Compression ratio	0.32*	0.05	-0.29*

Table 4: Correlation coefficients for simple textual features against survey ratings and cliché density. * indicates a significant result with $p \ll 0.001$.

Table 4 also shows the correlation coefficients of the number of clichés compared to the simple baseline features. All correlations are significant, and the results are in line with expectations: novels with longer sentences have less clichés, more dialogue and more simple vocabulary is associated with more clichés, and a novel that is more compressible (a low ratio) tends to have more clichés.

Since the simple features are correlated with the number of clichés, these features are not independent (i.e., they are collinear). On the other hand, the fact the clichés have a higher correlation with the literary ratings shows that clichés pick up on more than the above features. This suggests that in addition to the quantity of dialogue, the quality is also relevant, and the number of clichés appears to be a proxy for the latter. Concretely, literary and non-literary authors exhibit a different rate of clichés given the same amount of dialogue—literary authors tend to use less cliché expressions.

It could also be the case that the different genres employ different kinds of clichés. To investigate this, we inspected the top 10 most common clichés for each genre, and contrasted their frequencies. We normalize the frequencies, i.e,. the counts of each cliché are summed for each genre, and divided by the number of books, to obtain the expected frequency per novel in the genre. The clichés occurring in Fiction novels are common across all genres. A few clichés are common in both Suspense and Romantic, but not Fiction:

(4) a. Waar heb je het over?
         What are you talking about?
     b. Is dat zo?
         Is that true?

Only the Romantic genre has several characteristic clichés that are rare in the two other genres:

(5) a. Dat meen je niet!
         You can't be serious!
     b. Dacht ik al.
         I already thought so.
     c. Doe niet zo raar.
         Don't act so strange.
     d. Ik red me wel.
         I can take care of myself.

We conclude that, except for these outliers, the types and frequencies of clichés attested in the different genres are generally comparable.

An interesting question beyond the scope of this paper is whether certain novels may deliberately use clichés for certain parts or characters, as opposed to the clichés being part of the general style of the novel.

6   The n-gram distribution of clichés

Our approach of relying on a list of cliché expressions can be contrasted with Cook and Hirst (2013), who present an automated method of assessing whether a text is clichéd, using n-gram frequencies as a proxy. Their method uses n-gram frequencies from a large reference corpus and does not require an explicit list of cliché expressions. This implies that their method can only confirm a high density of cliché expressions, but not inspect the expressions themselves or analyze the number of types and counts for each expression. We will test their method to see if the results hold up with our cliché lexicon and corpus.

The method of Cook and Hirst (2013) is a corpus-based heuristic for cliché density based on the distribution of n-gram frequencies. We replicate their results on Dutch using n-gram counts from the 700 million word Lassy Large corpus (Van Noord, 2009); only counts of 2 and higher are included. The n-gram counts were extracted using Colibri (van Gompel and van den Bosch, 2016). Note that our reference corpus is significantly smaller than the one used by Cook and Hirst (2013), which consists of 1 trillion words.

We will use this reference corpus to compare three samples of text. The first two are written and spoken text from Lassy small and CGN. The third sample of text is the set of cliché expressions, i.e., a sample with 100 % cliché density. Since the cliché dataset itself consists of templates containing variable and optional elements, we extract n-gram counts from a list of 2457 cliché occurrences as attested in our corpus of novels.

Figure 3 shows a comparison of n-grams from the list of clichés versus samples from the spoken and written reference corpora. The plots are histograms, shown as line plots to facilitate comparison. Each histogram shows the absolute counts in a text sample (y-axis) of all n-gram tokens with a certain log count in the large reference corpus (x-axis). Only counts of 2 and up are shown (i.e., hapax legomena and

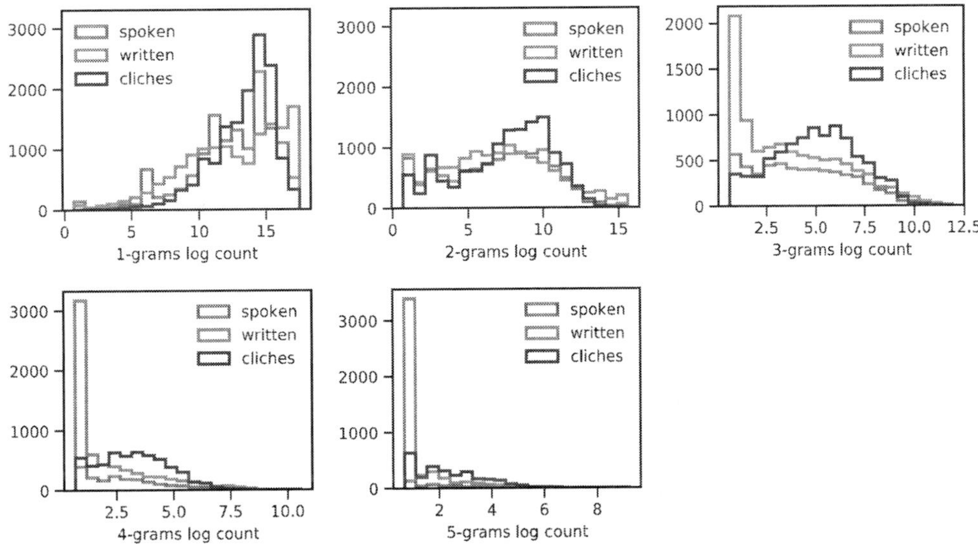

Figure 3: Histogram plots of *n*-gram distributions across several text samples. The x-axis bins the *n*-grams according to their frequency in a large reference corpus; the y-axis compares the absolute counts in several text samples.

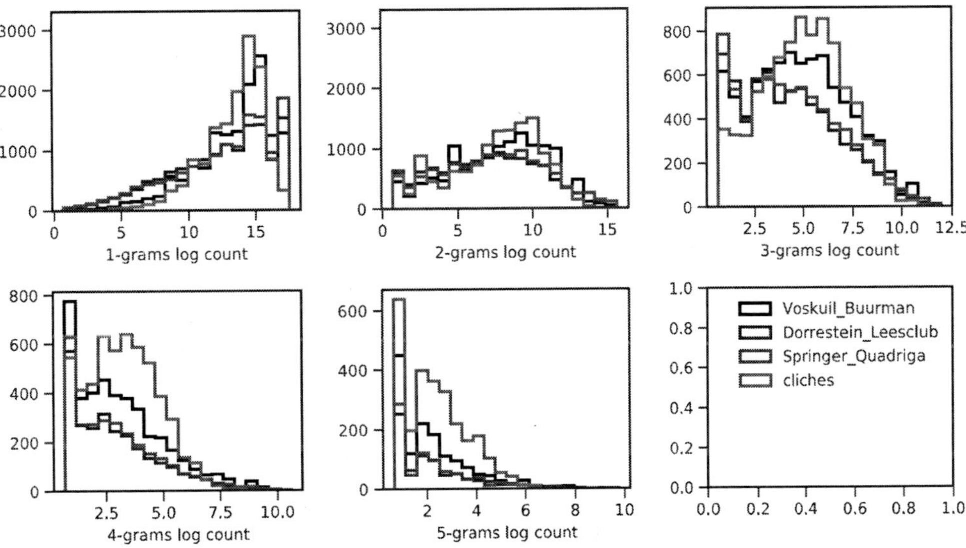

Figure 4: Histogram plots for the log count of *n*-grams in two novels without cliché matches (Dorrestein, Springer), one literary novel with many clichés (Voskuil), and the cliché lexicon.

n-grams not found in the reference corpus are not plotted). Each text sample, written, spoken, and clichés, contains approximately the same number of tokens, to ensure that the *n*-gram counts are comparable.

We observe characteristic peaks for the clichés in the mid to high frequency range, similar to those reported by Cook and Hirst (2013); this is most clearly visible for 2–4 grams. The distributions of the *n*-gram frequencies in the text samples are significantly different according to a Wilcoxon rank sum test ($p \ll 0.001$).

Differences with the graphs of Cook and Hirst (2013) are attributable to the fact that they use a larger corpus, and use only *n*-gram counts of 40 and up, while we use a threshold of 2 on a smaller corpus. Despite the differences clichés do appear to exhibit a readily identifiable frequency profile with *n*-grams s.t. $n > 1$.

Cook and Hirst (2013) argue that the *n*-gram heuristic is better because it is not possible to say whether the sample of 1,988 English clichés at their disposal has sufficient coverage. However, this is a precision-recall trade-off. A manually curated dataset may have limited recall, but will yield higher precision (i.e., will contain fewer false positive). Moreover, the *n*-gram technique cannot be used to detect whether a particular set of clichés is present in a large text, and the clichés cannot be located; the *n*-gram method is therefore coarse grained. Finally, while the *n*-gram distributions can be used as a proxy for detecting clichéd language, it is not clear whether the peaks reflect clichéd language specifically, or perhaps more generally informal and colloquial language.

In Section 4, we found that two novels do not have any matches from the cliché lexicon at all. To confirm that this is not caused by a lack of coverage in the cliché lexicon, we use the *n*-gram distribution method to confirm that these novels do not contain clichéd language. Cf. Figure 4 for the histograms of the two novels without cliché matches, a highly literary novel with many clichés, and the cliché dataset itself. The two novels without cliché matches indeed do not show the characteristic peaks of clichés, while the novel with many clichés has a similar shape as the cliché lexicon.

7   Conclusion

We conducted a large-scale corpus study of cliché expressions in novels and reference texts. We confirmed the intuition that novels judged as more literary tend to use less cliché expressions, and found a relatively robust effect. Clichés predominantly occur as part of dialogue and consist of short sentences with simple language. The cliché density of a text is correlated with several textual features such as sentence length, common words, and amount of dialogue, but the overlap is partial and the density of clichés is a better predictor of literariness than these other textual features. Non-literary genres such as suspense and romantic novels were found to contain more clichés.

The collection of Dutch cliché expressions exhibits a distinctive *n*-gram frequency profile, confirming results of previous research. Individual (unigram) word counts of clichés are unremarkable compared to reference texts, but higher order *n*-grams show a markedly different frequency profile.

Several interesting open questions remain. In general, what makes a particular expression a cliché expression? While we identified some basic characteristics of clichéd language, it would be interesting to try to model clichéhood directly. In the particular case of literariness, it is interesting to dive deeper into specific qualitative aspects, such as in what situations a cliché may be more or less desirable stylistically.

Acknowledgments

We are grateful to Wouter van Wingerden and Pepijn Hendriks for providing us with their dataset of clichés. Kim Jautze collaborated in this research at an earlier stage. Corina Koolen and three anonymous reviewers provided valuable comments. This work is part of The Riddle of Literary Quality, a project supported by the Royal Netherlands Academy of Arts and Sciences through the Computational Humanities Program. In addition, part of the work on this paper was funded by the German Research Foundation DFG (*Deutsche Forschungsgemeinschaft*).

References

Chris Baldick. 2008. Literariness. In *The Oxford Dictionary of Literary Terms*. Oxford University Press, USA.

Pierre Bourdieu. 1996. *The rules of art: Genesis and structure of the literary field*. Stanford University Press.

Mathieu Constant, Gülşen Eryiğit, Johanna Monti, Lonneke van der Plas, Carlos Ramisch, Michael Rosner, and Amalia Todirascu. 2017. Multiword expression processing: A survey. *Computational Linguistics*, 43(4):837–892.

Paul Cook and Graeme Hirst. 2013. Automatically assessing whether a text is clichéd, with applications to literary analysis. In *Proceedings of the 9th Workshop on Multiword Expressions*, pages 52–57.

Andreas van Cranenburgh and Rens Bod. 2017. A data-oriented model of literary language. In *Proceedings of EACL*, pages 1228–1238.

Rudolph Flesch. 1948. A new readability yardstick. *Journal of applied psychology*, 32(3):221.

Maarten van Gompel and Antal van den Bosch. 2016. Efficient n-gram, skipgram and flexgram modelling with Colibri Core. *Journal of Open Research Software*, 4(1):e30.

Nidhi Kulkarni and Mark Alan Finlayson. 2011. jMWE: A java toolkit for detecting multi-word expressions. In *Proceedings of the Workshop on Multiword Expressions: from Parsing and Generation to the Real World*, pages 122–124.

Jan Mukarovsky. 1964. Standard language and poetic language. *A Prague School reader on aesthetics, literary structure, and style*, pages 17–30.

Gertjan Van Noord. 2009. Huge parsed corpora in Lassy. In *Proceedings of TLT7*, Groningen, The Netherlands. LOT.

Wouter van Wingerden and Pepijn Hendriks. 2015. *Dat Hoor Je Mij Niet Zeggen: De allerbeste taalclichés*. Thomas Rap, Amsterdam. Transl.: You didn't hear me say that: The very best linguistic clichés.

Ton van der Wouden, Heleen Hoekstra, Michael Moortgat, Bram Renmans, and Ineke Schuurman. 2002. Syntactic analysis in the spoken Dutch corpus (CGN). In *Proceedings of LREC*, pages 768–773.

Analysis of Rhythmic Phrasing: Feature Engineering vs. Representation Learning for Classifying Readout Poetry

Timo Baumann
Language Technologies Institute
Carnegie Mellon University
Pittsburgh, USA
tbaumann@cs.cmu.edu

Hussein Hussein and **Burkhard Meyer-Sickendiek**
Department of Literary Studies
Free University of Berlin
Berlin, Germany
{hussein,bumesi}@zedat.fu-berlin.de

Abstract

We show how to classify the phrasing of readout poems with the help of machine learning algorithms that use manually engineered features or automatically learnt representations. We investigate modern and postmodern poems from the webpage *lyrikline*, and focus on two exemplary rhythmical patterns in order to detect the rhythmic phrasing: The *Parlando* and the *Variable Foot*. These rhythmical patterns have been compared by using two important theoretical works: The *Generative Theory of Tonal Music* and the *Rhythmic Phrasing in English Verse*. Using both, we focus on a combination of four different features: The grouping structure, the metrical structure, the time-span-variation, and the prolongation in order to detect the rhythmic phrasing in the two rhythmical types. We use manually engineered features based on text-speech alignment and parsing for classification. We also train a neural network to learn its own representation based on text, speech and audio during pauses. The neural network outperforms manual feature engineering, reaching an f-measure of 0.85.

1 Literary Motivation and Introduction

Many theorists of modern poetry claim that accounts of meter touch on only a very limited part of the rhythmic structures and effects of modern and postmodern poems. For this reason, existing tools for the digital analysis of meter in poetry (Metricalizer (Bobenhausen, 2011)) do not capture the whole range of rhythmic features of modern poetry. Mainly the theory of Rhythmic Phrasing in English Verse (RPEV), developed by Richard Cureton, offers a detailed formalization of these rhythmic features, including a set of rules and a number of scanned examples. The RPEV draws heavily on music theory, mainly the *Generative Theory of Tonal Music* (GTTM), conceived by music theorist Fred Lerdahl and linguist Ray Jackendoff (Lerdahl and Jackendoff, 1983). Deeply influenced by Chomsky's generative grammar, they developed a musical grammar based on similar tree structure-style hierarchical organization uniting musical "phrase groupings". Such a grouping distinguishes the notion of phrases as relatively closed, self-contained musical units from that of the articulated phrasing associated with performance. An example of such a group is the *musical phrase*: "the smallest musical unit that conveys a more or less complete musical thought. Phrases vary in length and are terminated at a point of full or partial repose, which is called a cadence." (White, 1976, pp. 43-44).

Richard Cureton's theory on *Rhythmic Phrasing in English Verse* is truly the most important application of GTTM to poetry. This becomes evident in the hierarchical system used in both theories. The GTTM from Lerdahl and Jackendoff is based on four hierarchical systems that shape our musical intuitions: (1) The *Grouping structure* is based on the hierarchical segmentation of the musical piece into motives and phrases. (2) The *Metrical structure* identifies the regular alternation of strong and weak beats at a number of hierarchical levels, differing between the beat and the time span between two beats. Both structures explain the so-called "time-span segmentation". (3) The *Time-span reduction* combines the information gleaned from these metrical and grouping structures. This is illustrated in a tree structure-style hierarchical organization uniting time-spans at all temporal levels. (4) The *Prolongational reduction* provides our "psychological" awareness of tensing and relaxing patterns in a given musical piece: In a strong prolongation, the roots, bass notes, and melodic notes are identical which effects the feeling

Proceedings of Workshop on Computational Linguistics for Cultural Heritage, Social Sciences, Humanities and Literature, pages 44–49
Santa Fe, New Mexico, USA, August 25, 2018.

of continuity and progression, caused by a movement towards relaxation. Following this hierarchical system by Lerdahl and Jackendorff, Richard Cureton has divided the poetic rhythm into three (not four) components: meter, grouping and prolongation (Cureton, 1992, pp. 124). The meter contains the perception of beats in regular patterns, the grouping refers to the linguistic units gathered around a single climax or peak of prominence, and the prolongation refers to the anticipation and overshooting of a goal, the experience of anticipation and arrival, such as the end of a line in an enjambment. Rhythmic prolongation is a matter of connected, goal-oriented motion, for example in the prosodic phrasing of an enjambment, where the line-break is felt as a linear extension of the sentence before the end of the sentence is reached in the next line.

Cureton's rhythm theory involves the interrelationship of these three components within a strictly hierarchical structure. A rhythm consists of a series of local events or units that are perceived as more or less prominent elements within longer events or units, which in turn are perceived as more or less prominent elements within even longer events or units, and so on to the entire poem. The analysis of phrase movements for Cureton involves examining the interaction of grouping and prolongation in a hierarchical organization. Cureton represents grouping hierarchies by a tree diagram (borrowed from linguistics) or an equivalent bracketing around each group. One of the examples he examines at length is a passage from W. C. Williams' poem Paterson. In *Paterson V* (1958) as well as in his late volumes *The Desert Music* (1954), and *Journey to Love* (1955), Williams developed the "triadic line," also known as the *Variable Foot*. It is based on the idea that, despite the different number of syllables per line, all the lines are isochronic, because all lines are based on a similar phrase/clause. In his readings, Williams emphasized the isochronicity of the lines by interrupting each by a regular breathing pause.

1.1 Applying Rhythmic Phrasing to Readout Poetry Analysis

In our research, we analyzed a large number of German poems following this rhythmical type. One example is the following poem of Ernst Jandl – *Beschreibung eines Gedichts* (Jandl, 1982, pp. 129) – which uses the *Variable Foot* and is shown in Figure 1a:

> bei geschlossenen lippen
> ohne bewegung in mund und kehle
> jedes einatmen und ausatmen
> mit dem satz begleiten
> langsam und ohne stimme gedacht
> ich liebe dich
> so daß jedes einziehen
> der luft durch die nase
> sich deckt mit diesem satz
> jedes ausstoßen der luft durch die nase
> das ruhige sich heben
> und senken der brust

Jandl uses the *Variable Foot* and its breath-controlled line, which divides the syntax into a phrase or clause per line. That each line corresponds to exactly one single breath unit, causing a short break – a breathing space – at the end of each line, can be seen in Figure 1a: There is a characteristic gap at the end of the first line.

With regards to similar "phrase groupings" in modern and postmodern poetry, we compared the *Variable Foot* with a distinct but similar pattern, also using a sub-category below the sentence-level, that is a phrase/clause in each line. This second rhythmical pattern is called the *Parlando*, which was also very common in postwar German poetry. It was developed by the German poet Gottfried Benn. The *Parlando* is a prosodic style similar to the litany, using a similar orientation towards everyday speech in order to express the speaker's spontaneous feelings. A prominent example is Benn's poem "Teils-Teils" (Benn, 2006, pp. 317) which is shown in Figure 1b:

> In meinem Elternhaus hingen keine Gainsboroughs
> wurde auch kein Chopin gespielt

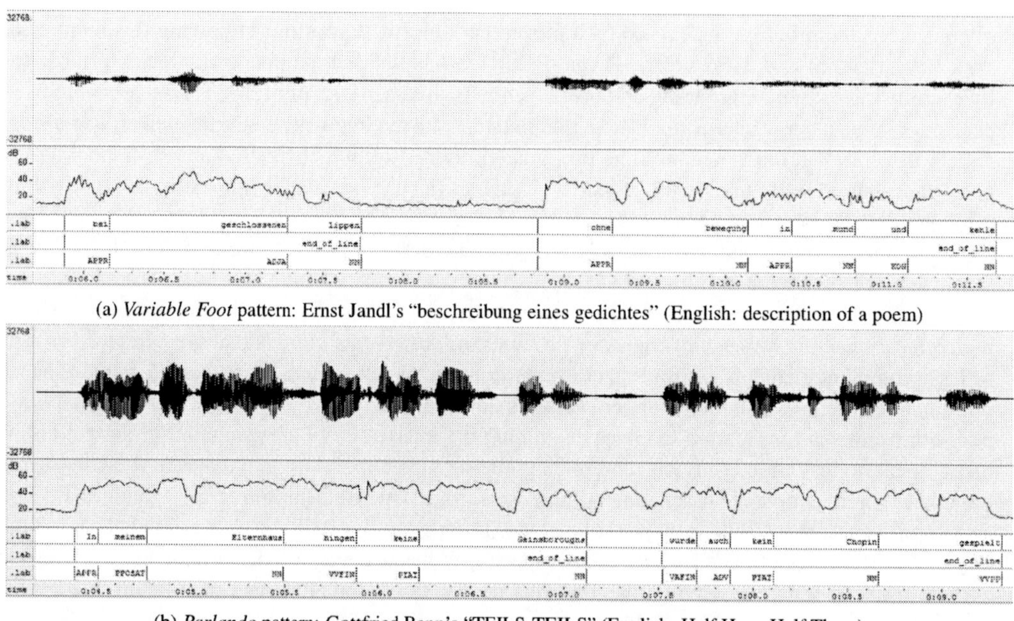

(a) *Variable Foot* pattern: Ernst Jandl's "beschreibung eines gedichtes" (English: description of a poem)

(b) *Parlando* pattern: Gottfried Benn's "TEILS-TEILS" (English: Half Here, Half There)

Figure 1: Two examples of the styles: poem text on the left, visualization of the first two lines on the right.

ganz amusisches Gedankenleben
mein Vater war einmal im Theater gewesen
Anfang des Jahrhunderts
Wildenbruchs »Haubenlerche«
davon zehrten wir
das war alles.

Both patterns – *Variable Foot* and *Parlando* – use a similar line arrangement, based on a colon in each line, as long as nearly each line has an enjambment: However, the *Parlando* makes no use of the breath-controlled line. Both patterns had a strong impact on German poetry beginning in the same period, the 1960s and 1970s. The exemplary analysis is particularly devoted to the GTTM, respectively to RPEV (Cureton, 1992) which is based on the GTTM. The GTTM and the RPEV both offer a very fruitful framework for the manual and digital analysis of these rhythmic patterns and for the specific "tonality" of (post-)modern poems. Given this theory, both poetic patterns use a similar line arrangement and a similar kind of prolongation, caused by the incomplete syntax at the end of nearly each line: the meaning runs over from one poetic line to the next. But in the *Parlando* style the poet does not emphasize the stops at the end of each line, in difference to those poets using the *Variable Foot* pattern. This can be clearly observed when listening to the audio recordings of both patterns.

With regards to the two patterns Cureton offered a new insight by "defining these line-terminal syntactic expectations as mid-level prolongational energies" (Cureton, 1992, pp. 153): Both patterns involve the experience of anticipating a goal at the end of each line, caused by the enjambment and its connection to the second part of the sentence in the following line. So both patterns use prolongation in nearly every line. But only the *Parlando* ignores this prolongation and its enjambment by arriving immediately at the goal in the next line. Only in the *Parlando*, the authors reading includes a time-span reduction.

1.2 Research Question and Hypothesis

We focus on structural similarities between tonality and cadences in music as well as poetic languages by using hermeneutical and computational methods. Our aim is to detect the tonality-like features of rhythmical patterns in a corpus of modern readout poetry and to use such features for classification.

Given that literary theory establishes contrastive features that differentiate the given styles (as outlined above and to be detailed below), we expect that we can automatically extract such features from the poems using language and speech processing tools and use them for classification. We contrast this approach to one where a hierarchical neural network (NN) learns its own representations based on the poetic source (text, speech, and pause between lines), rendering manual feature engineering and extraction unnecessary.

2 Database

In the project *Rhythmicalizer* (www.rhythmicalizer.net), we want to offer a theoretical as well as digital framework for the automatic recognition of rhythmical patterns in modern and postmodern poetry. We use a large collection of modern and postmodern readout poetry taken from our partner *lyrikline* (www.lyrikline.org) which hosts contemporary international poetry as audio files (read by the authors themselves) and texts (original versions & translations). The digital material covers more than $10,800$ poems by more than $1,200$ international poets from 80 different languages. This work investigates only poems written in German. The philological scholar (third author) in our project collected from the website poems written in German that belonged to either of the two patterns based on his experience in literary study and analysis. The total number of poems in this study is 68 from 24 poets (34 poems in each class). To deal with the low amounts of data, we use 10-fold cross-validation in the experiments reported below.

3 Classification Based on Manually Engineered Features

Our manually engineered features make use of a number of speech and text processing tools: We use a text-speech aligner (Baumann et al., 2018b), which implements a variation of the SailAlign algorithm (Katsamanis et al., 2011) to create an alignment of the written poems and spoken recordings in order to extract temporal features, in particular pauses. While overall the alignment coverage of the tool is quite high, we did not check the accuracy of the alignments.

On the textual side, we detected the syntactic features, in particular the words' Part-of-Speech (PoS), in order to identify those poems (*Parlando* and *Variable Foot*) using a "dismemberment of the line"(Berry, 1997, pp. 880) by separating the sentences into a nominal phrase and a verbal phrase. We use the Stanford parser (Rafferty and Manning, 2008) to parse the written text of poems, parsing each line in isolation. Poems are difficult material due to the absence of punctuation, special characters, and unexpected upper-/lowercasing which all introduce errors in the parsing process.

As could be seen in Figure 1, *Variable Foot* introduces longer pauses between lines. Different features including pause and parser information used in the classification process. Three feature sets are utilized: The **pause** feature set contains two features (the the average pause length at the end of each line as well as between words). Based on the parser output, we compute three features (the poem's number of lines, number of lines with a finite verb, and number of lines with punctuation) as the **parser** feature set. The **pause+parser** feature set includes five features which are a combination of pause as well as parser features. We experimented with several classification algorithms (*AdaBoostM1*, *IBk*, *SimpleLogistic*, and *RandomTree*) in the WEKA toolkit (Hall et al., 2009) and settled for *AdaBoostM1* (Freund and Schapire, 1996) which yielded the best results (see (Hussein et al., 2018) for more details).

4 Neural Network-based Representation Learning

We train a neural network that learns to derive and represent features relevant for differentiating the patterns on its own. Inspired by Yang et al. (2016; Tsaptsinos (2017), we build a hierarchical attention network that encodes each line of a poem using a bidirectional recurrent network based on gated recurrent units (Cho et al., 2014) and *inner attention* (Liu et al., 2016). The result for each line is then combined by another bidirectional recurrent layer into a poem representation that is used for the final classification layer. Our model is implemented in *dyNet* (Neubig et al., 2017). Further details on the model are available in (Baumann et al., 2018a).

We use three variants for the input into the network: (a) only the text character sequence of each line, (b) we add acoustics of each line based on MFCCs and encoded similarly to the characters, and (c) we

Table 1: Results (weighted f-measure) for both approaches.

classifier and feature engineering			NN and representation learning		
pause	parser	pause+parser	text	text+speech	text+speech+pause
0.59	0.69	0.62	0.65	0.85	0.85

add acoustics of the *pause* following the line before the next line.

This method only requires a line-by-line text-audio alignment and no further text processing tools. While characters are not informative by themselves, the model is theoretically able to learn textual features such as the ones identified in manual feature engineering based on their character sequences.

5 Results and Discussion

In the *Parlando* subcorpus, we find per average 37 lines, 18 lines with finite verbs, and 25 lines using a punctuation. In the *Variable Foot* subcorpus, the same distribution is 20, 10, and 11. This indicates that the poetic lines in both classes do hardly contain complete sentences and that these poems belong to both classes: *Parlando* and *Variable Foot*. The results of classifying poems as dominated by *Parlando* or *Variable Foot* are presented in Table 1. As can be seen, the classifier using manually engineered features yielded the best results by using only the parser information (f-measure is 0.69) which is unexpected given that pauses identify the *Variable Foot* pattern, according to theory. The classification results indicate that the method based on neural networks outperforms the manually engineered features, in particular when taking speech (and pausing) into account. The NN that uses only text is inferior to manual parsing features. This indicates that the neural network is better able to make use of information contained in the speech audio than can be captured by traditional feature-engineering approaches.

6 Conclusion and Future Work

We presented an experiment for the classification of rhythmical patterns in modern and postmodern poetry by analyzing a corpus of readout poems using machine learning techniques (using manually engineered feature or representation learning). We compared these rhythmical features with rhythmic phrasing in readout poetry and focused on two important rhythmical patterns (*Parlando* and *Variable Foot*). We used different sets of manually engineered features based on pause and parser information for classification. We found that parser features outperform pause features, although the latter should have been favored based on theoretical insight. Furthermore, we find that the feature-less neural networks-based approach outperforms the methods based on manually derived features. This indicates that elaborate feature engineering can be offset by representation learning capabilities of neural networks.

In the future, we hope to understand better the *aspects* of a poem that are encoded in its representation. A total of 18 rhythmical patterns are defined till now by the philological scholar. We want to analyze and classified other rhythmical patterns.

Acknowledgements

The work is funded by the Volkswagen Foundation in the announcement 'Mixed Methods in the humanities? Funding possibilities for the combination and the interaction of qualitative hermeneutical and digital methods'.

References

Timo Baumann, Hussein Hussein, and Burkhard Meyer-Sickendiek. 2018a. Style detection for free verse poetry from text and speech. In *Proceedings of the 27th International Conference on Computational Linguistics (COLING 2018)*, Santa Fe, New-Mexico, USA.

Timo Baumann, Arne Köhn, and Felix Hennig. 2018b. The Spoken Wikipedia Corpus Collection: Harvesting, Alignment and an Application to Hyperlistening. *Language Resources and Evaluation*.

Gottfried Benn. 2006. *Sämtliche Gedichte / Künstlerische Prosa - Band 1*. Klett-Cotta, Stuttgart.

Eleanor Berry. 1997. The Free Verse Spectrum. *College English*, 8(59):873–897.

K. Bobenhausen. 2011. The Metricalizer – Automated Metrical Markup of German Poetry. In C. Küper, editor, *Current Trends in Metrical Analysis*, pages 119—131.

Kyunghyun Cho, Bart van Merrienboer, Caglar Gulcehre, Dzmitry Bahdanau, Fethi Bougares, Holger Schwenk, and Yoshua Bengio. 2014. Learning phrase representations using rnn encoder–decoder for statistical machine translation. In *Proceedings of the 2014 Conference on Empirical Methods in Natural Language Processing (EMNLP)*, pages 1724–1734, Doha, Qatar, October. Association for Computational Linguistics.

R.D. Cureton. 1992. *Rhythmic Phrasing in English Verse*. Longman.

Yoav Freund and Robert E. Schapire. 1996. Experiments with a New Boosting Algorithm. In *Thirteenth International Conference on Machine Learning*, pages 148–156, San Francisco. Morgan Kaufmann.

M. Hall, E. Frank, G. Holmes, B. Pfahringer, P. Reutemann, and I. H. Witten. 2009. The WEKA Data Mining Software: An Update. *SIGKDD Explorations*, 11(1):10–18.

H. Hussein, B. Meyer-Sickendiek, and T. Baumann. 2018. Tonality in Language: The "Generative Theory of Tonal Music" as a Framework for Prosodic Analysis of Poetry. In *Proceedings of the Sixth International Symposium on Tonal Aspects of Languages*, Berlin, Germany, June.

Ernst Jandl. 1982. *der gelbe Hund. Gedichte*. Luchterhand Verlag, Darmstadt und Neuwied.

Athanasios Katsamanis, Matthew Black, Panayiotis G Georgiou, Louis Goldstein, and S Narayanan. 2011. SailAlign: Robust Long Speech-Text Alignment. In *Proc. of Workshop on New Tools and Methods for Very-Large Scale Phonetics Research*.

Fred Lerdahl and Ray Jackendoff. 1983. *A Generative Theory of Tonal Music*. Cambridge, Mass.: MIT Press.

Yang Liu, Chengjie Sun, Lei Lin, and Xiaolong Wang. 2016. Learning natural language inference using bidirectional LSTM model and inner-attention. *CoRR*, abs/1605.09090.

Graham Neubig, Chris Dyer, Yoav Goldberg, Austin Matthews, Waleed Ammar, Antonios Anastasopoulos, Miguel Ballesteros, David Chiang, Daniel Clothiaux, Trevor Cohn, Kevin Duh, Manaal Faruqui, Cynthia Gan, Dan Garrette, Yangfeng Ji, Lingpeng Kong, Adhiguna Kuncoro, Gaurav Kumar, Chaitanya Malaviya, Paul Michel, Yusuke Oda, Matthew Richardson, Naomi Saphra, Swabha Swayamdipta, and Pengcheng Yin. 2017. Dynet: The dynamic neural network toolkit. *arXiv preprint arXiv:1701.03980*.

Anna N. Rafferty and Christopher D. Manning. 2008. Parsing Three German Treebanks: Lexicalized and Unlexicalized Baselines. In *Proceedings of the Workshop on Parsing German*, PaGe '08, pages 40–46, Stroudsburg, PA, USA. Association for Computational Linguistics.

Alexandros Tsaptsinos. 2017. Lyrics-based music genre classification using a hierarchical attention network. In *Proceedings of the 18th International Society for Music Information Retrieval Conference (ISMIR 2017)*, pages 694–701.

John D. White. 1976. *The Analysis of Music*. New York: Prentice-Hall, Inc.,.

Zichao Yang, Diyi Yang, Chris Dyer, Xiaodong He, Alex Smola, and Eduard Hovy. 2016. Hierarchical attention networks for document classification. In *Proceedings of the 2016 Conference of the North American Chapter of the Association for Computational Linguistics: Human Language Technologies*, pages 1480–1489.

Cross-Discourse and Multilingual Exploration of Textual Corpora with the DualNeighbors Algorithm

Taylor Arnold
University of Richmond
Mathematics and Computer Science
28 Westhampton Way
Richmond, VA, USA
tarnold2@richmond.edu

Lauren Tilton
University of Richmond
Rhetoric and Communication Studies
28 Westhampton Way
Richmond, VA, USA
ltilton@richmond.edu

Abstract

Word choice is dependent on the cultural context of writers and their subjects. Different words are used to describe similar actions, objects, and features based on factors such as class, race, gender, geography and political affinity. Exploratory techniques based on locating and counting words may, therefore, lead to conclusions that reinforce culturally inflected boundaries. We offer a new method, the DualNeighbors algorithm, for linking thematically similar documents both within and across discursive and linguistic barriers to reveal cross-cultural connections. Qualitative and quantitative evaluations of this technique are shown as applied to two cultural datasets of interest to researchers across the humanities and social sciences. An open-source implementation of the DualNeighbors algorithm is provided to assist in its application.

1 Introduction

Text analysis is aided by a wide range of tools and techniques for detecting and locating themes and subjects. Key words in context (KWiC), for example, is a method from corpus linguistics for extracting short snippets of text containing a predefined set of words (Luhn, 1960; Gries, 2009). Systems for full text queries have been implemented by institutions such as the Library of Congress, the Social Science Research Network, and the Internet Archive (Cheng). As demonstrated by the centrality of search engines to the internet, word-based search algorithms are powerful tools for locating relevant information within a large body of textual data.

Exploring a collection of materials by searching for words poses a potential issue. Language is known to be highly dependent on the cultural factors that shape both the writer and subject matter. As concisely described by Foucault (1969), "We know perfectly well that we are not free to say just anything, that we cannot simply speak of anything, when we like or where we like; not just anyone, finally, may speak of just anything." Searching through a corpus by words and phrases reveals a particular discourse or sub-theme but can make it challenging to identify a broader picture. Collections with multilingual data pose an extreme form of this challenge, with the potential for important portions of a large corpus to go without notice when using traditional search techniques.

Our works build off of recent research in word embeddings to provide a novel exploratory recommender system that ensures recommendations can cut across discursive and linguistic boundaries. We define two similarity measurements on a corpus: one based on word usage and another based on multilingual word embeddings. For any document in the corpus, our DualNeighbors algorithm returns the nearest neighbors from each of these two similarity measurements. Iteratively following recommendations through the corpus provides a coherent way of understanding structures and patterns within the data.

The remainder of this article is organized as follows. In Section 2 we first give a brief overview of prior work in the field of word embeddings, recommender systems, and multilingual search. We then provide a concise motivation and algorithmic description of the DualNeighbors algorithm in Sections 3 and 4. Next, we qualitatively (Section 5) and quantitatively (Section 6) assess the algorithm as applied

Proceedings of Workshop on Computational Linguistics for Cultural Heritage, Social Sciences, Humanities and Literature, pages 50–59
Santa Fe, New Mexico, USA, August 25, 2018.

English	French	Spanish	Dutch	Korean	Chinese
school	école	escuela	school	학교	中学校
schools	lycée	colegio	middelbare	학교의	小学校
university	collège	bachillerato	jongensschool	학교인	中学
elementary	écoles	preparatoria	schoolonderwijs	고등학교인	学校
preparatory	scolarisé	escuelas	privéschool	예원학교	私立中学
baccalaureate	school	school	meisjesschool	중학교와	女学校
prekindergarten	scolarité	bachilleratos	businessschool	학교는	高等院校
preparatory	élèves	escolar	cadettenschool	학교를	文理学院
highschool	scolarise	preuniversitario	basisschool	학교와	神学校
kindergarten	collèges	preuniversitarios	scholen	학교에는	盲聾學校

Table 1: Nearest neighbors of the English word "school" in a multilingual embedding space.

to (i) a large collection of captions from an iconic archive of American photography, and (ii) a collection of multilingual Twitter news feeds. Finally, we conclude with a brief description of the implementation of our algorithm.

2 Related Work

2.1 Word Embeddings

Given a lexicon of terms L, a word embedding is a function that maps each term into a p-dimensional sequence of numbers (Mikolov et al., 2013b). The embedding implicitly describes relationships between words, with similar terms being projected into similar sequences of numbers (Goldberg and Levy, 2014). Word embeddings are typically derived by placing them as the first layer of a neural network and updating the embeddings by a supervised learning task (Joulin et al., 2017). General purpose embeddings can be constructed by using a generic training task, such as predicting a word as a function of its neighbors, over a large corpus (Mikolov et al., 2013a). These embeddings can be distributed and used as an input to other text processing tasks. For example, the pre-trained fastText embeddings provide 300-dimensional word embeddings for 157 languages (Grave et al., 2018).

While there is meaningful information in the distances between words in an embedding space, there is no particular significance attached to each of its dimensions. Recent work has drawn on this degree of freedom to show that two independently trained word embeddings can be aligned by rotating one embedding to match another. When two embeddings from different languages are aligned, by way of matching a small set of manual translations, it is possible to embed a multilingual lexicon into a common space (Smith et al., 2017). Table 1 shows the nearest word neighbors to the English term 'school' in six different languages. The closest neighbor in each language is an approximate translation of the term; other neighbors include particular types of schools and different word forms of the base term.

2.2 Word Embedding Recommendations

The ability of word embeddings to capture semantic similarities make them an excellent choice for improving query and recommendation systems. The word movers distance of Kusner et al. (2015) uses embeddings to describe a new document similarity metric and Li et al. (2016) uses them to extend topic models to corpora containing very short texts. Works by Ozsoy (2016) and Manotumruksa et al. (2016) utilize word embeddings as additional features within a larger supervised learning task. Others have, rather than using pre-trained word embeddings, developed techniques for learning item embeddings directly from a training corpus (Barkan and Koenigstein, 2016; Vasile et al., 2016; Biswas et al., 2017).

Our approach most closely builds off of the query expansion techniques of Zamani and Croft (2016) and De Boom et al. (2016). In both papers, the words found in the source document are combined with other terms that are close within the embedding space. Similarity metrics are then derived using standard probabilistic and distance-based methods, respectively. Both methods are evaluated by comparing the recommendations to observed user behavior.

2.3 Multilingual Cultural Heritage Data

Indexing and linking multilingual cultural heritage data is an important and active area of research. Much of the prior work on this task has focused on the use of semantic enrichment and linked open data, specifically through named entity recognition (NER). Named entities are often written similarly across languages, making them relatively easy points of reference to link across multilingual datasets (Pappu et al., 2017). De Wilde et al. (2017) recently developed MERCKX, a system for combining NER and DBpedia for the semantic enrichment of multilingual archive records, built off of a multilingual extension of DBpedia Spotlight (Daiber et al., 2013). To the best of our knowledge, multilingual word embeddings have not been previously adapted to the exploration of cultural heritage datasets.

3 Goal and Approach

Our goal is to define an algorithm that takes a starting document within a corpus of texts and recommends a small set of thematically or stylistically similar documents. One can apply this algorithm to a particular text of interest, select one of the recommendations, and then re-apply the algorithm to derive a new set of document suggestions. Following this process iteratively yields a method for exploring and understanding a textual corpus. Ideally, the collection of recommendations should be sufficiently diverse to avoid getting stuck in a particular subset of the corpus.

Our approach to producing document recommendations, the DualNeighbors algorithm, constructs two distinct similarity measurements over the corpus and returns a fixed number of closest neighbors from each similarity method. The first measurement uses a standard TF-IDF (term-frequency, inverse document frequency) matrix along with cosine similarity. We call the nearest neighbors from this set the *word neighbors*; these assure that the recommendations include texts that are very similar and relevant to the starting document. In the second metric we replace terms in the search document by their closest M other terms within a word embedding space. The transformed document is again compared to the rest of the corpus through TF-IDF and cosine similarity. The resulting *embedded neighbors* allow for an increased degree of diversity and connectivity within the set of recommendations. For example, using Table 1, the embedding neighbors for a document using the term "school" could include texts referencing a "university" or "kindergarten".

The DualNeighbors algorithm features two crucial differences compared to other word-embedding based query expansion techniques. Splitting the search explicitly into two types of neighbors allows for a better balance between the connectivity and diversity of the recommended documents. Also, replacing the document with its closest word embeddings, rather than augmenting as other approaches have done, significantly improves the diversity of the recommended documents. Additionally, by varying the number of neighbors displayed by each method, users can manually adjust the balance between diversity and relevance in the results. The effect of these distinctive differences are evaluated in Table 3 and Section 6.

4 The DualNeighbors Algorithm

Here, we provide a precise algorithmic formulation of the DualNeighbors algorithm. We begin with a pre-determined lexicon L of lemmatized word forms. For simplicity of notation we will assume that words are tagged with their language, so that the English word "fruit" and French word "fruit" are distinct. Next, we take a (possibly multilingual) p-dimensional word embedding function, as in Section 2.1. For a fixed neighborhood size M, we can define the neighborhood function as a function f that maps each term in L to a set of new terms in the lexicon by associating each word in L with its M closest (Euclidiean) neighbors. The DualNeighbors algorithm is then given by:

1. **Inputs**: A textual corpus C, document index of interest $\tilde{i}$, a lexicon L, word neighbor function f, and desired number word neighbors N_w and embedded neighbors N_e to return.

2. First, apply tokenization, lemmatization, and part-of-speech tagging models to each element in the input corpus C. Filter the word forms to those found in the set L. Then write the corpus C as

$$C = \{c_i\}_{i=1}^{n}, \quad c_i = \{w_{i,k_i}\}_{k_i}, \quad w_{i,k_i} \in L, \quad 1 \le k_i \le |L| \tag{1}$$

3. For each document i and element j in the lexicon, compute the $n \times |L|$ dimensional binary term frequency matrix Y and TF-IDF matrix X according to

$$Y_{i,j} = \begin{cases} 1, & l_j \in c_i \\ 0, & \text{else} \end{cases} \qquad\qquad X_{i,j} = Y_{i,j} \times \log \frac{n}{\sum_i Y_{i,j}}. \tag{2}$$

4. Simlarly, compute the embedded corpus E as

$$E = \{e_i\}, \quad e_i = \bigcup_{k_i} f(w_{k_i}). \tag{3}$$

Define the the embedded binary term frequency matrix Y^{emb} and TF-IDF matrix X^{emb} as

$$Y_{i,j}^{emb} = \begin{cases} 1, & l_i \in e_i \\ 0, & \text{else} \end{cases} \qquad\qquad X_{i,j}^{emb} = Y_{i,j}^{emb} \times \log \frac{n}{\sum_i Y_{i,j}}. \tag{4}$$

5. Compute the $n \times n$ document similarity matrices S and S^{emb} using cosine similarity, for $i \neq i'$, as

$$S_{i,i'} = X_{i'} X_i^t / \sqrt{X_i^t X_i} \qquad\qquad S_{i,i'}^{emb} = X_{i'}^{emb} X_i^t / \sqrt{X_i^t X_i}, \tag{5}$$

where X_i is the ith row vector of the matrix X and $S_{i,i}$ and $S_{i,i}^{emb}$ are both set to zero.

6. **Output**: The recommended documents associated with document $\tilde{i}$ are given by:

$$\texttt{TopN}\left(N_w, S_{i,\tilde{i}}\right) \bigcup \texttt{TopN}\left(N_e, S_{i,\tilde{i}}^{emb}\right) \tag{6}$$

where $\texttt{TopN}(k, x)$ returns the indices of the largest k values of x.

In practice, we typically start with Step 2 of the algorithm to determine an appropriate lexicon L and cache the similarity matrices S and S^{emb} for the next query. In implementation and examples, the multilingual fastText word embeddings of (Grave et al., 2018) used. Details of the implementation of the algorithm are given in Section 7.

5 Qualitative Evaluation

5.1 FSA-OWI Captions

Our first example applies the DualNeighbors algorithm to a corpus of captions attached to approximately ninety thousand photographs taken between 1935 and 1943 by the U.S. Federal Government through the Farm Security Administration and Office of War Information (Baldwin, 1968). The collection remains one of the most historically important archives of American photography (Trachtenberg, 1990). The majority of captions consist of a short sentence describing the scene captured by the photographer. Photographic captions mostly come from notes taken by individual photographers; the style and lexicon is substantially variable across the corpus.

An example of the connections this method gives are shown in Table 2. For example, the word neighbors of the caption about the farming of carrots consists of other captions related to carrots. The embedding neighbors link to captions describing other vegetables, including pumpkins, cucumbers and turnips. Because of the correlation between crop types and geography, the embedding neighbors allow the search to extend beyond the U.S. South into the Northeast. Similarly, the caption about fiestas (a Spanish term often used to describe events in Hispanic/Latino communities) becomes linked to similar festivals in other locations by way of its embedding neighbors. By also including a set of word neighbors, we additionally see other examples of events within various communities across the Southwestern U.S..

Figure 1 shows the images along with the captions for a particular starting document. In the first row, the word neighbors show depictions of two older African American midwives, one in rural Georgia by

Figure 1: Example visualization of the DualNeighbors algorithm. Item 1 is the starting point, items 2-4 are the first three word neighbors, and 5-8 are the first four embedding neighbors.

Jack Delano in 1941 and another by Marion Post Walcott in 1939. The second row contains captions and images of embedding neighbors. Among these are two Fritz Henle photographs of white nurses training to assist with an appendectomy, taken in New York City in 1943. These show the practice of medicine in the U.S. from two different perspectives. Using only straightforward TF-IDF methods, there would otherwise have been no obvious link between these two groups of images. The two sets were taken over a year apart by different photographers in different cities. None of the key terms in the two captions match each other. It would be difficult for a researcher looking at either photograph to stumble on the other photograph without sifting through tens of thousands of images. The embedding neighbors solves this problem by linking the two related but distinct terms used to describe the scenes. Both rows together reveal the wide scope of the FSA-OWI corpus and the broad mandate given to the photographers. The DualNeighbors algorithm, therefore, illuminates connections that would be hidden by previous word-based search and recommender systems.

5.2 News Twitter Reports

Our second corpus is taken from Twitter, consisting of tweets by news organizations in the year 2017 (Littman et al., 2017). We compare the center-left British daily newspaper *The Guardian* and the center-right daily French newspaper *Le Figaro*. Twenty thousand tweets were randomly selected from each newspaper, after removing retweets and anything whose content was empty after removing hashtags and links. We used a French parser and word embedding to work with the data from *Le Figaro* and an English parser and embedding to process *The Guardian* headlines (Straka et al., 2016).

In Table 2 we see two examples of the word and embedding nearest neighbors. The first tweet shows

Caption	Top-3 Word Neighbors	Top-3 Embedding Neighbors
Grading and bunching **carrots** in the **field**. Yuma County, Arizona	• Bunching **carrots** in the **field**. Yuma County, Arizona • Bunching **carrots**. Imperial County, California • Bunching **carrots**, Edinburg, Texas	• Roadside display of **pumpkins** and **turnips** and other vegetables near Berlin, Connecticut • Hartford, Connecticut... Mrs. Komorosky **picking cucumber**s • Pumpkins and **turnip**s near Berlin, Connecticut
Brownsville, TX. Charro Days **fiesta**. **Children**.	• Brownsville, Texas. Charro Days **fiesta**. • Visitor to Taos **fiesta**, New Mexico • Bingo at **fiesta**, Taos, New Mexico	• **Picnic** lunch at May Day-Health Day festivities... • Spectators at **childrens** races, Labor Day **celebration** ... • Detroit, Michigan. Child in **toddler** go-cart
Imperial Brands **shareholders** revolt over CEO's pay rise	• Evening Standard urged to declare Osborne's job with Uber **shareholder** • Uber **CEO** Travis Kalanick should have gone years ago • £37bn paid to **shareholders** should have been invested	• Bruno Le Maire Wall Street pour attirer les **investisseur**s ... • Pierre Berg : Le Monde perd l'un de ses **actionnaires** • Le pacte d'**actionnaires** de STX France en question
Cannes 2017: Eva Green and Joaquin Phoenix on the **red carpet**	• Five looks to know about from the SAG **red carpet** • Baftas 2017: the best of the **red carpet** fashion • Emmys 2016 fashion: the best looks on the **red carpet**	• Festival de Cannes 2017: Bella Hadid, **rouge** écarlate sur le **tapis** • À New York, **tapis rouge** pour Kermit la grenouille • Sur **tapis rouge**

Table 2: Two FSA-OWI captions and two tweets from the *Guardian* versus *Le Figaro* corpora along with the top-3 word and embedding neighbors.

how the English word "shareholders" is linked both to its closest direct translation ("actionnaires") as well as the more generic "investisseur". In the next example the embedding links the search term to its most direct translation. "Red carpet" becomes "tapis rouge". Once translated, we see that the themes linked to by both newspapers are similar, illustrating the algorithm's ability to traverse linguistic boundaries within a corpus. Joining headlines across these two newspapers, and by extension the longer articles linked to in each tweet, makes it possible to compare the coverage of similar events across national, linguistic, and ideological boundaries. The connections shown in these two examples were only found through the use of the implicit translations given by the multilingual word embeddings as implemented in the DualNeighbors algorithm.

6 Quantitative Evaluation

6.1 Connectivity

We can study the set of recommendations given by our algorithm as a network structure between documents in a corpus. This is useful because there are many established metrics measuring the degree of connectivity within a given network. We will use five metrics to understand the network structure induced by our algorithm: (i) the algebraic connectivity, a measurement of whether the network has any bottlenecks (Fiedler, 1973), (ii) the proportion of document pairs that can be reached using edges, (iii) the average minimum distance between connected pairs of documents, (iv) the distribution of in-degrees, the number of other documents linking into a given document (Even and Tarjan, 1975), and (v) the dis-

	N_w	N_e	FSA-OWI					Twitter				
			λ_2	u.c.	dist	$d^{in}_{0.9}$	$\text{ego}_{0.1}$	λ_2	u.c.	dist	$d^{in}_{0.9}$	$\text{ego}^{(3)}_{0.1}$
	12	0	0.002	25.1%	9.8	27	17	.	57.6%	7.3	25	16
Q. Replacement	11	1	0.011	15.7%	8.4	26	77	0.028	11.1%	7.3	26	84
	10	2	0.023	15.5%	8.1	25	124	0.046	11.0%	7.2	27	110
	9	3	0.038	16.3%	7.9	24	158	0.056	12.2%	7.1	28	129
	8	4	0.047	17.8%	7.8	23	189	0.070	14.6%	7.0	29	134
	7	5	0.056	20.4%	7.8	22	217	0.077	17.0%	7.0	29	139
	6	6	0.061	23.8%	7.8	20	238	0.085	20.6%	7.0	30	137
Q. Expansion	11	1	0.002	26.8%	9.2	26	50	0.028	21.0%	8.2	25	61
	10	2	0.002	31.7%	9.3	25	53	0.024	31.7%	8.9	25	68
	9	3	0.002	35.5%	9.6	24	56	0.020	42.5%	10.2	26	65
	8	4	0.002	40.8%	9.8	22	59	0.010	54.2%	15.8	26	61
	7	5	0.003	47.0%	10.8	21	62	0.013	59.9%	2.3	26	56
	6	6	0.004	52.9%	10.4	20	64	0.014	60.3%	1.5	25	51

Table 3: Connectivity metrics for similarity graphs. All examples relate each item to twelve neighbors, with N_w word neighbors and N_e embedding neighbors. For comparison, we show the results using both query replacement (as described in the DualNeighbors algorithm) and with the query expansion method suggested in the papers discussed in Section 2.2. The metrics give the (undirected) spectral gap λ_2, the proportion of directed pairs of items that are unconnected across directed edges (u.c.), the average distance (dist) between connected pairs of items, the 90th percentile of the in-degree ($d^{in}_{0.9}$), and the 10th percentile of the number of neighbors within three links ($\text{ego}^{(3)}_{0.1}$).

tribution of third-degree ego scores, the number of documents that can be reached by moving along three or fewer edges (Everett and Borgatti, 2005). The algebraic connectivity is defined over an undirected network; the other metrics take the direction of the edge into account.

Table 3 shows the five connectivity metrics for various choices of N_w and N_e. All of the examples use a total of 12 recommendations for consistency. Generally, we see that adding more edges from the (query expansion) word embedding matrix produces a network with a larger algebraic connectivity, lower average distance between document pairs, and larger third-degree ego scores. The distribution of in-degrees becomes increasingly variable, however, as more edges get mapped to a small set of hubs (documents linked to from a very large number of other documents). These two effects combine so that the most connected network using both corpora have 10 edges from word similarities and 2 edges from the word embedding logic. Generally, including at least one word embedding edges makes the network significantly more connected. The hubness of the network slowly becomes an issue as the proportion of embedding edges grows relative to the total number of edges.

To illustrate the importance of using query replacement in the word embedding neighbor function, the table also compares our approach (query replacement) to that of query expansion. That is, what happens if we retain the original term in the embedding neighbor function f, as used in Equation 3, rather than replacing it. Table 3 shows that the query replacement approach of the DualNeighbors algorithm provides a greater degree of connectivity across all five metrics and any number of embedding neighbors N_e. Therefore, this modification serves as an important contribution and distinguishing feature of our approach.

6.2 Relevance

It is far more difficult to quantitatively assess how relevant the recommendations made by our algorithm are to the starting document. The degree to which an item is relevant is subjective. Also, our goal is to find links across the corpus that share thematic similarities but also cut across languages and discourses, so a perfect degree of similarity between recommendations is not necessarily ideal. In order to make a quantitative assessment of relevancy, we constructed a dataset of $3,000$ randomly collected links be-

Pos.	FSA-OWI		Twitter	
	TF-IDF	Emb.	TF-IDF	Emb.
1-3	0.88%	2.66%	6.34%	9.52%
4-8	1.27%	2.54%	9.09%	10.32%
9-12	5.17%	3.16%	9.40%	13.55%

Table 4: Taking a random sample of 3000 links from each corpus, the proportion of links between terms that were hand-coded as 'invalid' organized by corpus, neighbor type, and the position of the link in the list of edges. See Section 6.2 for the methodology used to determine validity.

tween documents from each of our two corpora. We hand-labelled whether or not the link appeared to be 'valid'. This was done according to whether the links between any of the terms used to link the two texts together used the terms in the same word sense. For example, we flagged as an invalid connection a link between the word "scab" used to describe a skin disease and "scab" as a synonym for strikebreaker. While a link being 'valid' does not guarantee that there will be an interesting connection between two documents, it does give a relatively unambiguous way of measuring whether the links found are erroneous or potentially interesting.

The results of our hand-tagged dataset are given in Table 4, with the proportion of invalid links grouped by corpus, edge type, and the position of the edge within the list of possible nearest neighbors. Overall, we see that the proportion of valid embedding neighbors is nearly as high as the word neighbors across both corpora and the number of selected neighbors. This is impressive because there are many more ways that the word embedding neighbors can lead to invalid results. The results of Table 4 illustrate, however, that the embedding neighbors tend to find valid links that use both the source and target words in the same word sense. This is strong evidence that the DualNeighbors algorithm increases the connectivity of the recommendations through meaningful cross-discursive and multilingual links across a corpus.

7 Implementation

To facilitate the usage of our method in the exploration of textual data, we provide an open-source implementation of the algorithm in the R package **cdexplo**.[1] The package takes raw text as an input and produces an interactive website that can be used locally on a user's computer; it therefore requires only minimal knowledge of the R programming language. For example, if a corpus is stored as a CSV file with the text in the first column, we can run the following code to apply the algorithm with N_w equal to 10 and N_e equal to 2:

```
library(cdexplo)
data <- read.csv("input.csv")
anno <- cde_annotate(data)
link <- cde_dual_neigh(anno, nw = 10, ne = 2)
cde_make_page(link, "output_location")
```

The source language and presence of metadata, including possible image URLs, will be automatically determined from the input, but can also be manually specified. The image in Figure 1 is a screen-shot from the output of the package applied to the FSA-OWI caption corpus.

8 Conclusions

We have derived the DualNeighbors algorithm to assist in the exploration of textual datasets. Qualitative and quantitative analyses have illustrated how the algorithm cuts across linguistic boundaries and improves the connectivity of the recommendation algorithm without a significant decrease to the relevancy of the returned results.

Language is impacted by cultural factors surrounding the writer and their subject. Syntactic and lexical choices serve as strong signals of class, race, education, and gender. The ability to connect and transcend the boundaries constructed by language while exploring textural data offers a powerful new

---

[1]The package can be downloaded and installed from https://github.com/statsmaths/cdexplo

approach to the study of cultural datasets. Our open-source implementation assists in the application of the DualNeighbors approach to new corpora. Furthermore, the computed recommendations can be directly adapted as a recommendation algorithm for digital public projects, allowing the exploratory benefits afforded by our technique to be available to a wider audience.

One avenue for extending the DualNeighbors algorithm is to further refine the process of constructing a lexicon and corresponding word embedding. Most of the errors we detected in the experiment in Section 6.2 were the result of proper nouns and noun phrases that do not make sense when embedding each individual word. Recent work has shown that better pre-processing can alleviate some of these difficulties Trask et al. (2015). We also noticed, particularly over the jargon-heavy Twitter news corpus, that many key phrases were missing from our embedding mapping. Research on sub-word Bojanowski et al. (2017) and character level embeddings Santos and Zadrozny (2014); Zhang et al. (2015) could be used to address terms that are outside of the specified lexicon.

Acknowledgements

We thank an anonymous reviewer whose comments suggested an additional motivation for our work. These suggestions have been incorporated into the final version of the paper.

References

Sidney Baldwin. 1968. Poverty and politics; the rise and decline of the farm security administration.

Oren Barkan and Noam Koenigstein. 2016. Item2vec: neural item embedding for collaborative filtering. In *Machine Learning for Signal Processing (MLSP), 2016 IEEE 26th International Workshop on,* pages 1–6. IEEE.

Arijit Biswas, Mukul Bhutani, and Subhajit Sanyal. 2017. Mrnet-product2vec: A multi-task recurrent neural network for product embeddings. In *Joint European Conference on Machine Learning and Knowledge Discovery in Databases,* pages 153–165. Springer.

Piotr Bojanowski, Edouard Grave, Armand Joulin, and Tomas Mikolov. 2017. Enriching word vectors with subword information. *Transactions of the Association for Computational Linguistics,* 5:135–146.

Brenton Cheng. Searching through everything. *Internet Archive Blog,* (26 October 2016).

Joachim Daiber, Max Jakob, Chris Hokamp, and Pablo N Mendes. 2013. Improving efficiency and accuracy in multilingual entity extraction. In *Proceedings of the 9th International Conference on Semantic Systems,* pages 121–124. ACM.

Cedric De Boom, Steven Van Canneyt, Thomas Demeester, and Bart Dhoedt. 2016. Representation learning for very short texts using weighted word embedding aggregation. *Pattern Recognition Letters,* 80:150–156.

Max De Wilde, Simon Hengchen, et al. 2017. Semantic enrichment of a multilingual archive with linked open data. *Digital Humanities Quarterly.*

Shimon Even and R Endre Tarjan. 1975. Network flow and testing graph connectivity. *SIAM journal on computing,* 4(4):507–518.

Martin Everett and Stephen P Borgatti. 2005. Ego network betweenness. *Social networks,* 27(1):31–38.

Miroslav Fiedler. 1973. Algebraic connectivity of graphs. *Czechoslovak mathematical journal,* 23(2):298–305.

Michel Foucault. 1969. *L'archéologie du savoir.* Gallimard, Paris, France.

Yoav Goldberg and Omer Levy. 2014. word2vec explained: Deriving mikolov et al.'s negative-sampling word-embedding method. *arXiv preprint arXiv:1402.3722.*

Edouard Grave, Piotr Bojanowski, Prakhar Gupta, Armand Joulin, and Tomas Mikolov. 2018. Learning word vectors for 157 languages. In *Proceedings of the International Conference on Language Resources and Evaluation (LREC 2018).*

Stefan Th Gries. 2009. *Quantitative corpus linguistics with R: A practical introduction.* Routledge, London, England.

Armand Joulin, Edouard Grave, Piotr Bojanowski, and Tomas Mikolov. 2017. Bag of tricks for efficient text classification. In *Proceedings of the 15th Conference of the European Chapter of the Association for Computational Linguistics: Volume 2, Short Papers*, pages 427–431. Association for Computational Linguistics.

Matt Kusner, Yu Sun, Nicholas Kolkin, and Kilian Weinberger. 2015. From word embeddings to document distances. In *International Conference on Machine Learning*, pages 957–966.

Chenliang Li, Haoran Wang, Zhiqian Zhang, Aixin Sun, and Zongyang Ma. 2016. Topic modeling for short texts with auxiliary word embeddings. In *Proceedings of the 39th International ACM SIGIR conference on Research and Development in Information Retrieval*, pages 165–174. ACM.

Justin Littman, Laura Wrubel, Daniel Kerchner, and Yonah Bromberg Gaber. 2017. News outlet tweet ids.

Hans Peter Luhn. 1960. Key word-in-context index for technical literature (kwic index). *Journal of the Association for Information Science and Technology*, 11(4):288–295.

Jarana Manotumruksa, Craig Macdonald, and Iadh Ounis. 2016. Modelling user preferences using word embeddings for context-aware venue recommendation. *arXiv preprint arXiv:1606.07828*.

Tomas Mikolov, Kai Chen, Greg Corrado, and Jeffrey Dean. 2013a. Efficient estimation of word representations in vector space. *arXiv preprint arXiv:1301.3781*.

Tomas Mikolov, Ilya Sutskever, Kai Chen, Greg S Corrado, and Jeff Dean. 2013b. Distributed representations of words and phrases and their compositionality. In *Advances in neural information processing systems*, pages 3111–3119.

Makbule Gulcin Ozsoy. 2016. From word embeddings to item recommendation. *arXiv preprint arXiv:1601.01356*.

Aasish Pappu, Roi Blanco, Yashar Mehdad, Amanda Stent, and Kapil Thadani. 2017. Lightweight multilingual entity extraction and linking. In *Proceedings of the Tenth ACM International Conference on Web Search and Data Mining*, pages 365–374. ACM.

Cicero D Santos and Bianca Zadrozny. 2014. Learning character-level representations for part-of-speech tagging. In *Proceedings of the 31st International Conference on Machine Learning (ICML-14)*, pages 1818–1826.

Samuel L Smith, David HP Turban, Steven Hamblin, and Nils Y Hammerla. 2017. Offline bilingual word vectors, orthogonal transformations and the inverted softmax. *arXiv preprint arXiv:1702.03859*.

Milan Straka, Jan Hajic, and Jana Straková. 2016. Udpipe: Trainable pipeline for processing conll-u files performing tokenization, morphological analysis, pos tagging and parsing. In *LREC*.

Alan Trachtenberg. 1990. *Reading American Photographs: Images as History-Mathew Brady to Walker Evans.* Macmillan, London, England.

Andrew Trask, Phil Michalak, and John Liu. 2015. sense2vec-a fast and accurate method for word sense disambiguation in neural word embeddings. *arXiv preprint arXiv:1511.06388*.

Flavian Vasile, Elena Smirnova, and Alexis Conneau. 2016. Meta-prod2vec: Product embeddings using side-information for recommendation. In *Proceedings of the 10th ACM Conference on Recommender Systems*, pages 225–232. ACM.

Hamed Zamani and W Bruce Croft. 2016. Estimating embedding vectors for queries. In *Proceedings of the 2016 ACM International Conference on the Theory of Information Retrieval*, pages 123–132. ACM.

Xiang Zhang, Junbo Zhao, and Yann LeCun. 2015. Character-level convolutional networks for text classification. In *Advances in neural information processing systems*, pages 649–657.

The Historical Significance of Textual Distances

Ted Underwood
School of Information Sciences and Department of English
University of Illinois, Urbana-Champaign
`tunder@illinois.edu`

Abstract

Measuring similarity is a basic task in information retrieval, and now often a building-block for more complex arguments about cultural change. But do measures of textual similarity and distance really correspond to evidence about cultural proximity and differentiation? To explore that question empirically, this paper compares textual and social measures of the similarities between genres of English-language fiction. Existing measures of textual similarity (cosine similarity on tf-idf vectors or topic vectors) are also compared to new strategies that strive to anchor textual measurement in a social context.

1 Introduction

Computational methods appeal to humanists partly because they promise to shed light on long-standing questions about the pace and direction of historical change. One popular approach to this topic begins by measuring the similarities between documents (or document parts). Researchers then interpret textual similarity as evidence of social continuity, and textual distance as evidence of change.

Distance has been measured in a range of ways. Researchers often topic model their corpus first—hoping, perhaps, to produce a measure of distance fitted to the patterns of a specific corpus. Once texts are translated into topic vectors, the vectors may be compared using cosine similarity or KL divergence. These methods have recently been used to make arguments about literary and political influence (Jockers, 2013; Barron et al., 2018) and about the pace of change in popular music (Mauch et al., 2015).

The key link in these arguments is the premise that measurements of textual (or acoustic) distance can be used as a proxy for human judgments about social difference. The assumption is not baseless: researchers have shown that simple textual models can detect cultural categories like genre (Kessler et al., 1997; Kim et al., 2017). So we do know that social differences leave a textual trace. But the converse proposition is less well supported: we don't know that all textual differences will be relevant to a given cultural or political question. The rise of contractions in the 18th century, for instance, is not usually considered a revolution in English literature.

To make its historical significance clearer, textual distance could be measured in relation to specific reference points that define a space of socially meaningful variation. This is easy to achieve when researchers are interested in a single category. To measure divergence from a particular paradigm of science fiction, for instance, researchers can just train a model of the genre using novels that 1950s reviewers labeled "science fiction." If the model is accurate, we know it has defined a space of textual differences that mattered in relation to one point of reference.

But in practice, historians are often more interested in changes that transform the reference points themselves. Genres are not stable. A scholar might wonder, for instance, whether fantasy and science fiction are more distinct today than they were before *The Lord of the Rings*. Since questions of this kind involve the relative positions of multiple generic reference points, it is not immediately obvious how they would be solved with a supervised model. Instead, scholars have to fall back on generalized distance measures, hoping that those measures will roughly correspond to socially meaningful differences.

Proceedings of Workshop on Computational Linguistics for Cultural Heritage, Social Sciences, Humanities and Literature, pages 60–69
Santa Fe, New Mexico, USA, August 25, 2018.

This paper aims to test that assumption. How rough is the "rough correspondence" between textual similarity and social proximity? The paper will:

1. Introduce evidence about the social proximity of genres in nineteenth- and twentieth-century fiction.

2. Use that evidence to ask whether prevailing measures of textual distance correspond to anything outside the text.

3. And finally, introduce new measures of distance that rely on the triangulation of multiple social reference points instead of generalized comparisons between text vectors.

To avoid misunderstanding: the "distances" discussed here will be statistical distances, but not often distance metrics in a strict sense (Cha, 2007). They may not, for instance, be limited to positive values.

2 Data

The underlying data for this paper comes from HathiTrust Digital Library, which contains more than 16 million volumes. Using a mixture of metadata and predictive modeling, we identified 210,305 of those volumes as English-language fiction. Over the course of the past century or so, those books were assigned to subject and genre categories by librarians, using a controlled vocabulary maintained by the Library of Congress. But the controlled vocabulary governing categorization has changed enormously over the last century.

2.1 Mutability of genre categories

Computational methods are often tested on a limited context—say, newsgroups in the 1990s—where categories can be treated as stable. But in many domains that interest historians, this is not true.

The categorization of fiction is a good example. This article will measure the textual differences between "genres." But the concept of genre lacks a consensus definition. Linguists like Biber and Conrad (2009) may describe genres by enumerating the "expected textual conventions" that define them (144). But sociologists often bracket textual content, in order to understand genres simply as "sets of artworks classified together on the basis of perceived similarities" (DiMaggio, 1987). The social act of classification itself is foregrounded, and the hypothesis that those classifications are founded on real formal characteristics is left as a conjecture.

Both approaches to genre have validity; a researcher needn't make a final decision between them. But it is important to recognize that genre is a multifaceted concept that has been used differently in different communities. This slipperiness only increases as we move back in time. In fact, it has not always been clear that the category of genre should be central to the classification of books. By the late 19th century, "subject headings" had become common in libraries (Stone, 2000). But it took longer for librarians to start categorizing books by genre. At first, genres were often treated as subjects (Miller, 2000). Instead of describing works of early-20th-century fiction as *examples* of "Historical fiction" or "Love stories," for instance, catalogers described them as books *about* "History" or "Man-woman relationships"—as if they were nonfiction. In the past thirty years, catalogers have applied genre labels to fiction more consistently, but books cataloged earlier usually still have subject headings rather than genre labels. Audience designations ("Juvenile fiction") and forms ("Short stories") are also still promiscuously mixed with genre categories.

In short, genres are typical of the categories that interest humanists: they are tangled up with time, for reasons that have as much to do with the history of observers as with the history of the object. A fuller history of genre might draw on a wider range of sources—publishers, for instance, and book reviewers. But the underlying challenge would remain the same: different observers have divided the world of fiction in different ways. We may strongly suspect that novels under the subject heading "Detectives" will resemble those later assigned to the genre category "Mystery fiction." But this is an empirical question about the continuity of social practices.

2.2 Social proximity

One way to test the affinities of genres is to measure the overlap between categories in the library itself. Books can carry multiple tags for genre and subject; if certain tags tend to be assigned to the same books, we might infer that those pairs of categories are related in practice. A loosely similar approach is adopted in Wu et al. (2010). Digital libraries provide plenty of overlapping categories, because they often include multiple copies of a book, cataloged in different libraries. After deduplication, the 210,305 volumes we began with boil down to 138,164 distinct titles, each of which might carry tags assigned by several different hands.

To quantify the tendency to overlap, we calculated pointwise mutual information for every combination of categories a and b. PMI is often used to measure the strength of collocations. In this context, however, it potentially overlooks the problem that categories may have disjoint chronological distributions. If the subject category "History" was only assigned before 1980, and then got replaced by the genre category "Historical fiction," the two categories might rarely coincide, and appear unrelated.

We addressed this problem in several ways. First, we calculated the probabilities that are components of PMI only *within* a random sample t of volumes selected to have the same chronological distribution as $a \cup b$. We also added a small constant (0.1) to the counts of (a, b) for Laplace smoothing, since the distance from a count of zero to a count of one can be very large in sparse data. The net effect of these changes was to increase PMI for chronologically disjoint categories.

$$pmi(a; b) = log \frac{p(a, b|t)}{p(a|t)p(b|t)} \tag{1}$$

Finally, we supplemented empirical evidence with strong priors about pairs of categories where a genre term and a subject term were identical or closely related. (We expect the subject heading "Horror," for instance, to be closely related to the genre category "Horror.")

Even after this adjustment, there are reasons to doubt that we can capture all the relations between genres by measuring the intersection of categories in a library. Two genres in themselves very different might happen to hybridize a lot, producing anomalously high PMI. Moreover, collisions between genres are sparse: in 223 of 496 comparisons, there was no overlap at all between a and b.

So PMI based on library metadata should not be taken as ground truth about the real relations between genres. No single oracle can be trusted on that question. Rather, we have many different ways to compare genres, and we want to inquire about the degree of correlation between them. The advantage of a measure based on cataloging practices is simply that it doesn't rely directly on the text; it thus gives us a yardstick plausibly independent from the textual measures we want to evaluate.

2.3 Textual evidence

While social proximity was calculated using the entire set of 138,164 titles, textual distances were calculated for a smaller sample, balanced so we would have the same number of examples of each category. We selected twenty genre categories and twelve subject headings, for a total of 32 categories. For each category, we randomly drew 100 volumes as a primary sample.

Because genre categories intersect, it often happened that some volumes randomly selected as "War fiction" also carried the tag "Love stories." The intersection of genres is a real social fact, and researchers shouldn't ignore it. But because our measure of social proximity was explicitly based on the size of this intersection, we didn't want textual comparisons to be dominated by the same factor: in that case, we might no longer have two independent measures of similarity. To permit comparison between strictly non-overlapping samples, we selected supplementary groups of books tagged (for instance) "War-Not-Love" and "Love-Not-War," which could be used to replace books carrying both tags.

We also selected two completely random samples of fiction to be used as contrast sets in predictive modeling. Adding together all of these samples, we had 6846 volumes of fiction.

Word frequencies for all these books (even for books under copyright) are publicly available from HathiTrust Research Center (Capitanu et al., 2016). Because works of fiction sometimes begin with nonfiction introductions, we ignored the first 10% and last 5% of pages in each volume. A few categories of individually rare tokens were consolidated into a single collective feature: for instance, all Arabic numbers became "#arabicnumber."

3 Methods

We evaluated three different measures of the textual distance between genres, looking in each case at the correlation with social evidence of genre proximity.

3.1 Tf-idf vectors

One well-established measure of the distance between documents multiplies the frequency of each term by its inverse document frequency (Jones, 1972). Distance is usually measured by taking the cosine between the vectors thereby constructed.

We adapted this to make comparisons between genres by summing the term frequencies of all 100 volumes in the primary sample for each genre to produce a collective term-frequency vector. The top 10,000 words, by document frequency, were considered.

3.2 Topic vectors

It has recently become more common for researchers to estimate cultural change by topic modeling a corpus and comparing topic vectors (Jockers, 2013; Barron et al., 2018). This is in part simply a dimension-reduction strategy, but researchers may also hope that topic vectors will produce a more significant measure of distance. However, it is not entirely clear what kind of significance is being maximized. The generative logic of LDA doesn't in itself guarantee that topics will be optimal for any particular discriminative task (Lacoste-Julien et al., 2009). Social evidence about genre similarity allows us to ask how much is really added by the topic modeling step.

We used the scikit-learn implementation of Latent Dirichlet Allocation (Pedregosa et al., 2011). Removing a standard list of English stopwords gave us a lexicon of 28,443 words. A model with 100 topics was selected. Topic vectors were then constructed in several different ways:

1. A naïve approach simply summed the topic vectors for the 100 volumes in the primary sample for each genre; this was analogous to the construction of tf-idf vectors, although it tended to weight books more evenly (where the tf-idf method had given more weight to longer volumes).

2. To more carefully ensure that our measure of similarity was not defined by the size of the intersection between genres, we also made comparisons between the symmetric differences of genre sets. This required constructing a different topic vector for each comparison. For instance, we had to exclude volumes bearing the tag "War fiction" when "Love stories" were compared to that genre, but then exclude a different set of books when "Love stories" were compared to "Bildungsromans."

3. We also constructed a third set of genre vectors where the topic vector for each volume was first centered by subtracting the running average vector for its position on the timeline. This allowed us to factor out differences produced purely by chronology, and compare genres in terms of their *difference* from the prevailing norm in each period.

3.3 Comparing the predictions of supervised models

So far we have envisioned cultural "distances" as comparisons between vectors in a single shared space. The angle between "Bildungsromans" and "Short stories" may differ from the angle between "Bildungsromans" and "Juvenile fiction," but both comparisons are made in a space defined by the same set of features (whether topics or words). However, the assumption of a shared space might not be justified. The features that distinguish novels from short stories could simply stop mattering when we turn to the orthogonal contrast between adult and juvenile audiences. One way to acknowledge this is to train a different supervised model for each genre. By assigning different weights to features, supervised models acknowledge that distances are measured, not just in different directions, but in different spaces.

Predictive models could be used to measure distance in several ways. One approach would train a separate model to distinguish each pair of categories, and interpret accuracy (or AUC) as a form of

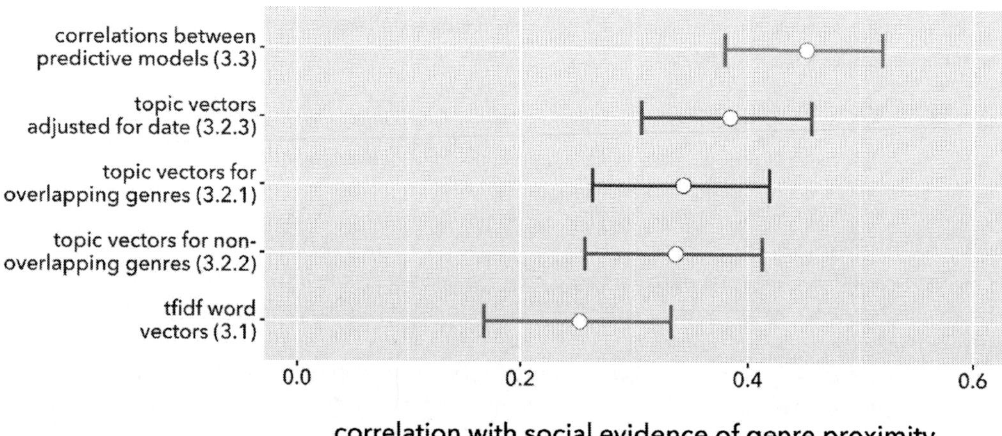

Figure 1: Pearson correlation between textual similarity and evidence of social proximity. Error bars cover a 95% confidence interval (Zuo, 2018; Wickham, 2009).

distance. But this approach has several disadvantages. Accuracy and social differentiation seem unlikely to have a linear relationship: it could be much harder to go from 90% to 95% accuracy than from 50% to 55%. Also, a direct comparison between categories would make it difficult to factor out confounding variables, as we factored out the time axis in 3.2.3 above.

So we chose instead to "center" all models on a random sample of fiction with the same distribution across time as the genre category being modeled. Model A (of genre a) learns to distinguish short stories from a random sample of fiction; model B (of genre b) learns to distinguish juvenile fiction from another random sample (with a different chronological distribution). The number of features and regularization constant for regularized logistic regression are tuned by grid search. Then we apply each model to the works used in the other, and compare the way they rank the books by probability of belonging to a or b. This produces two Spearman correlation coefficients; before they can be averaged, they need to undergo Fisher's z-transformation—in effect, $arctanh$. So the distance d between a and b is

$$d(a;b) = -\frac{1}{2}(arctanh(spearman(p(a|A), p(a|B))) + arctanh(spearman(p(b|B), p(b|A)))) \quad (2)$$

Initial experiments on a toy sample revealed that this measure has a linear relationship to random dilution of data. So Fisher's z-transformation is not just a convenience for averaging; it gives correlation coefficients an unbounded distribution that may be appropriate for a measure of statistical distance. However, other measures might be equally appropriate. For instance, given a well-calibrated probabilistic model, Pearson correlation can be substituted for Spearman in equation (2).

4   Results

The measures discussed in Section 3 were used to estimate textual distances for all distinct pairings of the 32 categories selected in Section 2—except self-comparisons, which were ignored. (Subtracting self-comparisons, $n = 496$.) Different measures of textual distance were compared to the estimates of social distance produced by calculating PMI on genre labels. (Since PMI is actually a measure of proximity, we reversed the sign to interpret it as a distance.)

The Pearson correlations of different textual measures with our social benchmark are shown in Figure 1. This is admittedly an imperfect evaluative strategy. To understand how these results might confirm or weaken specific methodological priors, details need to be inspected more closely.

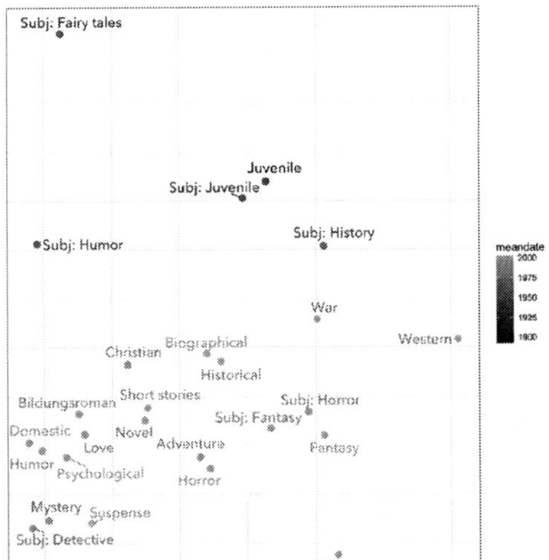

Figure 2: Multidimensional scaling on distances inferred from topic vectors (3.2.2). Genres colored by mean publication date.

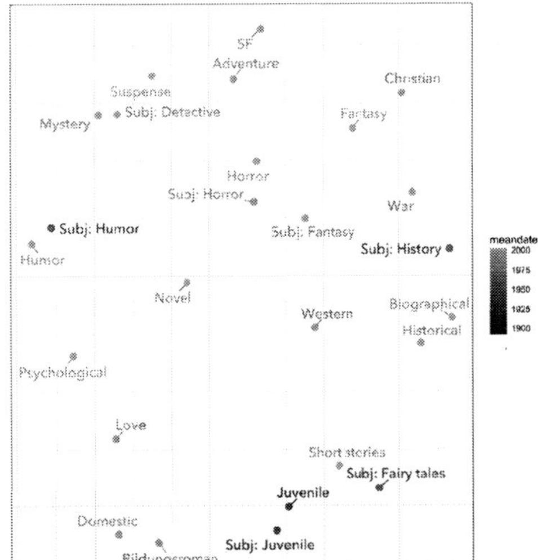

Figure 3: Multidimensional scaling on distances inferred from predictive models (3.3). Genres colored by mean publication date.

4.1 Social and textual measures of distance do correlate

Prevailing practice in cultural analytics relies on comparisons between topic vectors (Jockers, 2013; Barron et al., 2018; Mauch et al., 2015). These measures correlated with social measures of distance at $r = .33$ to $r = .38$, a moderately strong effect size. It is difficult to say exactly how pleased or concerned we should be by correlations around .35, because the social evidence itself is sparse and fallible. We don't know that it's a gold standard, and thus don't know how closely textual distances should be approximating it. But it would certainly have been concerning to discover that social and textual measures didn't correlate at all!

4.2 Overlapping genres did not significantly distort results

Excluding the intersection of genres—to avoid potential circularity in our comparisons—greatly complicated this study. But in the end, this precaution made little difference. Allowing genres to overlap gave one method (3.2.1) a slight advantage, but the effect was dwarfed by date adjustment or predictive modeling on non-overlapping genres.

4.3 Topic modeling did make a difference

Cosine similarity on raw tf-idf vectors performed significantly worse than the other methods. It appears that topic modeling does tend to foreground lexical choices that have social significance. However, this effect might depend as much on corpus construction as it does on the algorithm. In this case, for instance, topics were inferred from a corpus that had been selected to represent generic differences with evenly-sized samples. Many genres would not have been well represented in a purely random sample, and topics inferred from that sample might not have been as well suited to the discrimination of genres.

Note also that a goal of even coverage may not entirely resolve this problem: some empirical evidence suggests that topic models covering a long timeline tend to give a finer-grained description of documents toward the center of the timeline, exaggerating distances there. If this turns out to be a general pattern, it would be a significant problem for diachronic research, deserving further investigation.

4.4 Limiting the form of distance being measured is vital for historical significance

The question posed in this experiment concerned differences between genres. We couldn't assume that those differences were entirely independent of time; e.g. Westerns came along almost a century after historical novels, so the difference between those categories may be partly chronological. But we had reason to suspect that transformation of the English language would often be a confounding variable, obscuring the textual similarities between categories with generic kinship.

For instance, the subject category "Humor" contains volumes with a mean publication date of 1925; it's one of the earlier categories applied to fiction. But the genre category "Humor" has a mean date of 1990; as we mentioned in Section 2, genres don't get described *as genres* until relatively late in the history of cataloging. The mere passage of time will create many linguistic differences between these groups of books, yet our priors would probably place the categories relatively close to each other.

As you can see on the left side of Figure 2, distances inferred from topic vectors (3.2.2) don't succeed in placing "Humor" and "Subj: Humor" next to each other. Instead, this space looks suspiciously dominated by a chronological gradient.

By contrast, distances inferred from predictive models place "Humor" close to "Subj: Humor" and "Historical" novels close to "Subj: History." Because our predictive models always use a random contrast set that matches the chronological distribution of the genre category being modeled, the confounding variable of time is partly factored out of distance measurements. Something similar can be achieved by adjusting topic vectors for time (3.2.3).

Note, however, that this choice doesn't compel us to ignore chronological differences. Some genres do change more across time than others. In Figure 3 you may notice that "Fantasy" and "Subj: Fantasy" are relatively remote, compared to, say, "Mystery" and "Subj: Detective." Existing literary scholarship already suggests that the detective story crystallized earlier than the modern fantasy genre, and remained more stable across the last two centuries (Rachman, 2010). 19th-century fantasy, for instance, can be difficult to distinguish from children's literature (Levy and Mendlesohn, 2016). When a genre changes rapidly, different samples will differ from a random contrast set in different ways, even though the contrast sets always match the chronological distribution of the genre. Genres that change rapidly should thus be expected to cover a lot of space in our map.

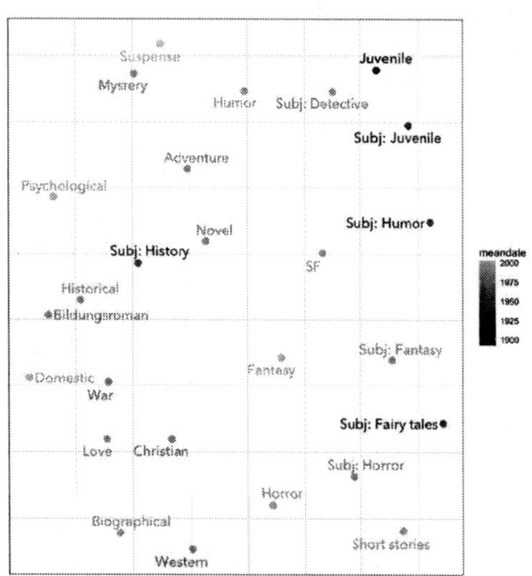

Figure 4: Multidimensional scaling on distances inferred from PMI on labels assigned by librarians.

This sort of detailed inspection is an essential supplement to the quantitative evaluation in Figure 1. Social distances inferred from library metadata are perhaps best understood as an initial sanity check; if those measures of social contiguity didn't correlate with textual distances at all, we would need to reconsider this whole research program. But it is not safe to assume that any sample of social evidence constitutes firm ground truth about the real similarities of genres.

In fact, readers might also want to skeptically inspect the social evidence we have been using as a benchmark for textual distances. Figure 4 makes this possible. Casual inspection is vulnerable to confirmation bias, but in the present author's judgment this map is clearly preferable to Figure 2. For instance, "Novel" and "Short stories" ought to be fairly remote categories; Figure 2 put them too near each other. On the other hand, it is far from clear that Figure 4 fits our priors better than Figure 3. Categories like "Mystery" and "Subj: Detective" ought to be closer than they appear in the social map.

Ironically, Figure 4 is based on priors specifying, for instance, that "Mystery" and "Subj: Detective" should be relatively close. But they were only priors, and therefore had to compromise with the evidence provided by library metadata. Figure 3, which relies purely on textual evidence and not on our priors, actually conforms to those priors more closely. Moreover, it provides surprises that retrospectively make sense (e.g. "Bildungsroman" is close to "Juvenile" fiction.) Evidence of this kind tends to demonstrate that predictive models provide reliable guidance about the relationships between genres. One can have roughly the same amount of confidence in time-adjusted topic vectors (the method described in 3.2.3). The value of the other three measures of textual distance is more dubious. On inspection, it seems likely that those distance matrices are dominated by a chronological gradient that doesn't correspond to readers' intuitions about the relationships between categories. In other words, the gap between the top two methods in Figure 1, and the bottom three methods, may be bigger than it appears.

Problems of this kind are fairly common. Researchers inquiring about textual distance often tacitly expect to measure certain *kinds* of distance, and tacitly expect other kinds to be factored out. Measurement will become more reliable if those tacit assumptions are made explicit. In this case, time was the problem—and time is definitely a common problem in historical inquiry. But other research projects, inquiring about the pace of stylistic change for instance, may confront a converse problem. Time might become the topic of interest, and the distribution of texts across genres might become the confounding variable. The solutions explored here would still be applicable. For instance, to factor generic differences out of a question about time, one wouldn't necessarily have to hold genre distribution constant across the timeline (and risk distorting the corpus). Instead, one could train predictive models where the genre distribution of the random contrast set matches the genre distribution of the decade modeled. That strategy can reduce confounds while still acknowledging that genre and time are interwoven.

5 Conclusions

This paper asks whether the assumptions underpinning contemporary work in cultural analytics hold up to empirical scrutiny. Broadly, it has answered "yes." Textual distances do correlate with independent measures of social affinity. And topic modeling a corpus probably does improve that correlation.

On the other hand, there are also reasons for caution here. Figure 2 suggests that topic modeling cannot in itself replace reflection on confounding variables. Unless researchers explicitly limit the range of differences that interest them, general measurements of "stylistic change" may indiscriminately register linguistic drift, the rise of a new genre, or a shift in the underlying gender balance of authorship.

This paper has not prescribed a particular response to the problem; two different methods performed well in this experiment, and other solutions are imaginable. However, the strong performance of supervised models ($r = .45$) does hint that they have under-exploited potential as measures of distance.

Supervised learning is usually explained as if it aimed simply to reproduce existing ground truth. If this were true, supervised models would find little application in the humanities. Humanists are often posing questions where reliable ground truth is not yet available (and perhaps never will be). "Accuracy" would be a naïve goal.

However, predictive models don't need to be contained in that naïve frame. In this paper, for instance, models of science fiction were applied to fantasy—not because we expected them to be right, but to measure divergent assumptions. Training a predictive model can translate a static set of examples into a measure of distance, and thereby put concepts in dialogue with each other.

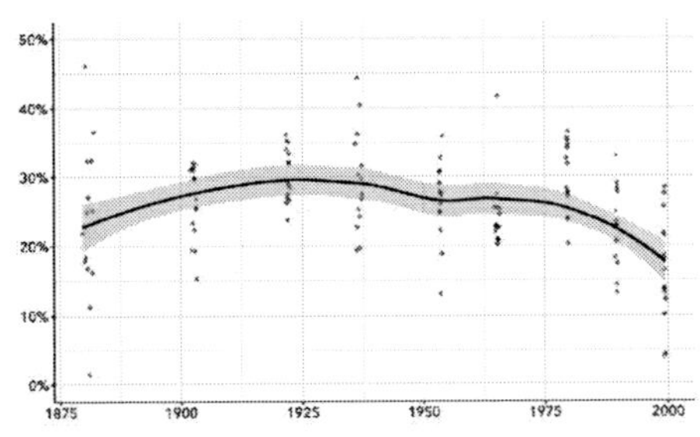

Figure 5: Distance between models of fantasy and science fiction, expressed as a percentage of the text that would need to be randomly altered to produce the measured loss of correlation.

Our goal in this experiment was simply to develop a measure of the distance between genres that corresponds to literary intuition, because it uses evidence about the genres themselves to define "distance." But once we have done that, it becomes possible to pose questions where we don't have intuitive answers. Figure 5, borrowed from a forthcoming project, hints that the genres of science fiction and fantasy have been converging in the last thirty years.

Predictive models can also give scholars a way of comparing different perspectives on genre. Instead of taking library metadata as authoritative, we can draw lists of examples from the conflicting practices of critics or reviewers, and compare the resulting models.

How widely could this method be applied? The history of genre may initially appear to be an odd special case, where we happen to have labeled categories. The methods that work for genre may seem unlikely to be useful for more open-ended questions about historical change.

But labels come in many forms. Time itself is a label. For instance, one might ask, "How quickly has science fiction changed over the last century?" and answer by comparing models of the genre trained on different segments of the timeline.

The task of measuring distance in a supervised way, triangulating from multiple reference points, needs better computational solutions. We readily admit that the solution offered in this paper was improvised empirically and uses Spearman correlation as duct tape. It works, but it has awkward limitations: for instance, to put models on an equal footing, all categories have to be limited to an equal number of examples. A more integrated and principled approach is imaginable, patterned perhaps on supervised topic modeling (Lacoste-Julien et al., 2009; Zhu et al., 2009), but with the goal of inferring distances (of a particular social character) rather than latent topics.

6 Open code and data

Code used in this paper is available both on GitHub `https://github.com/tedunderwood/genredistance`, and more archivally at Zenodo (Underwood, 2018a). Data used in the paper has also been archived (Underwood, 2018b).

Acknowledgments

The research undertaken here was supported by the NovelTM project, funded by Canada's Social Sciences and Humanities Research Council and directed by Andrew Piper. HathiTrust Research Center was also a crucial resource, and some work was supported by the Andrew W. Mellon Foundation via the WCSA+DC grant to HTRC, directed by J. Stephen Downie. At an early stage of the project, crucial advice came from Jacob Eisenstein; conversation with David Mimno and Laure Thompson guided some of my thinking about topic models.

References

Alexander T. J. Barron, Jenny Huang, Rebecca L. Spang, and Simon DeDeo. 2018. Individuals, institutions, and innovation in the debates of the French Revolution. *Proceedings of the National Academy of Sciences*.

Douglas Biber and Susan Conrad. 2009. *Register, Genre, and Style*. Cambridge University Press, Cambridge.

Boris Capitanu, Ted Underwood, Peter Organisciak, Timothy Cole, Maria Janina Sarol, and J. Stephen Downie. 2016. The HathiTrust Research Center extracted feature dataset (1.0).

Sung-Hyuk Cha. 2007. Comprehensive survey on distance/similarity measures between probability density functions. *International Journal of Mathematical Models and Methods in Applied Sciences*, 1(4):300–307.

Paul DiMaggio. 1987. Classification in art. *American Sociological Review*, 52:440–455.

Matthew L. Jockers. 2013. *Macroanalysis: Digital Methods and Literary History*. University of Illinois Press, Urbana.

Karen Spärck Jones. 1972. A statistical interpretation of term specificity and its application in retrieval. *Journal of Documentation*, 28(1):11–21.

Brett Kessler, Geoffrey Nunberg, and Hinrich Schütze. 1997. Automatic detection of text genre. In *Proceedings of the Eighth Conference on European Chapter of the Association for Computational Linguistics*, EACL '97, pages 32–38, Stroudsburg, PA, USA. Association for Computational Linguistics.

Evgeny Kim, Sebastian Padó, and Roman Klinger. 2017. Investigating the relationship between literary genres and emotional plot development. In *Proceedings of the Joint SIGHUM Workshop on Computational Linguistics for Cultural Heritage, Social Sciences, Humanities, and Literature*, pages 17–26. Association for Computational Linguistics.

Simon Lacoste-Julien, Fei Sha, and Michael I. Jordan. 2009. DiscLDA: Discriminative learning for dimensionality reduction and classification. In D. Koller, D. Schuurmans, Y. Bengio, and L. Bottou, editors, *Advances in Neural Information Processing Systems 21*, pages 897–904. Curran Associates, Inc.

Michael Levy and Farah Mendlesohn. 2016. *Children's Fantasy Literature: An Introduction*. Cambridge University Press, Cambridge.

Matthias Mauch, Robert M. MacCallum, Mark Levy, and Armand M. Leroi. 2015. The evolution of popular music: USA 1960–2010. *Royal Society Open Science*, 2(5).

David P. Miller. 2000. Out from under: Form/genre access in LCSH. *Cataloging and Classification Quarterly*, 29(1/2):169–188.

F. Pedregosa, G. Varoquaux, A. Gramfort, V. Michel, B. Thirion, O. Grisel, M. Blondel, P. Prettenhofer, R. Weiss, V. Dubourg, J. Vanderplas, A. Passos, D. Cournapeau, M. Brucher, M. Perrot, and E. Duchesnay. 2011. Scikit-learn: Machine learning in Python. *Journal of Machine Learning Research*, 12:2825–2830.

Stephen Rachman. 2010. Poe and the origins of detective fiction. In Catherine Ross Nickerson, editor, *The Cambridge Companion to American Crime Fiction*, pages 17–28. Cambridge University Press, Cambridge.

Alva T. Stone. 2000. The LCSH century: A brief history of the Library of Congress subject headings, and introduction to the centennial essays. *Cataloging and Classification Quarterly*, 29(1/2):1–15.

Ted Underwood. 2018a. Code to support "The historical significance of textual distances". `https://zenodo.org/record/1300934#.WzaQvSOZNBw`.

Ted Underwood. 2018b. Data on the historical significance of textual distances. `http://hdl.handle.net/2142/100119`.

Hadley Wickham. 2009. *ggplot2: Elegant Graphics for Data Analysis*. Springer-Verlag New York.

Zhili Wu, Katja Markert, and Serge Sharoff. 2010. Fine-grained genre classification using structural learning algorithms. In *Proceedings of the 48th Annual Meeting of the Association for Computational Linguistics*, pages 749–759. Association for Computational Linguistics.

Jun Zhu, Amr Ahmed, Eric P. Xing, Jun Zhu, Amr Ahmed, Eric P. Xing, and David Blei. 2009. MedLDA: Maximum margin supervised topic models for regression and classification. In *In Leon Bottou and Michael Littman, editors, International Conference on Machine Learning (ICML)*, pages 1257–1264.

Zhiya Zuo. 2018. Calculate Pearson correlation interval in python. `https://zhiyzuo.github.io/Pearson-Correlation-CI-in-Python/`.

One Size Fits All? A simple LSTM for Non-literal Token- and Construction-level Classification

Erik-Lân Do Dinh, Steffen Eger, and Iryna Gurevych
Ubiquitous Knowledge Processing Lab (UKP-TUDA)
Department of Computer Science, Technische Universität Darmstadt
`http://www.ukp.tu-darmstadt.de`

Abstract

We tackle four different tasks of non-literal language classification: token and construction level metaphor detection, classification of idiomatic use of infinitive-verb compounds, and classification of non-literal particle verbs. One of the tasks operates on the token level, while the three other tasks classify constructions such as "hot topic" or "stehen lassen" (*to allow sth. to stand* vs. *to abandon so.*). The two metaphor detection tasks are in English, while the two non-literal language detection tasks are in German. We propose a simple context-encoding LSTM model and show that it outperforms the state-of-the-art on two tasks. Additionally, we experiment with different embeddings for the token level metaphor detection task and find that 1) their performance varies according to the genre, and 2) Mikolov et al. (2013) embeddings perform best on 3 out of 4 genres, despite being one of the simplest tested models. In summary, we present a large-scale analysis of a neural model for non-literal language classification (i) at different granularities, (ii) in different languages, (iii) over different non-literal language phenomena.

1 Introduction

Computational research of non-literal phenomena, e.g., metonymy, idiom, and prominently metaphor detection (Veale et al., 2016), has been plentiful. For metaphor detection, most works name the Conceptual Metaphor Theory (Lakoff and Johnson, 1980) as their underlying framework, in which metaphors are modeled as cognitive mappings of concepts from a source to a target domain. However, the datasets created and used in these works often follow no unified annotation guidelines (compare Steen et al. (2010) and Tsvetkov et al. (2014)), or even no disclosed guidelines at all, e.g., Heintz et al. (2013), or annotate metaphors at different levels of granularity (Steen et al., 2010; Gutierrez et al., 2016). This is also true for many works in more general non-literal language detection. Consequently, methods are seldom compared on related tasks.

Neural networks have been successfully applied to various natural language processing tasks, but few have applied them to metaphor detection (Do Dinh and Gurevych, 2016; Rei et al., 2017) or detection of non-literal and figurative language in general. In this paper, we test whether the same simple generic neural network approach is effective for four different non-literal language detection tasks: token and construction level metaphor detection, idiom classification and classification of literal and non-literal German particle verbs. We train a neural model using LSTMs to encode the context of a metaphor candidate or non-literal compound. We show that our approach outperforms existing state-of-the-art models on two tasks, while producing competitive results on another task, independent of the mode of classification (e.g., token vs. construction classification). In demonstrating the applicability of the same, simple neural network architecture to different non-literal language tasks, we lay the foundation for a more integrative approach. A joint modeling of these tasks, through data concatenation and multi-task learning, is investigated in Do Dinh et al. (2018).

Given enough training data, our model renders many of the handcrafted features employed in previous work unnecessary. This includes e.g., abstractness values to model source and target concepts (Tsvetkov

Proceedings of Workshop on Computational Linguistics for Cultural Heritage, Social Sciences, Humanities and Literature, pages 70–80
Santa Fe, New Mexico, USA, August 25, 2018.

et al., 2014; Turney and Assaf, 2011), selectional preference violations (Wilks, 1978; Shutova, 2013) or topic modeling (Heintz et al., 2013; Beigman Klebanov et al., 2014). In contrast, because they are the only external resource we utilize, we investigate the influence of an important hyper-parameter of our network—different pre-trained embeddings—on the token-level metaphor detection task and show the genre-specific effects of these embedding models.

2   Related work

Classification and detection of non-literal language has largely focused on metaphor detection. Another prominent task is the detection of idiomatic language. Similar features have been employed in those tasks, even though the specific phenomena differ. However, since the datasets used for these tasks are annotated differently, it is difficult to compare methods across the different tasks (or even subtasks of, e.g., metaphor detection). For some tasks, feature-based approaches are still superior to neural models. For many, more general, non-literal language tasks, neural models have not yet been applied. While distributed word representations have been used even in feature-based methods, a comparison regarding the influence of different pre-trained embeddings on these tasks has not been carried out so far.

Tsvetkov et al. (2014) classify adjective-noun pairs and subject-verb-object constructions. Their features include imageability, abstractness ratings, supersenses and low-dimensional word representations trained using an LSA variant. They train their system on English, and test it on four different languages— English, Russian, Farsi and Spanish—with the help of bilingual dictionaries. Similar, Gutierrez et al. (2016) examine adjective-noun compounds, specifically those for which the interaction between the components is sufficient to determine metaphoricity. To this end, they adapt a compositional distributional semantic model (CDSM) approach, representing adjectives as matrices and nouns as vectors. By computing distinct representations for literal and metaphorical use of adjectives they introduce a separation of literal and metaphorical meaning in the CDSM.

Do Dinh and Gurevych (2016) also investigate metaphor detection, however in contrast to the previously described works on a token level. Specifically, they use a multi-layer perceptron to classify metaphoric tokens using concatenated pre-trained word embeddings. Their approach is language-agnostic as it does not use additional features. However, they only test it on English data, on which it compares favorably to a simple SVM baseline and an existing feature-based method. A more complex neural model is proposed by Rei et al. (2017). They implement a similarity network in which they modulate the word representation of a token in a possibly metaphoric construction based on the remaining construction tokens. Further, they introduce a mapping from the vector space of the pre-trained embeddings to a metaphor-specific vector space. While their system performs well, it cannot beat the feature-based system by Tsvetkov et al. (2014) on adjective-noun constructions.

Zhang and Gelernter (2015) investigate metonymy identification, i.e. identification of instances where entities replace other associated entities. For example in the sentence "Washington and Beijing enter new trade talks", *Washington* and *Beijing* are used to refer to the US and Chinese governments. Zhang and Gelernter (2015) reuse many features commonly used for the metaphor detection task, such as imageability and abstractness ratings. They further test different word representations—word embeddings, LSA, and one-hot-encoding—to detect metonymy using an SVM.

A different non-literal language task is investigated by Horbach et al. (2016), in which they classify literal and idiomatic use of different German infinitive-verb compounds based on their context. They employ Naive Bayes and various features—including local skip-n-grams, POS tags, automatically obtained subject and object information, selectional preferences, and manually annotated topic information.

Köper and Schulte im Walde (2016) classify literally and non-literally used German particle verbs across 10 particles. Using a random forest classifier and various features (e.g., unigrams, affective ratings, distributed word representations), they achieve an accuracy of 85% over all particle verbs, and find that taking into account particle information additionally increases performance.

Task	dataset	size	M	lang	example
Token level metaphor detection	VUAMC	103,865	15%	en	Along with Sir James he **found** the US much more **attractive**, [...]
Construction level metaphor detection	Tsvetkov et al. (2014)	1,738	47%	en	Wind and wave power providing the **green energy** of the future.
Classification of idiomatically used verb compounds	Horbach et al. (2016)	5,249	64%	de	„Auch eine Uhr, die **stehen geblieben** ist, geht zweimal am Tag richtig", sagt er. ("A clock that has **stopped running** is correct two times a day, too," he says.)
Classification of non- literally used particle verbs	Köper and Schulte im Walde (2016)	6,436	35%	de	Auf Decken sitzt man ums Feuer und lässt den ereignisreichen Tag **nachklingen**. (One sits on blankets around the fire and lets the day **linger on** [lit.: ring on].)

Table 1: Investigated tasks and datasets. *Size* describes labeled tokens in case of token level metaphor detection (content tokens), and labeled constructions for the other tasks respectively, *M* denotes percentage of non-literal labels. Non-literal use of tokens/constructions in the examples is marked bold.

3   Tasks

To investigate if our generic network can successfully tackle different non-literal language detection tasks, we consider token level metaphor detection, construction level metaphor detection, classification of idiomatically used infinitive-verb compounds, and classification of particle verbs into literal and non-literal usage. Table 1 gives an overview along with examples. The corpora differ in size, percentage of non-literal instances, and language.

For **token-level metaphor detection** we use the VU Amsterdam metaphor corpus (VUAMC) (Steen et al., 2010), a subset of the BNC Baby covering four genres: *academia, conversation, fiction,* and *news*. Metaphors are annotated on a token level using MIPVU (Steen et al., 2010), which in short specifies that all tokens which are not used in their most basic (concrete, bodily-related, or historically older) sense are to be labeled as metaphorical if the contextual meaning of the token can be understood in comparison with its basic sense. Inter-annotator agreement of 0.84 Fleiss' κ has been reported for this dataset. Our network is trained on each genre of the VUAMC separately; for each subcorpus we use a random subset of 76% of the data for training, 12% as a development set and 12% as a test set, reproducing the experimental setup of Do Dinh and Gurevych (2016). We re-implement their state-of-the-art approach on this dataset to compare both architectures.

We also examine **metaphor detection on construction level** utilizing the English data set created by Tsvetkov et al. (2014), specifically the literal and metaphorical adjective-noun (AN) samples, which were also used in the neural model by Rei et al. (2017). Originally these were explicitly selected for their context-independence (i.e., they should be distinguishable as metaphorical or literal based on the construction's tokens, without help from their context). We augment the published training set (i.e., the constructions) by randomly selecting for each construction a sentence containing it from the British National Corpus (BNC Consortium, 2007) and ukWac (Baroni et al., 2009). In this way, we attain 1538 sentences in total, on which we train using 10-fold cross validation. For testing, we use the 200 sentences from the original test set, which was labeled by 5 annotators achieving a Fleiss' κ of 0.74. The metaphor definition is broader than for the VUAMC; the annotators where asked to mark all tokens which "in your opinion, are used non-literally in the following sentences."

Idiom classification is the task of deciding whether a given phrase is used idiomatically or literally. As a figurative language classification problem, and because determining whether a given phrase is used

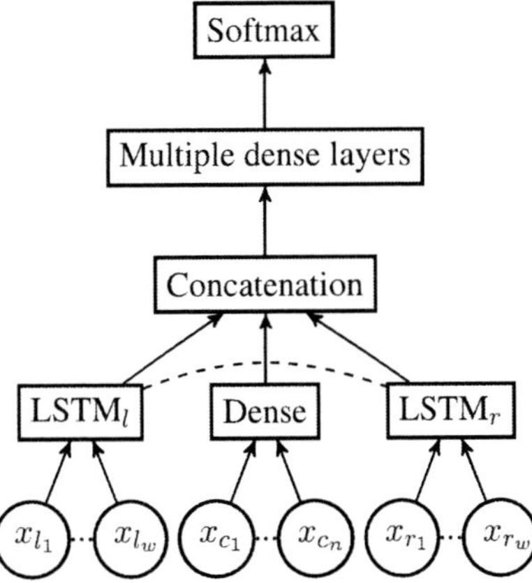

Figure 1: The basic structure of our LSTM, starting with pre-trained word embeddings x_i. Hyper-parameters include number of dense layers before applying softmax, whether or not the same LSTM layer is being used for encoding the context (i.e., $\text{LSTM}_l = \text{LSTM}_r$), and layer sizes. Center size n is determined by the corpus (e.g., $n = 1$ for token classification or $n = 2$ for adjective-noun classification).

idiomatically is largely context-dependent, this task is closely related to metaphor detection. We use the corpus introduced by Horbach et al. (2016), comprising 5,249 sentences containing literal and idiomatic uses of 6 different German infinitive-verb compounds, stemming from the Wahrig corpus (Krome (2010), covering newspaper and magazine articles). Cohen's κ for two expert annotators is reported to range between 0.63 and 0.87, with no explicit guidelines set other than to annotate the compounds as being used literally or idiomatically in a given context sentence. We run experiments on the 6 compounds separately and set up the data in a similar way as Horbach et al. (2016), i.e., we directly report accuracy scores on 10-fold cross validation experiments (averaged over 50 randomly sampled hyper-parameter configurations), without using a separate test set.

We also evaluate our approach on another task using German data: **classification of German particle verbs** into literal and non-literal cases, proposed by Köper and Schulte im Walde (2016). They compiled a corpus using 159 German particle verbs across 10 particles, extracting up to 50 sentences for each particle verb from DECOW14AX (Schäfer and Bildhauer, 2012; Schäfer, 2015). Annotators were asked to label instances on a 6-point scale from "clearly literal" to "clearly non-literal". Inter-annotator agreement of the binarized labels is reported as 0.70 Fleiss' κ for 3 annotators. We use the same setup as in the original paper and perform cross validation on the complete dataset; again we report average accuracy and F_1 over 50 randomly sampled hyper-parameter configurations. We compare our results to their follow-up paper (Köper and Schulte im Walde, 2017), in which they investigate multi-sense embeddings for this task.

4 Architecture

Our approach separately encodes the context of potential metaphorical tokens or constructions (Figure 1). More specifically, our neural network is designed to encode the left and right context of tokens/constructions using Long-Short Term Memory layers (LSTMs), to reduce the influence of the context tokens compared to just concatenating their corresponding word embeddings. This design decision stems from preliminary experiments in which we included the complete sentence context. However, this amount of context was too large to obtain reasonable results. Still, we encode the context using LSTMs rather than fully connected layers, since this provides a more concise model with fewer parameters. The *center* consists of one or two embeddings (depending on the task), which are encoded using a fully connected layer. The output of left context LSTM, center dense layer, and right context LSTM are then concatenated, before being fed to additional fully connected layers. We experiment with different network variations: shared/separate embedding layers (with re-trainable embeddings), shared/separate weights

	Token level metaphor detection		Construction level metaphor detection		Classification of idiomatically used infinitive-verb compounds		Classification of non-literally used particle verbs	
	D	LSTM	R	LSTM	H	LSTM	K	LSTM
A	**0.87**	0.86	**0.83**	0.81	0.86	**0.89**	–	0.89
F_1	0.56	**0.59**	**0.81**	0.79	–	0.90	**0.88**	0.85

Table 2: Accuracy (A) and F_1-score of existing methods (D = Do Dinh and Gurevych (2016), R = Rei et al. (2017), H = Horbach et al. (2016), K = Köper and Schulte im Walde (2017)) and LSTM on the four investigated tasks. For both metaphor detection tasks, these are results on the test set of the best systems as determined by dev set (token level) or cross validation (construction level); for the classification of idiomatically used verb-compounds and the classification of non-literally used particle verbs these are averages over 50 configurations, since the original papers only report performance on cross validation. For subcorpus specific results see Table 3 (token level metaphor detection) and Table 4 (classification of idiomatically used infinitive-verb compounds).

for the context-LSTMs, different context representation sizes, and differing number and size of the fully-connected layers.

We adapt the input for our network to each corpus, since the context can differ depending on the task. For example, for the infinitive-verb classification, the annotated instance can consist of two tokens, thus we can have two *center* embeddings. To illustrate, consider the example:

> "Kinder sollten nicht mehr **sitzen bleiben** müssen, sondern gefördert werden."

In this sentence, we use (*Kinder,sollten,nicht,mehr*) as left context, (*sitzen,bleiben*) as center, and (*müssen,sondern,gefördert,werden*) as right context (see Figure 1).

For the tasks with German data we use the word embeddings of Reimers et al. (2014). For construction level metaphor detection we employ the embeddings of Komninos and Manandhar (2016) as preliminary cross validation experiments on the training set show that they work well. On the other hand, preliminary experiments on the development set for token level metaphor detection show an advantage of the Google News word2vec embeddings (Mikolov et al., 2013) for this task, which is why we use them to work on the VUAMC (a more in-depth analysis validates our decision, Section 6). We conduct our experiments using Keras[1] and Theano[2]. We make our code publicly available[3].

5 Results

The main results are laid out in Table 2, results broken down into subcorpora are shown in Table 3 (token level metaphor detection) and Table 4 (classification of particle verbs). We see that our LSTM model outperforms the existing approaches on both token-level metaphor detection and classification of idiomatically used infinitive-verb compounds. The results on the remaining two tasks are slightly below the state-of-the-art, but are comparable despite not using handcrafted features. The results for the two German tasks are generally higher for all approaches, because multiple instances—both for non-literal and literal use—of each construction are available in these datasets. Further, they only consider few given terms/phrases. In contrast, the English datasets provide annotations for many more different tokens (or constructions). For a closer analysis, we look into the best system for each task.

5.1 Token level metaphor detection

For the token level metaphor detection task, our LSTM yields better results on all subcorpora compared to the re-implemented MLP approach (Table 3). This is not only a matter of choosing the right hyper-parameter combination, as displayed in the much larger spread for the MLP (an example shown for the *news* subcorpus in Figure 2), which is similarly large for both *academia* and *fiction* subcorpora.

[1] v2.0.0, github.com/fchollet/keras
[2] v0.9.0, deeplearning.net/software/theano
[3] https://github.com/UKPLab/latech-cflf-2018-nonliteral

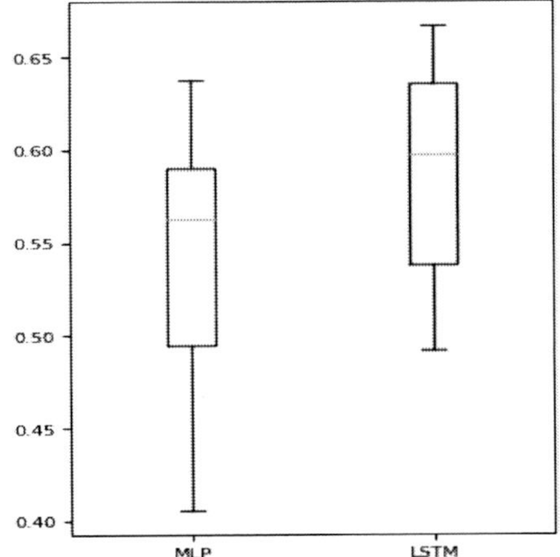

	Do Dinh and Gurevych (2016)	LSTM
academia	0.5916	**0.6341**
conversation	0.5023	**0.5410**
fiction	0.5259	**0.5555**
news	0.6251	**0.6448**
mean	0.5612	**0.5939**

Figure 2: **Token level metaphor detection.** Whisker plot comparing MLP and LSTM configurations performance spread according to development set F_1-score on the *news* subcorpus of the VUAMC. Whiskers extend to 1.5 interquartile range below the first and above the third quartile.

Table 3: **Token level metaphor detection.** F_1-score of the MLP and the LSTM on the genre-specific VUAMC test sets.

In contrast, both networks show comparably high variance for the *conversation* subcorpus. We attribute this to the often short sentence context in this subcorpus. For example, in 1/3 of the 159 instances in which both MLP and LSTM wrongly classify a token, sentence length is shorter than 9 tokens. This is only the case for roughly 1/9 of the correctly classified tokens. However, theoretically sufficient length does not guarantee sufficient context. Consider, e.g., the sentence

"you **see** put John, one of us start trussing early [...]" (metaphor in bold),

where ungrammaticality, omissions, and missing wider context make classification difficult, even for humans. This is true to a lesser extent also for the remaining corpus.

Investigating specific word forms indicates that in some cases the networks do not learn enough from the context. For example, 64 (out of 209) instances of the verb form "see" are annotated as being metaphorical in the training set, but the MLP seems unable to incorporate this information, labeling only 1 instance in the test set as metaphorical. In contrast, the LSTM labels only 1 instance of "take" as literal, even though the training set contains 50 (out of 119) literal examples.

5.2 Construction level metaphor detection

In this task, our generic model is slightly outperformed by a more complex task-tailored network (Rei et al., 2017). The original feature-based approach (Tsvetkov et al. (2014), F_1-score of 0.85) is still not in reach for both neural network approaches. However, since the original test set is quite small (200 instances), the results of all those approaches have to be interpreted carefully.

Our approach yields considerably lower recall (0.720) than precision (0.878) for this dataset. Ten constructions are wrongly labeled as metaphorical. Of those, four contain adjectives that are also part of wrongly literally labeled constructions: *honest opinion, unruly behavior, cool [dry] air, Clear [blue] skies* are wrongly labeled metaphorical. In contrast, *honest meal, unruly hair, cool feature, clear explanations* are misclassified as literal. Looking at nouns in the constructions, we observe that all pairs containing "voice" (*silky voice* (M), *shrill voices* (L), *quiet voice* (L)) are labeled as metaphor, while all the instances containing "brain" (*foggy brain, rusty brain*) are mislabeled as being literally used.

These examples illustrate that for construction level metaphor detection the interaction between the construction components is more important than the remaining context. Also, misclassified constructions appear at the beginning or end only in 24% of their containing sentences, compared to 28% of the correctly labeled ones. This further confirms that larger context is less important for this task than the immediate interaction between adjective and noun. Since we do not model this interaction explicitly, our network is outperformed by the approach of Tsvetkov et al. (2014) on the sparse amount of training data. However, even without this explicit modeling, our simple neural approach performs nearly as well as the much more specialized approach of Rei et al. (2017) which models this interaction specifically.

5.3 Classification of idiomatically used infinitive-verb compounds

For this task, we not only outperform the approach of Horbach et al. (2016) averaged over all infinitive-verb compounds, but for each individual compound. This is most pronounced for "hängen bleiben" and "liegen bleiben".

We examine the compounds on which our network performs best ("sitzen lassen" – *leave sitting*) and worst ("stehen bleiben" – *stay standing*) on average (Table 4). For "stehen bleiben" we see that for 48% of the instances which the LSTM mislabels the compound appears at the end of the sentence, meaning that basically no right context is available. This is only the case for 44% of the correctly labeled instances, indicating that further hyper-parameter optimization without changing the architecture can only increase performance to a degree. "sitzen lassen" has a highly skewed label distribution of only 44 of 881 instances being annotated as literal. The large number of false positive classifications in relation to actual literal instances (18 of the 44 literal instances are classified as non-literal) thus has only negligible impact on precision and F_1-score. 2/3 of those false positives contain the construction directly or very near the end of the sentence, highlighting again the problem with the windowed approach.

	Horbach et al. (2016)	LSTM
hängen+bleiben	0.836	**0.875**
liegen+bleiben	0.847	**0.881**
sitzen+bleiben	0.875	**0.904**
sitzen+lassen	0.946	**0.970**
stehen+bleiben	0.812	**0.817**
stehen+lassen	0.847	**0.861**
average	0.861	**0.885**

Table 4: **Classification of idiomatically used infinitive-verb compounds**. Accuracy values for Horbach et al. (2016) and LSTM (averaged over 50 configurations).

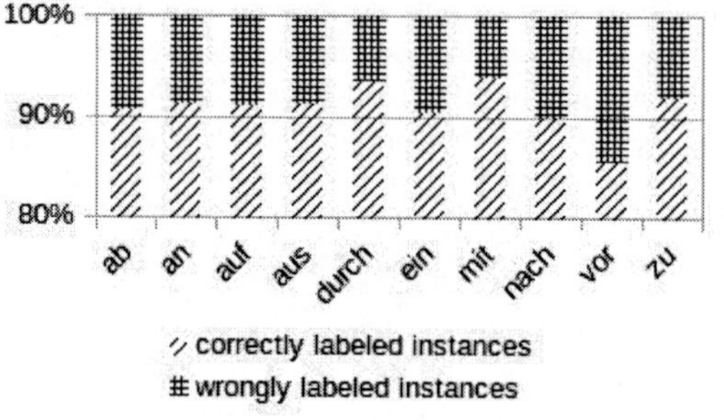

Figure 3: **Particle verb classification**. Accuracy across the ten different particles. Average macro-accuracy is 90.4%.

5.4 Classification of non-literal particle verbs

Classification error rates for the non-literal particle verbs are similar across the particles. Figure 3 shows that three particles stand out, namely: "durch" and "mit" exhibit a far lower error rate (6.8% and 6.3% respectively) and the particle "vor" higher (16.7%) than average (9.6%).

The corpus contains instances for two verbs that start with the particle "vor". While "vordrängen" (*to press forward*) is represented by mainly literal instances (91%), the distribution for "vorschalten" (*to prepose*) is rather balanced (literal: 46%). However, our model produces more classification errors for the former. For the particle "zu", "zustopfen" (*to plug*) is the only verb which also shows a fairly balanced label distribution. However, it also is responsible for almost half of the misclassifications made for verbs with "zu". Other balanced verbs show again different behavior; e.g., "einbrechen" (*to break in*) is misclassified only in 4 of 44 instances. We see that the amount of literal or non-literal training instances for one particular verb is not the deciding factor for classification accuracy. Instead, the network apparently manages to abstract over verbs, however, also introduces some errors in the process.

Embeddings	training data	type / method	coverage
word2vec (Mikolov et al., 2013)	Google News texts	skip-gram with negative sampling	87.6%
GloVe (Pennington et al., 2014)	Wikipedia, newswire	word-word co-occurrence statistics	92.0%
Conceptnet Numberbatch (Speer et al., 2017)	word2vec, GloVe, knowledge bases	combination of existing embeddings and knowledgebases using retrofitting	84.8%
Levy and Goldberg (2014)	Wikipedia	dependency-based	87.8%
Komninos and Manandhar (2016)	Wikipedia	dependency-based and token windows	89.6%

Table 5: Embeddings tested with classification, and their coverage of the VUAMC.

6 Effects of different embeddings

Next, we analyze more closely the effects of a special hyper-parameter on the detection of non-literal language: the pre-trained word embeddings used in our network. Our intuition is that embeddings trained on a similar domain as the test data lead to better results. To test this, we replicate the token level metaphor detection experiments using different word embedding models and sample ten hyper-parameter configurations, from which we choose the best performing (development set) respectively. We use the pre-trained embeddings detailed in Table 5 (all have 300 dimensions).

Coverage, i.e., how many of the tokens in the corpus have an embedding representation, only has a minimal effect on performance. This is illustrated, e.g., by the Glove embeddings, which have the highest coverage but by far the worst overall performance. Recall from Table 3 that metaphors from the *conversation* and *fiction* genres seem to be harder to detect in general, owing to larger context dependence, higher ambiguity, and in case of *conversation* to fragmented sentences and omission. Indeed, we find that *conversation* and *fiction* texts exhibit the largest differences and the worst results regardless of embeddings used. We note that arguably, those genres are the most different from the news texts and Wikipedia articles that the embeddings are trained on. Independently of the concrete embeddings used, the network performs consistently best on the *news* subcorpus, followed by the *academic* texts.

Looking more closely into the classifications on the *fiction* subcorpus, we observe a large performance difference between Glove and the remaining embeddings. This is mainly due to low recall (0.356, see also Table 6), especially compared to the word2vec embeddings (0.710). The results on the *conversation* subcorpus are similarly noteworthy, because here both embedding models that encode dependency information, from Levy and Goldberg (2014) and Komninos and Manandhar (2016), perform worse than the remaining models (also due to lower recall). This is in line with our findings from Section 5.1 where we note that our network struggles with omissions or ungrammatical sentences—as the structure of the conversation sentences is more likely to be irregular, including "correct" syntactic information can apparently be detrimental.

	academic			conversation			fiction			news			avg
	P	R	F_1	P	R	F_1	P	R	F_1	P	R	F_1	F_1
word2vec	.576	**.706**	**.634**	.567	.518	**.541**	.456	**.710**	**.555**	**.640**	.650	.645	**.592**
GloVe	.544	.594	.568	.470	**.584**	.521	.553	.356	.433	.598	.580	.589	.504
ConceptNet	.604	.654	.628	.595	.478	.530	**.570**	.486	.524	.621	.706	**.661**	.576
Levy	**.652**	.535	.588	.629	.439	.517	.485	.545	.513	.636	.645	.640	.553
Komninos	.634	.628	.631	**.652**	.396	.493	.511	.587	.547	.601	**.712**	.652	.569

Table 6: System precision (P), recall (R), and F_1-score for the VUAMC using different embeddings.

At the end, while e.g., the embeddings by Komninos and Manandhar (2016) perform close to the word2vec embeddings in most genres, the fact that they perform relatively poorly on the *conversation* transcripts make them a bad fit for general metaphor identification. The Conceptnet embeddings show better performance on the news subcorpus, however this is no substantial improvement over the generally better performing word2vec embeddings—which do not rely on further knowledgebases.

7 Conclusion

We conducted a large scale study on distinguishing literal from non-literal language on four different tasks, using a generic neural network. These tasks were: token level metaphor detection, construction level metaphor detection, classification of idiomatically used infinitive-verb compounds, and classification of literally or non-literally used particle verbs. Our tasks comprised two languages: English and German. We find that, while the tasks differ with regards to annotation scheme and supposed context dependence, and their respective datasets differ with regards to size and label balance, our generic simple neural model outperforms existing state-of-the-art models on two of four tasks using only pre-trained embeddings, and on the remaining tasks produces competitive results to more task-tailored or feature-based approaches.

Further, we investigated the influence of different pre-trained word embeddings for one of the tasks, token level metaphor classification. We find that performance depends less on the underlying genre than on the architecture used.

In future work, we want to explore how commonalities between the investigated and similar tasks can be exploited, e.g., using multi-task learning (Collobert and Weston, 2008), where we not only share the architecture, but also the parameters of the network among the investigated tasks.

Acknowledgements

This work has been supported by the German Federal Ministry of Education and Research (BMBF) under the promotional reference 01UG1816B (CEDIFOR).

References

Marco Baroni, Silvia Bernardini, Adriano Ferraresi, and Eros Zanchetta. 2009. The WaCky wide web: a collection of very large linguistically processed web-crawled corpora. *Language Resources and Evaluation*, 43(3):209–226.

Beata Beigman Klebanov, Chee Wee Leong, Michael Heilman, and Michael Flor. 2014. Different Texts, Same Metaphors: Unigrams and Beyond. In *Proceedings of the Second Workshop on Metaphor in NLP*, pages 11–17, Baltimore, MD, USA. Association for Computational Linguistics.

The BNC Consortium. 2007. The British National Corpus, version 3 (BNC XML Edition). Distributed by Oxford University Computing Services on behalf of the BNC Consortium.

Ronan Collobert and Jason Weston. 2008. A Unified Architecture for Natural Language Processing: Deep Neural Networks with Multitask Learning. In *Proceedings of ICML 2008*, pages 160–167, Helsinki, Finland. ACM.

Erik-Lân Do Dinh and Iryna Gurevych. 2016. Token-Level Metaphor Detection using Neural Networks. In *Proceedings of the Fourth Workshop on Metaphor in NLP*, pages 28–33, San Diego, CA, USA. Association for Computational Linguistics.

Erik-Lân Do Dinh, Steffen Eger, and Iryna Gurevych. 2018. Killing Four Birds with Two Stones: Multi-Task Learning for Non-Literal Language Detection. In *Proceedings of COLING 2018*, page (to appear), Santa Fe, NM, USA. ICCL.

Elkin Dario Gutierrez, Ekaterina Shutova, Tyler Marghetis, and Benjamin Bergen. 2016. Literal and Metaphorical Senses in Compositional Distributional Semantic Models. In *Proceedings of ACL 2016*, pages 183–193, Berlin, Germany. Association for Computational Linguistics.

Ilana Heintz, Ryan Gabbard, Donald S Black, Marjorie Freedman, Ralph Weischedel, and San Diego. 2013. Automatic Extraction of Linguistic Metaphor with LDA Topic Modeling. In *Proceedings of the First Workshop on Metaphor in NLP*, pages 58–66, Atlanta, GA, USA. Association for Computational Linguistics.

Andrea Horbach, Andrea Hensler, Sabine Krome, Jakob Prange, Werner Scholze-Stubenrecht, Diana Steffen, Stefan Thater, Christian Wellner, and Manfred Pinkal. 2016. A Corpus of Literal and Idiomatic Uses of German Infinitive-Verb Compounds. In *Proceedings of LREC 2016*, pages 836–841, Portorož, Slovenia. European Language Resources Association.

Alexandros Komninos and Suresh Manandhar. 2016. Dependency Based Embeddings for Sentence Classification Tasks. In *Proceedings of NAACL-HLT 2016*, pages 1490–1500, San Diego, CA, USA. Association for Computational Linguistics.

Sabine Krome. 2010. Die deutsche Gegenwartssprache im Fokus korpusbasierter Lexikographie. Korpora als Grundlage moderner allgemeinsprachlicher Wörterbücher am Beispiel des Wahrig Textkorpus digital. In Iva Kratochvílová and Norbert Richard Wolf, editors, *Kompendium Korpuslinguistik. Eine Bestandsaufnahme aus deutsch-tschechischer Perspektive*, pages 117–134. Heidelberg: Universitätsverlag Winter.

Maximilian Köper and Sabine Schulte im Walde. 2016. Distinguishing Literal and Non-Literal Usage of German Particle Verbs. In *Proceedings NAACL-HLT 2016*, pages 353–362, San Diego, CA, USA. Association for Computational Linguistics.

Maximilian Köper and Sabine Schulte im Walde. 2017. Applying Multi-Sense Embeddings for German Verbs to Determine Semantic Relatedness and to Detect Non-Literal Language. In *Proceedings of EACL 2017*, pages 535–542, Valencia, Spain. Association for Computational Linguistics.

George Lakoff and Mark Johnson. 1980. *Metaphors we live by*. University of Chicago Press, Chicago, IL, USA.

Omer Levy and Yoav Goldberg. 2014. Dependency-Based Word Embeddings. In *Proceedings of ACL 2014*, pages 302–308, Baltimore, MD, USA. Association for Computational Linguistics.

Tomas Mikolov, Ilya Sutskever, Kai Chen, Greg Corrado, and Jeffrey Dean. 2013. Distributed Representations of Words and Phrases and their Compositionality. In *Proceedings of NIPS 2013*, pages 3111–3119, Lake Tahoe, NV, USA. Curran Associates, Inc.

Jeffrey Pennington, Richard Socher, and Christopher D. Manning. 2014. GloVe: Global Vectors for Word Representation. In *Proceedings of EMNLP 2014*, pages 1532–1543, Doha, Qatar. Association for Computational Linguistics.

Marek Rei, Luana Bulat, Douwe Kiela, and Ekaterina Shutova. 2017. Grasping the Finer Point : A Supervised Similarity Network for Metaphor Detection. In *Proceedings of EMNLP 2017*, pages 1538–1547, Copenhagen, Denmark. Association for Computational Linguistics.

Nils Reimers, Judith Eckle-Kohler, Carsten Schnober, Jungi Kim, and Iryna Gurevych. 2014. GermEval-2014: Nested Named Entity Recognition with Neural Networks. In *Workshop Proceedings of the 12th Edition of the KONVENS Conference*, pages 117–120, Hildesheim, Germany. Universitätsverlag Hildesheim.

Roland Schäfer and Felix Bildhauer. 2012. Building Large Corpora from the Web Using a New Efficient Tool Chain. In *Proceedings of LREC 2012*, pages 486–493, Istanbul, Turkey. ELRA.

Roland Schäfer. 2015. Processing and querying large web corpora with the COW14 architecture. In *Proceedings of Challenges in the Management of Large Corpora 3 (CMLC-3)*, pages 28–34, Lancaster, UK. Institut für Deutsche Sprache.

Ekaterina Shutova. 2013. Metaphor Identification as Interpretation. In *Proceedings of *SEM*, pages 276–285, Atlanta, GA, USA. Association for Computational Linguistics.

Robert Speer, Joshua Chin, and Catherine Havasi. 2017. ConceptNet 5.5: An Open Multilingual Graph of General Knowledge. In *Proceedings of AAAI 2017*, pages 4444–4451, San Francisco, CA, USA. AAAI Press.

Gerard J. Steen, Aletta G. Dorst, J. Berenike Herrmann, Anna Kaal, Tina Krennmayr, and Trijntje Pasma. 2010. *A Method for Linguistic Metaphor Identification. From MIP to MIPVU*. John Benjamins, Amsterdam, Netherlands.

Yulia Tsvetkov, Leonid Boytsov, Anatole Gershman, Eric Nyberg, and Chris Dyer. 2014. Metaphor Detection with Cross-Lingual Model Transfer. In *Proceedings of ACL 2014*, pages 248–258, Baltimore, MD, USA. Association for Computational Linguistics.

Peter D Turney and Dan Assaf. 2011. Literal and Metaphorical Sense Identification through Concrete and Abstract Context. In *Proceedings of EMNLP 2011*, pages 680–690, Edinburgh, United Kingdom. Association for Computational Linguistics.

Tony Veale, Ekaterina Shutova, and Beata Beigman Klebanov. 2016. *Metaphor: A Computational Perspective.* *Synthesis Lectures on Human Language Technologies.* Morgan & Claypool, USA.

Yorick Wilks. 1978. Making Preferences More Active. *Artificial Intelligence*, 11(3):197–223.

Wei Zhang and Judith Gelernter. 2015. Exploring Metaphorical Senses and Word Representations for Identifying Metonyms. *arXiv preprint, arXiv:1508.04515.*

Supervised Rhyme Detection with Siamese Recurrent Networks

Thomas Haider
MPI for Empirical Aesthetics, Frankfurt
IMS, University of Stuttgart
thomas.haider@ae.mpg.de

Jonas Kuhn
IMS
University of Stuttgart
jonas.kuhn@ims-stuttgart.de

Abstract

We present the first supervised approach to rhyme detection with Siamese Recurrent Networks (SRN) that offer near perfect performance (97% accuracy) with a single model on rhyme pairs for German, English and French, allowing future large scale analyses. SRNs learn a similarity metric on variable length character sequences that can be used as judgement on the distance of imperfect rhyme pairs and for binary classification. For training, we construct a diachronically balanced rhyme goldstandard of New High German (NHG) poetry. For further testing, we sample a second collection of NHG poetry and set of contemporary Hip-Hop lyrics, annotated for rhyme and assonance. We train several high-performing SRN models and evaluate them qualitatively on selected sonnetts.

1 Introduction

Rhyme is a pervasive style device in historical poetry and Hip-Hop, but previous research has relied on small, handcrafted datasets. A reliable system for the detection of rhyme would allow large scale analyses, opening several directions for research. Given word pronunciations and a definition of rhyme, the problem is fairly easy. However, for domain specific or historical data, obtaining precise pronunciation information is a challenge (Katz, 2015). Also, a narrow definition of *perfect* rhyme[1] disregards frequently used and accepted deviations, as in imperfect rhyme (Primus, 2002) (Berg, 1990) or the related sonic devices assonance, consonance and alliteration. Information on the phonological similarity of two rhyme words can be used e.g. for the reconstruction of historical pronunciation (List et al., 2017) or the analysis of sonic pattern (McCurdy et al., 2015). A rhyme detection on grapheme strings is a step in this direction.

Previous research on the detection of rhyme is scarce. Reddy and Knight (2011) employed Expectation Maximization (EM) to predict (generate) the most probable scheme (e.g. *'abba'*) of a stanza. We use a supervised approach to rhyme detection to model the properties of rhyme itself. An accurate similarity measure between words would benefit an EM. Siamese Recurrent Networks are adept for rhyme, as they learn a (non-linear) similarity metric on variable length character sequences. This metric can be used to gauge the degree of imperfection in a rhyme, and by threshold, for a binary classification. We describe our architecture in section 3.2, followed by experiments and a qualitative error analysis to find the best detection system across languages (German, English, French) and domains (poetry, Hip-Hop).

We compiled three corpora with (gold) rhyme annotation, including (i) 116 German Hip-Hop lyrics, (ii) a diachronically balanced sample of 1.948 New High German poems, and (iii) 156 poems of school canon, covering the same period. Their sampling and annotation process will be discussed in section 2.

2 Rhyming Corpora

We describe the creation and annotation efforts of three corpora of lyric text 1.) DTR, a diachronically balanced sample of poems from the German text archive, containing 1,948 poems, 2.) ANTI-K, a very

---

[1]i.e. *identical* pronunciation of word segments starting from the last accented vowel (Fabb, 1997)

Proceedings of Workshop on Computational Linguistics for Cultural Heritage, Social Sciences, Humanities and Literature, pages 81–86
Santa Fe, New Mexico, USA, August 25, 2018.

| | #Poems | Stanzas | Verses | Words | Rhyme Pairs | Authors | Poems/Author | |
Corpus							avg.	median
HIPHOP	116	789	6,390	52,759	2,489	41	2.8	3
ANTI-K	156	731	3,603	20,412	1,440	50	3.1	1
DTR	1,948	8,147	40,523	251,730	13,785	57	33.5	31
DTL	28,275	74,523	507,663	3,557,632	?	75	377	139

Table 1: Size statistics of German poetry corpora

clean (and small) set of 156 poems of school canon, and 3.) HIPHOP, 116 Hip-Hop lyrics. All corpora were annotated for rhyme schema on stanza level. We extract rhyme pairs and non-rhyme pairs based on schema indices. Given a schema, matching indices ('aa') yield a rhyme pair, while non-matching indices ('ab') yield a non-rhyming pair. For a schema 'abba' we retrieve two rhymes and four non-rhymes. See table 1 for size statistics of the corpora. We will publish our datsets on github.[2]

2.1 DTR: German Text Archive Rhyme Gold

The German text archive (Deutsches Textarchiv[3], or **DTA**) is a corpus of New High German (NHG) texts. It is appealing because the editions are well curated, it contains gold POS (STTS) annotation, orthographic corrections and faksimiles, and the selection of authors and editions represents a small Canon for NHG poetry. DTA is balanced over four broad genres and includes 131 documents of *lyric poetry* (DTL). These documents span over 75 authors, where each document has only one author, typically in form of an anthology or collection. The DTL corpus contains in total 28,275 poems, stretching over 3,557,632 word token.

To create a rhyme schema goldstandard **DTR** we draw a diachronically balanced sample from DTL. We divide our timeline by 20-year wide slots (1630 - 1650, ..., 1790 - 1810, ..., 1890 - 1913), aiming at 500 stanzas per slot (allowing $\pm$ 10%). We left the original poems intact, sampling until the desired number of stanzas was fulfilled with complete poems. Additionally, an author needs to contribute enough poems within a std. deviation from the mean. No stanzas longer than one standard deviation over 12 lines (24) were allowed. DTR eventually contains 1,948 poems over 8,147 stanzas..

Students then annotated rhyme schema on stanza level (e.g. 'abba'). Annotators were instructed on rhyme, enumerating the most frequent imperfections (e.g. vowel rounding). For training and to inter-annotator agreement, each student annotated Georg Trakl's 1913 'Gedichte', 51 poems over 251 stanzas. Schemas were annotated directly in inline XML TEI P5, with the Oxygen XML editor to validate against RELAXng. Three annotators achieve .95–.97 Cohen κ among each other, measured on stanza label overlap. Reading stanzas vertically and annotating (typing) stanzas horizontally is prone to errors, generating false positives and negatives.

DTR yields 16,440 rhyme pairs. The list of these pairs was revisited. Out of 1.500 pairs, 244 did not actually rhyme (16% noise) and 17 instances were assonances. The remaining 1,200 pairs were split to a dev set and a untouched test set (both with neg. pairs from inverse schema indices). For further experiments, we clean the entire set which reduces the total set to 13,785 positive pairs.

2.2 ANTI-K: Lyrik.Antikoerperchen

The website `lyrik.antikoerperchen.de` provides a platform for students to upload essays about famous poems. These are neatly formatted in HTML, with clean line/stanza segmentation and reliable metadata, i.a. author, year, number of sentences, literary period, genre. The 156 poems (731 stanzas) are dispersed over 50 authors and over the NHG timeline. ANTI-K was was annotated by a competent student and re-checked. ANTI-K yields 1,440 rhyme pairs.

2.3 HIPHOP-R: Hip-Hop Rhyme

We collected 116 German Hip-Hop song texts and annotated them on rhyme and assonance (repetition of vowels). We retrieved the documents in plain text from `hiphoplyrics.de`, mainly covering the

---

[2] `github.com/thomasnikolaushaider`
[3] `deutschestextarchiv.de`

90's and 2000's, with 1–4 texts per author. Hip-Hop differs from lyric poetry in the regard that it makes heavy use of internal rhyme and assonance. As the annotation of internal rhyme is very time consuming, we confine our analysis to end-rhyme. Yet, assonances and rhymes often form a complex schema, so we decided to mark assonances with capital letters in the stanza level rhyme schema to extract them separately. We retrieve 2,489 rhyme pairs and 1,032 assonance pairs.

2.4 English and French Rhyme Gold

In order to analyze the similarity of rhymes within a graph structure, Sonderegger (2011) compiled a synchronous goldstandard of rhyme schema and their corresponding words. This dataset was modified to include diachronous variation and was used by Reddy and Knight (2011). The dataset includes 12,000 stanzas, yielding 54,000 rhyme pair token. The French rhyme standard includes 2,814 stanzas that yield 18,834 rhyme pair token.

3 Experiments

We introduce Siamese Recurrent Networks for supervised rhyme detection and it test it for English, French and for three German datasets. We ensure that no rhyme pair in the test sets occurs in the training set. We test on held out data (dev and test) from DTR (*dta*), on ANTI-K (*anti*), on Hip-Hop rhymes (only rhymes) (*hip*) plus assonances (*hipa*). We train several well performing models that then undergo a qualitative error analysis. We also include results from an EM baseline, although stanza and pair accuracy cannot be directly compared.

3.1 Schema inference with EM

We train Expectation maximization (EM) as described in Reddy and Knight (2011) on our two poetry corpora with the code provided by Sravana Reddy.[4] For certain experiments on English, they report accuracy up to .88 F1. Table 2 lists the results for two German corpora. When initialized orthographically, we achieve over .70 in accuracy. EM is initialized either uniformly (uni) or with orthographic overlap (orth) of potential rhyme words.

train	test	uni	orth
anti	anti	.63	.77
dta	anti	.37	.71

Table 2: Accuracy of EM on German stanzas

3.2 Siamese Networks

Siamese recurrent networks (SRN) have been successfully applied in NLP applications to measure the distance of texts, both on the level of characters and words. Neculoiu et al. (2016) use it for job title normalization, Mueller and Thyagarajan (2016) on sentence similarity and Das et al. (2016) for *Quora* question pair retrieval.

A SRN consists of two identical recurrent sub-networks that learn a vector representation from input pairs. The sub-networks each receive a rhyme word as character embedding vector and encode it through several layers of bidirectional Long Short Term Memory (biLSTM) Networks. The activations at each timestep of the final biLSTM layer are averaged to produce a fixed-dimensional output. This output is projected through a single densely connected feedforward layer. The respective dense layers are then connected at their outputs through an energy function. The energy of the model is then the similarity between the embeddings of x1 and x2. Our architecture, as that of Neculoiu et al. (2016) uses a cosine distance and a pair of three (later four) stacked biLSTM layers. The model learns through positive and negative examples and optimizes against accuracy and contrastive loss. Binary classification is carried out by setting a threshold of .5 for the cosine value (0-1). See figure (2) for an illustration of our architecture, as proposed by Neculoiu et al. (2016).

---

[4] https://github.com/sravanareddy/rhymediscovery

Our architecture is implemented in tensorflow. The initial codebase was provided by the github user *dhwajraj*.[5] Our parameter are as follows: *character embedding* is set to 100 dimensions. We experiment with the number of hidden units between the LSTM layers (20 – 100), settling on 50. We train 100 epochs, use a batch size of 64, leave dropout at 1.0 and L2 reg. at 0.0. Lastly, the system uses a random 80/20 train/dev split. Maximum document length is set to 30.

3.2.1 Binary Classification

In our initial setup we created only positive rhyme pairs and shuffled the words to generate negative examples at a ratio of 2:3 positive to negative examples.We train a model on the full DTR dataset of rhyme pair token (`token23`), i.e. pairs occur multiple times, and then removed redundant pairs and trained only on singular types (`type23`). We find that 5000 pairs already offer sufficient accuracy on DTA and ANTI (.96 on dta, .94 on anti). Both models are trained on three LSTM layers with 50 hidden units. We use this configuration to train models on 10,000 and 30,000 rhyme pairs from our English data and achieve .96 and .97 points accuracy on 5000 held out pairs (plus 5000 negative). We also train a 1:1 model on 12,000 French rhymes and test 3000 held out pairs (plus 3000 negative). Here, we also achieve .97 acc..

Subsequently, for German, we train on a 1:1 and a 1:4 ratio. (Neculoiu et al. (2016) report an ideal ratio of 1:4 for job title normalization). At 1:4, despite the large amount of data, the model only achieves .93 accuracy. For the 1:1 ratio, we first select 10.000 pairs (both positive and negative) to evaluate the number of LSTM layers, where four layers performed better overall than three or five layers. We train a model on four layers (`type11`) over the full dataset with 30 hidden units and achieve .98 acc. on the dta dev set, followed by the slightly noisier anti set (.96). We then gradually increase the training set to plot a learning curve against our four test sets. See figure (1) for the learning curve.

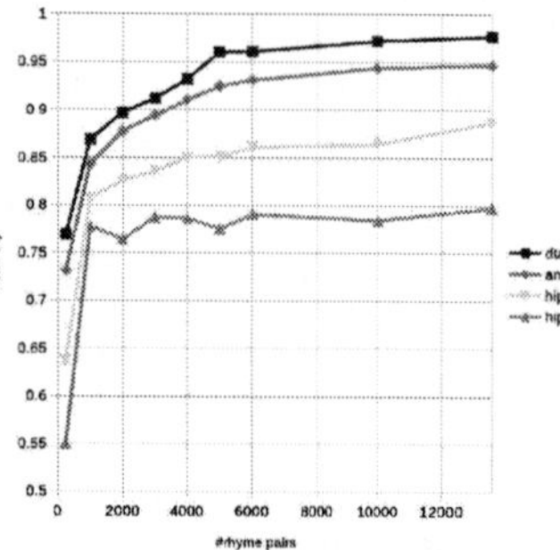

Figure 1: Learning rate of model `type11`

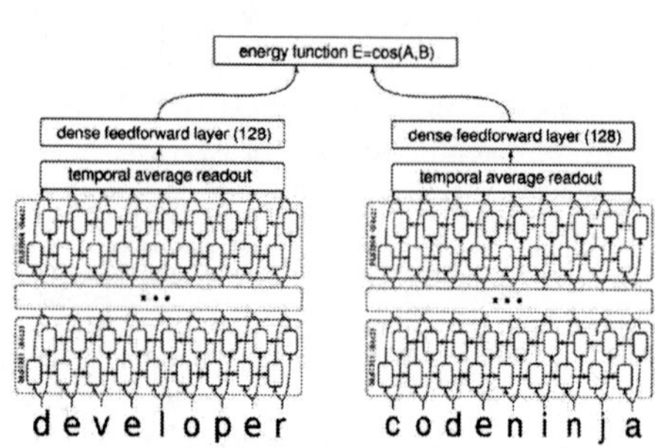

Figure 2: Siamese architecture, from (Neculoiu et al., 2016)

The reason why *anti* performs slightly worse is most likely owed to the noise introduced by wrong schema annotation. Training on dta and testing on Hip-Hop (hip) only achieves .88 accuracy. Generally, for a given test-set all three models exibit very similar performance. Hip-Hop rhyme is not detected that well from a model trained on historical poetry, as the language variety (slang, code switching) somewhat differs. Also, the bottom curve (hipa) indicates that assonances were not learned by this model, noticeably lacking in recall. Since the pairs retrieved from DTR included 16% noise, we decided to again manually correct the rhyme pair training set of DTR. We train another model (`clean11`) with the same parameters (but 50 hidden units), getting .98 accuracy.

3.2.2 Language & Domain Independence

We train two models with three and four layers and 50 epochs on all three languages (German, English, French). Each language contributes 20,000 pairs, evenly split for positive and negative examples. We report the 4-layer model in table 3 (`4indep`). Both models are on par with all previous approaches, in some cases even outperforming models trained on a single language. To further minimize the error

---

[5] `github.com/dhwajraj/deep-siamese-text-similarity`

on Hip-Hop, we include 4,000 (pos.+neg. 1:1) pairs from Hip-Hop into the lang. independent dataset and set aside the remaining 978 pairs for testing. We train on the same parameters (4indeph), and see improvement for Hip-Hop (.92 F1, .96 prec, .89 recall) while all other testsets remain stable and even slightly improve.

	dta_DE		anti_DE	hip_DE	ENG	FR
	dev	test				
Acc.	.976	.960	.961	.892	.965	.963
F1	.976	.960	.960	.885	.965	.963
Prec	.970	.954	.965	.948	.959	.960
Rec	.981	.967	.956	.830	.972	.966

Table 3: Lang. Independent Model 4indep

Schlegel			Gryphius			Kappus	
a	wieder		a	verheret		a	Klage
b	Reihen		b	Posaun		b	weh
b	zweien		b	Carthaun		b	Blütenschnee
a	nieder		a	gezehret		a	Tage
a	glieder		a	vmgekehret		a	Frage
b	dreien		b	zerhawn		b	geh
b	gedeihen		b	schawn		b	see
a	Lieder		a	durchfehret		a	wage
c	kränzen		c	blutt		c	trübe
d	dünket		c	flutt		d	Sommernächte
e	Gesetze		d	fortgedrungen		e	wann
d	winket		e	todt		c	Liebe
c	Gränzen		e	noth		d	möchte
e	Gegensätze		d	abgewzungen		e	kann

Table 4: Rhyme words and schema of three sonnetts

3.2.3 Qualitative Error Analysis

We conduct a small qualitative error analysis on three german sonnetts from different literary periods. They include a variety of imperfect rhymes and orthographic deviations. The first poem is by Schlegel, the second by Andreas Gryphius, and the third is by Franz Xaver Kappus. Table 4 lists the end words of these poems and the associated rhyme scheme. We generate pairs on all permutations of end words and evaluate our four models type23, token23 and token11, clean11 and the two independent models indep with and without Hip-Hop. When not mentioned for a poem, a model delivers perfect performance.

Schlegel clean11 and the indep models wrongly detect the mapping 'ei' → 'ä', therefore detecting (reihen, [g|k]ränzen), (zweien, [g|k]ränzen), etc..

Kappus type23 wrongly identifies (weh, Frage), (blütenschnee, Frage/wage), so it is probably matching on the final 'e'. type11 massively overgenerates on this poem with a precision .34 and perfect recall. This questions the overall sanity of this otherwise well performing model. The indephip model wrongly assigns very low cosine distance (<.1) to pairs that end with 'e', 'eh' or 'ee' such as (weh/geh, trübe/liebe), (Blütenschnee/See, trübe/liebe), e.g. (weh, trübe).

Gryphius The model type23 does not detect the historical spelling variation of the diphtong [aw] instead of [au] and consequently does not detect the following pair combinations: (posaun/carthaun, zerhawn/schawn). After manually correcting the words, the system does detect them. token23 additionally does not detect (schawn, zerhawn). Both indep models wrongly identify the combinations (blutt/flutt, todt/noth), probably matching on the 't'.

4 Conclusion

We have introduced three new poetry corpora for German and discussed their annotation with rhyme schema. Furthermore, we introduced a Siamese Recurrent Networks architecture to the detection of rhyme pairs and find that it learns this task with near perfect accuracy across languages. When switching domains from poetry to Hip-Hop we lose 10 points, and assonances are not that well detected. It is notable that SRNs can apparently compensate a noise level of 16% in the training set. Future research should determine the acceptable noise level. Finally, we have shown that a SRN can be trained on a dataset containing rhyme pairs of three languages and also a different domain without losing performance. But even though we achieve over 96% accuracy on pairs, each model exhibits individual errors in a qualitative error analysis, making it hard to determine an ideal model. While the independent models work well, they show some problems on particular character mappings.

References

Thomas Berg. 1990. Unreine reime als evidenz für die organisation phonologischer merkmale. *Zeitschrift für Sprachwissenschaft*, 9(1-2):3–27.

Arpita Das, Harish Yenala, Manoj Chinnakotla, and Manish Shrivastava. 2016. Together we stand: Siamese networks for similar question retrieval. In *Proceedings of the 54th Annual Meeting of the Association for Computational Linguistics (Volume 1: Long Papers)*, volume 1, pages 378–387.

Nigel Fabb. 1997. *Linguistics and literature: Language in the verbal arts of the world*. Blackwell.

Jonah Katz. 2015. Hip-hop rhymes reiterate phonological typology. *Lingua*, 160:54–73.

Johann-Mattis List, Jananan Sylvestre Pathmanathan, Nathan W Hill, Eric Bapteste, and Philippe Lopez. 2017. Vowel purity and rhyme evidence in old chinese reconstruction. *Lingua Sinica*, 3(1):5.

Nina McCurdy, Vivek Srikumar, and Miriah Meyer. 2015. Rhymedesign: A tool for analyzing sonic devices in poetry. In *Proceedings of the Fourth Workshop on Computational Linguistics for Literature*, pages 12–22.

Jonas Mueller and Aditya Thyagarajan. 2016. Siamese recurrent architectures for learning sentence similarity. In *AAAI*, pages 2786–2792.

Paul Neculoiu, Maarten Versteegh, and Mihai Rotaru. 2016. Learning text similarity with siamese recurrent networks. In *Proceedings of the 1st Workshop on Representation Learning for NLP*, pages 148–157.

Beatrice Primus. 2002. Unreine reime und phonologische theorie. *Sounds and Systems. Studies in Structure and Change. A Festschrift for Theo Vennemann. Berlin/New York*, pages 269–298.

Sravana Reddy and Kevin Knight. 2011. Unsupervised discovery of rhyme schemes. In *Proceedings of the 49th Annual Meeting of the Association for Computational Linguistics: Human Language Technologies: short papers-Volume 2*, pages 77–82. Association for Computational Linguistics.

Morgan Sonderegger. 2011. Applications of graph theory to an english rhyming corpus. *Computer Speech & Language*, 25(3):655–678.

Normalizing Early English Letters to Present-day English Spelling

Mika Hämäläinen, Tanja Säily, Jack Rueter, Jörg Tiedemann and Eetu Mäkelä
Department of Digital Humanities
University of Helsinki
`firstname.lastname@helsinki.fi`

Abstract

This paper presents multiple methods for normalizing the most deviant and infrequent historical spellings in a corpus consisting of personal correspondence from the 15th to the 19th century. The methods include machine translation (neural and statistical), edit distance and rule-based FST. Different normalization methods are compared and evaluated. All of the methods have their own strengths in word normalization. This calls for finding ways of combining the results from these methods to leverage their individual strengths.

1 Introduction

Working with historical texts is a challenging task for NLP. Whereas many off-the-shelf tools and libraries are available for the modern written standard of a majority language, these are not directly applicable to historical data. This is due to a wide variety in how words are spelled.

The problem of non-standard spelling is not an easy one to tackle because there is a multitude of reasons affecting orthography. Not only is there variation in spelling norms in different centuries but also individual variation affected by the dialect background of the writers, their command of the written norm, and the level of formality of the text among other factors. Orthography has also been influenced by editorial conventions at different stages of bringing the historical texts into a digital format.

The goal of this paper is to propose and compare methods of normalizing historical English automatically in the context of our CEEC corpus (*Corpora of Early English Correspondence*) (Nevalainen et al., 1998 2006), which consists of letters ranging from the 15th to the 19th century. The corpus consists of personal correspondence, which exhibits a great variety of non-standard spellings. The word *about* alone, for example, has over ten different spelling variants in our corpus such as *aboutt*, *aboute*, *abowt*, *abovt* and so on.

We will first normalize as much as possible of the CEEC with existing tools and methods. This will leave us with the most difficult cases of variant spelling to be dealt with using the methods we are presenting and evaluating in this paper. In other words, it is not in our interest to try to normalize something we can get the normalizations for already, but rather focus our efforts on the most deviant spelling forms.

Normalizing the CEEC will allow us to conduct more NLP research on the data in the future by using tools and libraries available for Present-day English. The primary motivation for our normalization efforts is studying neologisms and sociolinguistic variation in the letters. This means that we need to be able to normalize even the most difficult and infrequent spellings in our corpus.

2 Related Work

In the past, normalization of old texts has received some attention as an NLP task. There are ready-made tools available for normalization such as VARD2 (Baron and Rayson, 2008) and MorphAdorner (Burns, 2013). These tools, however, are not sufficient to solve the problem automatically for our corpus. Using VARD2 requires manual work and MorphAdorner does not provide enough coverage for our data.

Proceedings of Workshop on Computational Linguistics for Cultural Heritage, Social Sciences, Humanities and Literature, pages 87–96
Santa Fe, New Mexico, USA, August 25, 2018.

Using a string similarity metric such as edit distance has been used in the past for normalization. An example of such is the automatically produced diachronic dictionary of spelling variants for German (Amoia and Martinez, 2013). In building the dictionary, the authors used Levenshtein edit distance to cluster similar words together with their modern counterparts. This was facilitated by the fact that they were dealing with recipes, which thanks to their limited vocabulary, are easy to cluster. In addition, words can be clustered based on their semantics by looking at the shared contexts of the words.

Statistical machine translation models have also been used in solving the task by training a character based translation model using known historical spellings and their modern variants as training data. In (Samardzic et al., 2015) such a model was trained for normalizing Swiss German dialects to a standard variant. A similar SMT based approach has also been used in the context of historical text in (Pettersson et al., 2013).

Normalization has also been done by using deep learning. In (Bollmann and Søgaard, 2016), normalization is presented as a character-based sequence labeling task for bi-directional LSTMs. In their method a historical character does not need to be aligned with a single modern spelling character but can be aligned with a compound of characters in the training data.

3   The Corpus and Data Sources

The primary corpus we use is the CEEC (Nevalainen et al., 1998 2006). Compiled for the purposes of historical sociolinguistics, it is a corpus of personal correspondence in English representing a time span from the 15th to the 19th century. The letters have been selected from published original-spelling editions and digitized by the compilers, who have hand-corrected the OCR. The corpus comprises c. 5 million running words in 12000 letters written by more than 1000 individuals. The authors of the letters come from varied social backgrounds as reflected by the metadata in the CEEC, which contains, e.g., the socioeconomic status, gender, age, domicile and the relationship between the writer and recipient.

3.1   Preparing the Corpus

As a first step, we convert the CEEC into Unicode, remove punctuation, excluding apostrophes and hyphens, and tokenize the letters. After this step, we attempt to lemmatize each token with NLTK (Bird et al., 2009) by using the lemmatizer based on the Princeton WordNet. After this, we try to map each lemmatized token into the *Oxford English Dictionary* (OED). By doing so, we can filter out all the words that have a modern spelling in our corpus leaving out the ones with a non-standard spelling.

Our endeavor is to map as many words with non-standard spelling to the OED as possible. The most modern parts of the CEEC, namely those from the 16th to the 18th century, have been partially normalized with VARD2 in the past. These normalizations have been tagged in the CEEC in such a way that the original non-standard form has also been retained. We use this parallel list of non-standard and standard forms to map even more words to the OED by extending these normalizations to the whole corpus.

We run a tool called MorphAdorner on our corpus to produce more normalizations automatically. This allows us to map even more words to the OED. At this point, we have normalized all of the "easy" cases leaving out the words that have not been mapped into the OED utilizing these approaches. The number of unique unmapped word forms is 85298. The rest of the paper focuses on the normalization of these difficult word forms.

The fact that we were able to map some of the word forms to the OED has provided us with some parallel data specific to our corpus. We use the VARD2 normalizations and the MorphAdorner produced ones as a starting point for compiling a parallel corpus of non-normalized and normalized word forms. This corpus is extended with more parallel data in the next step, described in the following subsection of this paper.

3.2   Extracting Data from Other Sources

In order to normalize the old spellings in the CEEC, we use two lexicographical sources that link old spelling variants to their modern counterparts, namely the Oxford English Dictionary (OED, nd) and the

Middle English Dictionary (MED, nd), both of which we have in XML format. These two resources provide us with indispensable parallel data of non-standard and standard word forms.

We also use the British National Corpus (The BNC Consortium, 2007) as a language model for statistical machine translation. The BNC does not provide us with any parallel data since it does not have historical texts. We can, however, take the individual words out of the corpus to build a language model for the SMT system.

The OED stores alternative spellings in multiple parts of the hierarchical XML structure. To extract the non-standard and standard pairs from the OED, we use the information stored in the derivative lemmas of the lemma section as well as the forms and variant forms subsection of the inflection section, which stores only historical variants of the lemma. The latter section also contains valuable information about the centuries the word form was used in; we also store this information when we extend our initial parallel corpus with this new data. All of these sections contain variant forms that are relevant for our normalization efforts, because ultimately our goal is to map all the words in the CEEC to the OED entries.

We can get a similar historical–modern spelling parallel collection of words from the MED, the entries of which are Middle English word forms. The MED entries themselves do not contain a modern normalized version of the Middle English form, but the MED comes with a continuously developed XML[1] which contains links between some of the entries in the MED and in the OED. From this XML we can extend our parallel corpus with the historical MED headwords and their normalizations. The MED also provides us with the time period a given word form was in use, which we store as well. At this point, our parallel data consists of 183505 pairs of historical and modern spellings.

4 Methods for Normalization

In this part we present different methods for normalizing historical English words. The idea is to leverage each of their strengths by having all of them provide their own suggested normalizations. It is from this list of possibilities that the most likely normalization is picked.

4.1 VARD2 Rules

As previously mentioned, the most modern parts of the CEEC have been normalized to some extent with VARD2. As one possible normalization method, we apply these VARD2 rules to the list of non-normalized words in the CEEC. The VARD2 rules are simple replacement rules of character sequences given their position in the word. The position of a sequence can be anywhere, even at the beginning or the end of a word. All in all, we have a list of 58 unique replacement rules, such as "u → v anywhere".

We build a Finite-State Transducer (FST), using HFST (Lindén et al., 2013), based on the VARD2 rules. This allows multiple combinations of the VARD2 normalization rules to be applied for producing normalized forms. We define the LEXC file so that it consists of the lemmas from the OED. The normalization rules are defined with weighting to a spellrelax.regex file following a description in spelling (Beesley and Karttunen, 2003). The FST then applies the rules in all possible combinations to match the non-normalized forms to forms in the LEXC file. The weighting shows how many modifications were needed to reach normalization. We consider the candidate with least modifications required as the normalization candidate produced by this method.

4.2 Contextual Edit Distance

This method compares the non-normalized words to our extracted list of unique words from the BNC. First we list the possible normalization candidates by comparing the non-normalized words to the words in the BNC applying Levenshtein edit distance. The Levenshtein distance gives a score on the string similarity of two words, where each difference, such as addition or deletion of a character, increases the distance. In this way, we collect sets of normalization candidates for each non-normalized word consisting of candidate words with an edit distance score of 3 or lower.

---

[1]The version we use in this paper is dated 3/2018.

The list of normalization candidates is still too extensive and needs to be filtered down to fewer possibilities. This is done by looking at the shared context of the non-normalized words in the CEEC and the candidates in the BNC. In practice, for each non-normalized word and normalization candidate, we get the two words that precede and the two words that follow said word in each and every occurrence. Thus, we have built a list of contextual words together with information about their position in relation to each word, non-normalized and candidate alike. We then use these lists to further filter the normalization candidates, inspecting the intersection length of the lists for contextual words given their position. We only retain the normalization candidates exhibiting the highest number of contextually shared words with the non-normalized word.

Although the previous step narrows down the normalization candidates, we still need to filter them further. As a last step, we look at the pronunciation of the candidates and compare this with the pronunciation of the non-normalized words. Since we cannot produce an accurate pronunciation for the non-normalized words due to the fact that English orthography and pronunciation are not always clearly connected, we use Soundex[2] with the size of 6 to produce an estimated pronunciation.

4.3 Statistical Machine Translation (SMT)

Previous research has shown that SMT is a viable form of solving the problem of normalization. This is why we have decided to include an SMT based approach as a module in our system. We train a character based SMT model using the parallel data extracted earlier from the OED, MED and known normalizations in the CEEC. All the words are split into letters separated by a whitespace in order to make the SMT tool, Moses (Koehn et al., 2007), treat individual characters of a word as though they were words of a sentence. The parallel non-normalized to normalized word lists are aligned with GIZA++ (Och and Ney, 2003) as part of the machine translation process.

An SMT based system also requires a language model. Without it, the system would be more likely to produce non-words as output. As a language model, we use the list of words extracted from the BNC. Again, these words are split into characters by whitespaces. We build a 10-gram language model based on the BNC data with KenLM (Heafield et al., 2013) and use this model with Moses[3].

For tuning the model, we take a random sample of 2000 non-normalized and normalized word pairs from our parallel data set and run the tuning on that. We also tune century specific models with 2000 words from the era for the 15th and the 18th century to compare whether tuning for a given century yields better results for that century than a more generally tuned model.

4.4 Neural Machine Translation (NMT)

Neural machine translation can be used for normalization in a similar fashion to the SMT approach. We use OpenNMT (Klein et al., 2017) to train against a character based machine translation model by using the parallel data extracted earlier. For validation of the model, we use the same 2000 word parallel list as we did for the general SMT model.

For NMT, we train two different models for 13 epochs. The first model gets the same input as SMT, i.e. a parallel list of word forms. The second model has a specific input for the centuries in which certain non-normalized forms were used together with the actual word forms. This is done simply by appending the year of the century before each historical form in the data set. For some of the word forms, we do not have the information of the time period in which they were used. In such cases, we include the word forms without a year label.

For the model trained with year labels, we also add the year labels to the list of non-normalized word forms we input to the system for it to translate them. These years can be recovered from the letter metadata in the CEEC.

Additionally, we take the trained year aware model and continue training it separately for the 15th and the 18th century by feeding in the parallel data of only those centuries for an additional 10 epochs. For validation, we use a random sample of 2000 word pairs for the time periods. We do this to see whether by

---

[2] We use the implementation of the Fuzzy Python package (https://pypi.org/project/Fuzzy/).
[3] Note: Moses has to be built with a separate flag to allow language models that are the size of a 10-gram model.

continuing the training, the model can learn a more accurate normalization model specific to one century while still taking advantage of the normalizations for all the centuries.

4.5 Combining the Approaches

All the previously described approaches result in their own normalization candidates. In order to take advantage of them all, we need to pick out a normalization from all of the possibilities. Since we have an SMT and an NMT approach in use, some of the normalization candidates might be non-words as the machine translations can output words that are not part of the English language. First, we look up the normalization candidates in the OED. If they are not English words according to the OED, we ignore them and do not consider them to be selected.

For the remaining normalization candidates, we try two different approaches to picking out the correct one. The first one is a simple voting mechanism: the more approaches result in the same normalization, the more likely it is that correct normalization has been found. In the case of a tie in the voting, we pick a candidate at random out of the top ones.

The other approach is finding the normalization best fitting the context. We do this by training a first order Markov chain on the BNC. The chain learns the probability at which a given word follows another in a sentence. We can use this probability to pick the normalization that is the most likely to fit a given context.

When using the chain to pick out the best normalization, we look at a context window of 4 tokens on each side of the word to be normalized. Then we check whether all the words in the context are normalized, and replace them with their normalizations, if they are known. If, however, there are words that cannot be normalized in the context window, we will also look at the normalization candidates produced by our methods for those words. Then we count the probabilities for the chain by all the possible different combinations of normalizations and pick the likeliest one. For transitions of words that are not in the model, we add a probability of 1 over the number of possible transitions from that state.

5 Results and Evaluation

To evaluate the results produced by each individual method and the overall performance of combining them, we prepare three gold standards (Säily, 2018) by normalizing a random sample of 100 words by hand out of the non-normalized words in the CEEC for each of them. The first set has words randomly picked from all centuries and the other two consist of randomly picked 15th and 18th century words respectively. These normalizations are made by a linguist who is familiar with historical English texts.

5.1 Individual Methods

We compare the outputs of each of the methods to the gold standards presented earlier both directly and using NLTK WordNet Lemmatizer on the forms to see if the lemmas are the same. Since our ultimate goal is to map the words to the OED, we are more interested in matching to the right lemma rather than the exact inflectional form of the word. The results are shown in Table 1, where the columns represent the three different gold standards and the rows accuracies of each method. The last row shows the percentage of words that were correctly normalized by at least one method. This represents the upper boundary of accuracy that our system can achieve when selecting the best suitable normalization.

The first three NMT models are the ones with the century information fed into them during the training and the "NMT no years" is the one that received only words without their centuries as input. It is clear that the NMT model without the information about the century outperforms the three century specific ones.

Figure 1 shows the overlap of the correct normalizations produced by each method in a Venn diagram in the case of the general test set. The leftmost diagram shows a combination of the different SMT and century aware NMT models, while the differences in between the SMT and century aware NMT models are shown in the other two diagrams. The number in the bottom right corner shows the number of normalizations that were not produced correctly by any of the methods in the diagram.

Model	Generic	15th century	18th century
NMT	28%	43%	14%
NMT 18th	28%	43%	15%
NMT 15th	28%	43%	15%
NMT no years	46%	55%	25%
SMT	32%	31%	28%
SMT 18th	16%	14%	19%
SMT 15th	32%	28%	31%
Edit distance	31%	31%	31%
VARD2 rules	15%	10%	8%
At least one correct	*67%*	*71%*	*52%*

Table 1: Accuracy of each method

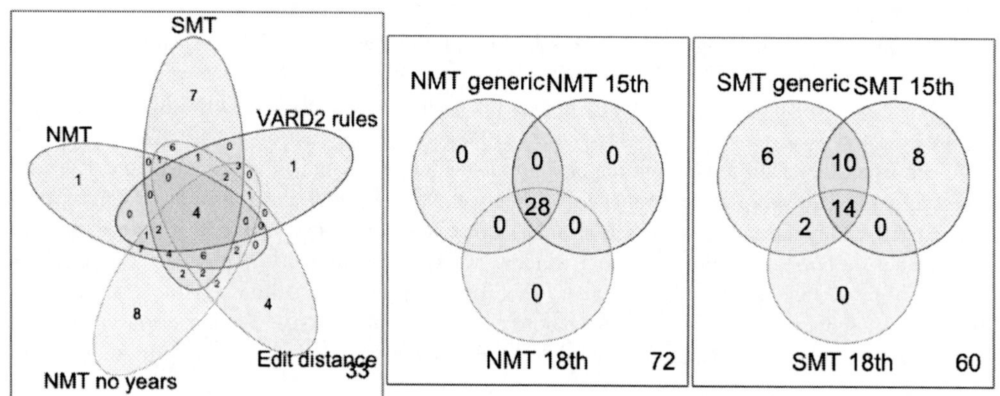

Figure 1: Overlap of correct normalizations in the general test set

We can see from Figure 1 that all of the methods have been able to correctly normalize words the other methods have not. There is also a reasonable overlap in the correct normalizations of multiple methods. This means that while a voting approach in picking the correct normalization out can work with a high precision, its recall will be lower due to the high amount of correct normalizations produced by only one method.

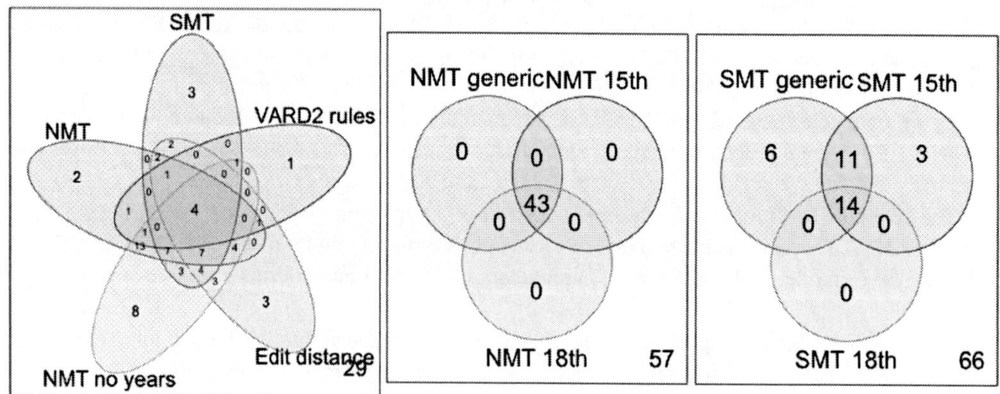

Figure 2: Overlap of correct normalizations in the 15th century test set

As for the century specific machine translation models, in the general dataset, all of the century aware NMT models produce the very same normalizations. In the case of the SMT models, both the generic one and the 15th century one find correct normalizations of their own, while the 18th century model fails to produce additional correct normalizations not produced by the other two.

Figure 2 depicts the overlap of correct normalizations in the 15th century test set. Again, all of the methods have managed to produce correct normalizations not captured by the other methods. The best one at producing correct normalizations not produced by the others is the NMT model that has not been trained with the century information, with its 8 unique correct normalizations.

Despite the high accuracy of the century aware NMT models, we can see in Figure 2 that no specialization has occurred in the 15th century NMT model to improve work for this century. In fact, all of the century-aware NMT models still produce the exact same normalizations.

As for the SMT models, we can see that the 15th century model is able to correctly normalize 3 words the other SMT models have not. What is more interesting is that despite the specialization for this century, the 15th century model has failed to correctly normalize 6 words the generic model was able to normalize.

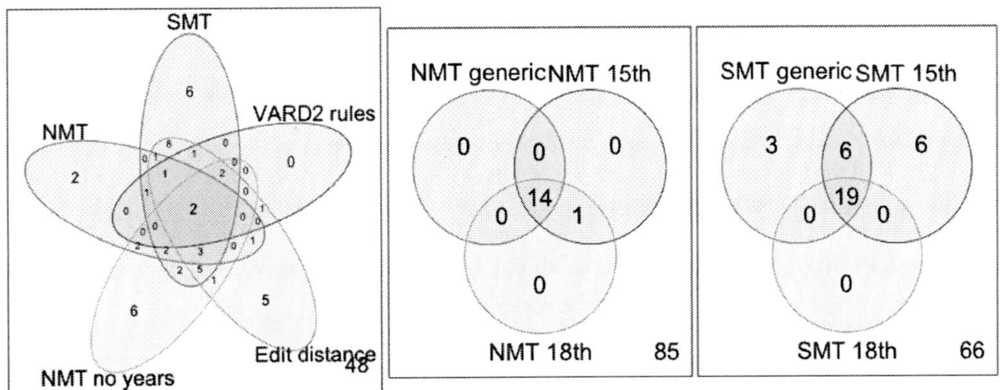

Figure 3: Overlap of correct normalizations in the 18th century test set

Finally, Figure 3 represents the overlapping correct normalizations for the 18th century. This time around, all methods except for the VARD2 rules have been able to produce correct normalizations of their own. The century aware NMTs are the weakest ones in this respect.

Interestingly, both of the century specific NMT models have been able to find the same additional correct normalization where the generic century-aware model has failed. Otherwise the normalizations produced by the models are the same.

Curiously, in the case of the SMT models, the one tuned for the 18th century seems to perform the worst, while the generic one and the 15th one are both able to produce unique normalizations of their own. In addition these two models both find the same 6 correct normalizations that the model tuned for the 18th century does not.

All in all, looking at the evaluations, it is contextual edit distance that seems to be the most consistent at finding the same amount of correct normalizations in each test set and always finding some unique ones. The same applies to the generic SMT model, which is slightly less consistent than the contextual edit distance. The VARD2 rewrite rules, unsurprisingly, perform the worst. And all the NMT models preform very differently in different test sets.

5.2 Picking the Best Normalization

In this part we present the results of the two ways for picking out the likeliest normalization from the normalization candidates produced using the different methods. These are voting and using the Markov chain trained earlier to pick out the likeliest normalization. We run the voting weighted with the accuracies of the individual methods so that the methods that have a higher accuracy have a higher vote. In addition, we run the voting unweighted so that every method has an equal vote.

	Generic	15th century	18th century
Voting no weights	41%	49%	23%
Voting weighted	45%	56%	22%
Markov chain	36%	40%	24%

Table 2: Accuracy of different ways to pick out the correct normalization

Table 2 shows that the weighted voting gives the highest results in picking the correct normalization candidate out of the possible ones in almost all the test sets. The Markov chain only outperforms it in the 18th century.

The reason for the poor performance of the Markov chain model is probably that we have narrowed this task down to the historical forms that are not trivially normalizable. This means that we are dealing with non-standard forms that occur in the CEEC only a handful of times in a context where other non-normalized word forms co-occur. This makes it difficult for a statistical model to pick out the most suitable normalization with only limited information available on the surrounding context.

6 Discussion and Future Work

The machine translation models were trained with the idea that the spelling variation follows similar tendencies within a century. Looking at the results, especially the ones obtained with SMT, it seems that the century is not necessarily a good enough variable to look at. While variation might not always be similar within a century, in the future we should look at the other variables recorded in the CEEC, such as the social class of the writer and the collection in which the letter has been published. Since this information is CEEC specific, however, having enough training data to train normalization for example for a certain social class becomes an issue.

In addition, we need to find a better way of making the NMT models specialize in a given category of variance, let it be the century as in the trials presented in this paper, or the social class of the author of the letter. Our results show that continuing the training with only the data for a particular century with a validation dataset of that century is not enough for the model to perform any better in its supposed century of specialization.

For NMT, feeding in century labels along with the historical word forms seems to even be harmful to the accuracy of the system. Finding better alternative ways to include additional information in the NMT model that will not make the accuracy decline is also a task for future research.

As for combining the results of the approaches, there is definitely room for improvement. Currently, the best performing method is weighted voting, but based on the Venn diagrams for the overlap of the correct normalizations by different methods, we can conclude that the voting approach will never reach the upper boundary of possible accuracy for the entire system: the number of correct normalizations that are unique to only one of the methods is too high, in which case voting will not suffice for selecting them. This is especially the situation if a method with a lower weight in its vote is the only one with the correct normalization.

In this paper, we have taken a naive approach thinking that two identical historical forms always normalize to the same standard form. This is true to a great extent in our case where we are dealing with the least frequent deviant forms, but there are still cases even in our set of non-normalized words where two identical historical spellings normalize into different modern English words. An example of such is *querry*, which is either *equerry* or *query* depending on the letter of appearance.

The ultimate goal of our normalization efforts is to facilitate the next step in our research, which is finding neologisms automatically in the CEEC. This is done by comparing the year of the letter where a neologism candidate is used with the earliest attestation recorded in the OED. This, of course, requires that we are able to map every single word in the CEEC to the OED. Due to the nature of neologisms, we are interested even in the least frequent words in the corpus.

7   Conclusions

In this paper, we have presented different approaches to normalized deviant infrequent historical spellings in the CEEC corpus. While all of the individual approaches have strengths of their own in terms of their facilitating the normalization of spelling variants other methods cannot, the single best individual method seems to be the NMT method without additional century labels.

Century has proven to be a poor variable to base tuning of the models on in the case of our corpus. This must be due to the fact that most of the spelling variation is due to other factors than the century of writing such as dialect background, social class and individual spelling mistakes.

Based on the findings presented in this paper, we have multiple different directions to continue our normalization efforts, all of which require further research and thus fall outside the scope of this paper.

Acknowledgements

This work was supported by the Academy of Finland grant 293009.

References

Marilisa Amoia and Jose Manuel Martinez. 2013. Using comparable collections of historical texts for building a diachronic dictionary for spelling normalization. In *Proceedings of the 7th workshop on language technology for cultural heritage, social sciences, and humanities*, pages 84–89.

Alistair Baron and Paul Rayson. 2008. VARD2: a tool for dealing with spelling variation in historical corpora. In *Postgraduate Conference in Corpus Linguistics*. Aston University, Birmingham.

Kenneth R. Beesley and Lauri Karttunen, 2003. *Finite-State Morphology*, pages 451–454. Stanford, CA: CSLI Publications.

Steven Bird, Ewan Klein, and Edward Loper. 2009. *Natural Language Processing with Python*. O'Reilly Media.

Marcel Bollmann and Anders Søgaard. 2016. Improving historical spelling normalization with bi-directional LSTMs and multi-task learning. *CoRR*, abs/1610.07844.

Philip R Burns. 2013. MorphAdorner v2: A Java library for the morphological adornment of English language texts. *Northwestern University, Evanston, IL.*

Kenneth Heafield, Ivan Pouzyrevsky, Jonathan H. Clark, and Philipp Koehn. 2013. Scalable Modified Kneser-Ney Language Model Estimation. In *Proceedings of the 51st Annual Meeting of the Association for Computational Linguistics*, pages 690–696, Sofia, Bulgaria, August.

Guillaume Klein, Yoon Kim, Yuntian Deng, Jean Senellart, and Alexander M. Rush. 2017. OpenNMT: Open-Source Toolkit for Neural Machine Translation. In *Proc. ACL*.

Philipp Koehn, Hieu Hoang, Alexandra Birch, Chris Callison-Burch, Marcello Federico, Nicola Bertoldi, Brooke Cowan, Wade Shen, Christine Moran, Richard Zens, et al. 2007. Moses: Open source toolkit for statistical machine translation. In *Proceedings of the 45th annual meeting of the ACL on interactive poster and demonstration sessions*, pages 177–180. Association for Computational Linguistics.

Krister Lindén, Erik Axelson, Senka Drobac, Sam Hardwick, Juha Kuokkala, Jyrki Niemi, Tommi A. Pirinen, and Miikka Silfverberg. 2013. HFST — A System for Creating NLP Tools. In Cerstin Mahlow and Michael Piotrowski, editors, *Systems and Frameworks for Computational Morphology*, pages 53–71, Berlin, Heidelberg. Springer Berlin Heidelberg.

MED. n.d. Middle English Dictionary. University of Michigan. https://quod.lib.umich.edu/m/med/.

Terttu Nevalainen, Helena Raumolin-Brunberg, Jukka Keränen, Minna Nevala, Arja Nurmi, Minna Palander-Collin, Samuli Kaislaniemi, Mikko Laitinen, Tanja Säily, and Anni Sairio. 1998–2006. CEEC, Corpora of Early English Correspondence. Department of Modern Languages, University of Helsinki. http://www.helsinki.fi/varieng/CoRD/corpora/CEEC/.

Franz Josef Och and Hermann Ney. 2003. A Systematic Comparison of Various Statistical Alignment Models. *Computational Linguistics*, 29(1):19–51.

OED. n.d. OED Online. Oxford University Press. http://www.oed.com/.

Eva Pettersson, Beáta Megyesi, and Jörg Tiedemann. 2013. An SMT approach to automatic annotation of historical text. In *Proceedings of the workshop on computational historical linguistics at NODALIDA 2013; May 22-24; 2013; Oslo; Norway. NEALT Proceedings Series 18*, number 087, pages 54–69. Linköping University Electronic Press.

Tanja Säily. 2018. Test set for Normalization of Historical English in CEEC, June. https://doi.org/10.5281/zenodo.1300332.

Tanja Samardzic, Yves Scherrer, and Elvira Glaser, 2015. *Normalising orthographic and dialectal variants for the automatic processing of Swiss German.* Proceedings of the 7th Language and Technology Conference. ID: unige:82397.

The BNC Consortium. 2007. The British National Corpus, version 3 (BNC XML Edition). Distributed by Bodleian Libraries, University of Oxford, on behalf of the BNC Consortium. http://www.natcorp.ox.ac.uk/.

Power Networks: A Novel Neural Architecture to Predict Power Relations

Michelle Lam*[1], Catherina Xu*[1], Angela Kong[1], and Vinodkumar Prabhakaran[1]

[1]Department of Computer Science, Stanford University, Stanford, CA, USA.
{mlam4, yuex, akong2, vinod}@cs.stanford.edu

Abstract

Can language analysis reveal the underlying social power relations that exist between participants of an interaction? Prior work within NLP has shown promise in this area, but the performance of automatically predicting power relations using NLP analysis of social interactions remains wanting. In this paper, we present a novel neural architecture that captures manifestations of power within individual emails which are then aggregated in an order-preserving way in order to infer the direction of power between pairs of participants in an email thread. We obtain an accuracy of 80.4%, a 10.1% improvement over state-of-the-art methods, in this task. We further apply our model to the task of predicting power relations between individuals based on the entire set of messages exchanged between them; here also, our model significantly outperforms the 70.0% accuracy using prior state-of-the-art techniques, obtaining an accuracy of 83.0%.

1 Introduction

With the availability and abundance of linguistic data that captures different avenues of human social interactions, there is an unprecedented opportunity to expand NLP to not only understand language, but also to understand the *people* who speak it and the *social relations* between them. Social power structures are ubiquitous in human interactions, and since power is often reflected through language, computational research at the intersection of language and power has gained interest recently. This research has been applied to a wide array of domains such as Wikipedia talk pages (Strzalkowski et al., 2010; Taylor et al., 2012; Danescu-Niculescu-Mizil et al., 2012; Swayamdipta and Rambow, 2012), blogs (Rosenthal, 2014) as well as workplace interactions (Bramsen et al., 2011; Gilbert, 2012; Prabhakaran, 2015).

The corporate environment is one social context in which power dynamics have a clearly defined structure and shape the interactions between individuals, making it an interesting case study on how language and power interact. Organizations stand to benefit greatly from being able to detect power dynamics within their internal interactions, in order to address disparities and ensure inclusive and productive workplaces. For instance, (Cortina et al., 2001) reports that women are more likely to experience incivility, often from superiors. It has also been shown that incivility may breed more incivility (Harold and Holtz, 2015), and that it can lead to increased stress and lack of commitment (Miner et al., 2012).

Prior work has investigated the use of NLP techniques to study manifestations of different types of power using the Enron email corpus (Diesner et al., 2005; Prabhakaran et al., 2012; Prabhakaran and Rambow, 2013; Prabhakaran and Rambow, 2014). While early work (Bramsen et al., 2011; Gilbert, 2012) focused on surface level lexical features aggregated at corpus level, more recent work has looked into the thread structure of emails as well (Prabhakaran and Rambow, 2014). However, both (Bramsen et al., 2011; Gilbert, 2012) and (Prabhakaran and Rambow, 2014) group all messages sent by an individual to another individual (at the corpus-level and at the thread-level, respectively) and rely on word-ngram

---

* Authors (listed in alphabetical order) contributed equally.

Proceedings of Workshop on Computational Linguistics for Cultural Heritage, Social Sciences, Humanities and Literature, pages 97–102
Santa Fe, New Mexico, USA, August 25, 2018.

based features extracted from this concatenated text to infer power relations. They ignore the fact that the text comes from separate emails, and that there is a sequential order to them.

In this paper, we propose a hierarchical deep learning architecture for power prediction, using a combination of Convolutional Neural Networks (CNN) to capture linguistic manifestations of power in individual emails, and a Long Short-Term Memory (LSTM) that aggregates their outputs in an order-preserving fashion. We obtain significant improvements in accuracy on the corpus-level task (82.4% over 70.0%) and on the thread-level task (80.4% over 73.0%) over prior state-of-the-art techniques.

2 Data and Problem Formulation

We use the version of the Enron Email corpus released by Agarwal et al. (2012) that captures the organizational power relation between 13,724 pairs of Enron employees, in addition to the reconstructed thread structure of email messages added by Yeh and Harnly (2006). We mask greetings and signature lines in the email content to prevent our model from being biased by the roles held by specific employees.

Entity type	# of Pairs	Train	Dev	Test
Per-Thread	15,048	7,510	3,578	3,960
Grouped	3,755	2,253	751	751

Table 1: Data instance statistics by problem formulation.

Prior work on NLP approaches to predict power in organizational email has used two different problem formulations — *Per-Thread* and *Grouped*. We investigate both formulations in this paper. Table 1 shows the number of data instances in each problem formulation.

Per-Thread: This formulation was introduced by Prabhakaran and Rambow (2014) in which, for a given thread t and a pair of related interacting participant pairs (A, B), the direction of power between A and B is predicted (where the assignment of labels A and B is arbitrary). The participants in these pairs are 1) *interacting*: at least one message exists in the thread such that either A is the sender and B is a recipient or vice versa, and 2) *related*: A and B are related by a dominance relation (either superior or subordinate) based on the organizational hierarchy. As in (Prabhakaran and Rambow, 2014), we exclude pairs of employees who are peers, and we use the same train-dev-test splits so our results are comparable.

Grouped: Here, we group all emails A sent to B across all threads in the corpus, and vice versa, and use these sets of emails to predict the power relation between A and B. This formulation is similar those in (Bramsen et al., 2011; Gilbert, 2012), but our results are not directly comparable since, unlike them, we rely on the ground truth of power relations from (Agarwal et al., 2012); however, we created an SVM model that uses word-ngram features similar to theirs as a baseline to our proposed neural architectures.

3 Methods

The inputs to our models take on two forms: **Lexical features:** We represent each email as a series of tokenized words, each of which is represented by a 100-dimensional GloVe vector pre-trained on Wikipedia and Gigaword (Pennington et al., 2014). We cap the email length at a maximum of 200 words. **Non-lexical features:** We incorporate the structural non-lexical features identified as significant by Prabhakaran and Rambow (2014) for the *Grouped* problem formulation. We used (1) the average number of recipients and (2) the average number of words in each email for each individual; these features were concatenated into a single input vector. We investigate the following three network architectures, in increasing order of complexity, to train our model:

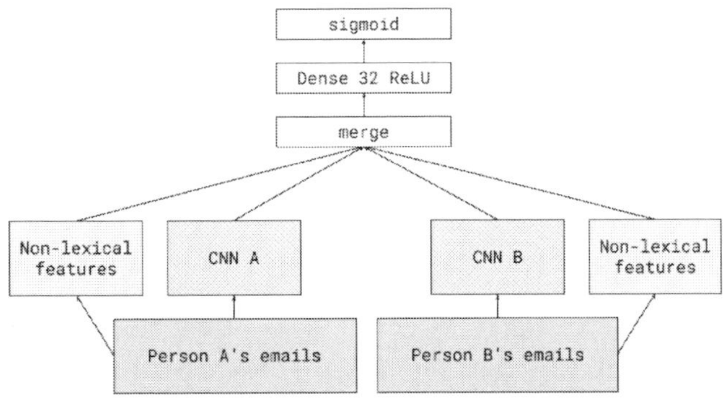

Figure 1: Batched emails (Batched-CNN)

Approach 1: Batched emails (Batched-CNN). In this model (see Figure 1), all of A's emails to B are batched and fed into a Convolutional Neural Network (CNN), and the same operation is performed for B's emails to A. The format of this input is described earlier in this section. This representation can be thought of as a neural equivalent of the SVM-based approaches in prior work, since they merge together all emails in either direction as a single unit. Then, the output of these two CNNs is merged with the non-lexical features from A's emails and B's emails, passed through a dense layer with rectified linear unit (ReLU) activation, and fed to a sigmoid classifier that predicts the power relation between A and B.

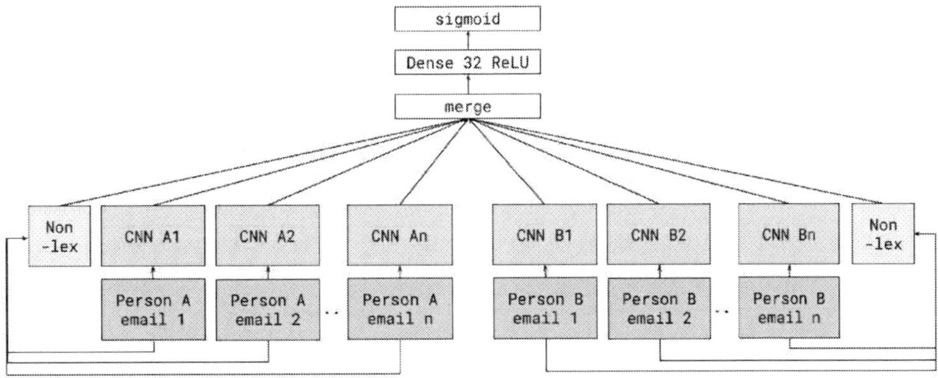

Figure 2: Separated emails (Separated-CNN)

Approach 2: Separated emails (Separated-CNN). In this model (see Figure 2), we capture the essence of individual emails by separating them in the model input. As in Batched-CNN, we separate A's and B's emails, but here we feed *each* email as input to a CNN. The motivation here is to first capture local patterns from individual emails. We then merge the output of these CNNs with the non-lexical features from A's and B's emails, pass this to a dense layer with ReLU activation, and pass the result to a sigmoid classifier that predicts the power relation.

Approach 3: Sequential emails (Sequential-CNN-LSTM). Finally, we use a third model where we account for the temporal order of emails, which may be important in the case of the *Per-Thread* formulation. In this model (see Figure 3), we separate each individual's emails, feed each email to a CNN, and pass the sequence of CNN outputs for each email to a Long Short-Term Memory network (LSTM) for that individual. We then merge the resulting output of the two LSTMs with the non-lexical features from each individual's emails, pass it on to a dense layer with ReLU activation, and then to a sigmoid classifier for the final prediction.

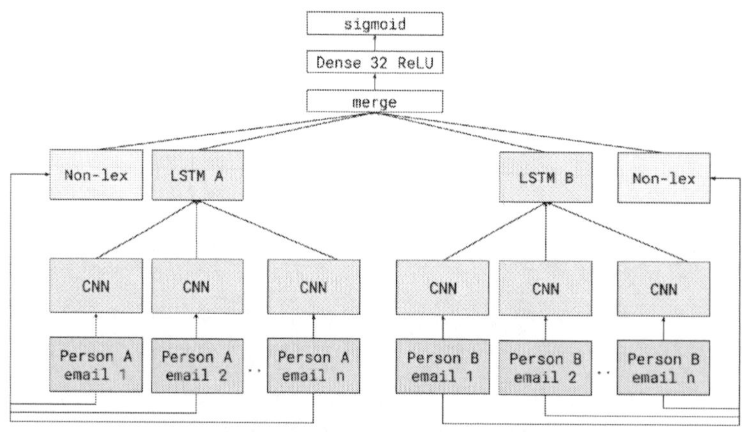

Figure 3: Sequential emails (Sequential-CNN-LSTM)

4 Experiments and Results

We use support vector machine (SVM) based approaches as our baseline, since they are the state-of-the art in this problem (Prabhakaran and Rambow, 2014; Bramsen et al., 2011; Gilbert, 2012). We use the performance reported by (Prabhakaran and Rambow, 2014) using SVM as baseline for the *Per-Thread* formulation (using the same train-dev-test splits) and implemented an SVM baseline for the *Grouped* formulation (not directly comparable to performance reported by (Bramsen et al., 2011; Gilbert, 2012)).

For each of our neural net models, we trained for 30-70 epochs until the performance on the development set stopped improving, in order to avoid overfitting. We used Hyperas to tune hyperparameters on our development dataset for the same set of parameter options for each task formulation, varying activation functions, hidden layer size, batch size, dropout, number of filters, and number of words to include per email.[1]

Table 2 presents the accuracy obtained using different models. All of our models significantly outperformed the SVM baseline in both task formulations. In the *Per-Thread* formulation, we obtained the best accuracy of 80.4% using the Sequential-CNN-LSTM approach, compared to the 73.0% reported by (Prabhakaran and Rambow, 2014). This is also a marked improvement over the simpler Batched-CNN and Separated-CNN models. This suggests that both temporal and local

Model	Per-Thread	Grouped
SVM Baseline	73.0	70.0
Batched-CNN	78.7	82.0
Separated-CNN	79.8	**83.0**
Sequential-CNN-LSTM	**80.4**	82.4

Table 2: Accuracy obtained using different models
SVM Baseline: (Prabhakaran and Rambow, 2014)

email features aid in the power prediction task within the *Per-Thread* formulation. In the *Grouped* formulation, the Separated-CNN model obtained the best accuracy of 83.0%, outperforming the Sequential-CNN-LSTM accuracy of 82.4%. We hypothesize that this is because the grouped formulation does not inherently have a temporal structure between emails, unlike the thread formulation where Sequential-CNN-LSTM is able to tap into the temporal structure.

Table 3 presents a few emails from our corpus, along with the true and predicted labels for the power relation between their sender and recipient(s). Our model seems to pick up on linguistic signals of lack of power such as relinquishing agency (*let me know who you'd like us to work with*), and status reports (*model is nearly completed*), as well as overt displays of power such as *I personally would like to see the*

---

[1]https://github.com/maxpumperla/hyperas

100

results and *we need to end all payments*. On the other hand, the model picks up on the phrasing in *don't use the ftp site* as displaying superiority while the superiority displayed here may have been derived from the expertise the subordinate has in file-transfer protocols. Similarly, the model may have misunderstood the overtly polite phrasings in the last email sent by a superior to be subordinate-like behavior. This sheds light on an important challenge in this task: superiors don't express their superiority in all emails, and subordinates may sometimes display power derived from other sources such as expertise. In such cases where text features alone are not informative enough, signals from additional non-lexical features may be key to accurate classification.

Text extracted from email	Actual	Predicted
Let me know who you'd like us to work with in your group. The Adaytum planning model is nearly completed.	Subordinate	Subordinate
Vince is hosting on Wharton and a project they are doing for us, I personally would like to see the results of that before doing more with Wharton.	Superior	Superior
We need to end all payments as of December 31, 2001.	Superior	Superior
Don't use the ftp site while I am away [...] I will check my messages when I return.	Subordinate	Superior
Here is the draft letter for your consideration. Please distribute this to the members of the legal team at Enron. Thank you for your assistance, and have a happy holiday season.	Superior	Subordinate

Table 3: Example power labels from Separated-CNN on the Grouped formulation. For *correct* labels, text segments that may signal the power relation are underlined in green; for *incorrect* labels, potentially confusing power signals are underlined in red. (text segments chosen based on our qualitative judgment).

5   Concluding Discussions

In this paper, we investigated the intersection between language and power in the corporate domain via neural architectures grounded in an understanding of how expressions of power unfold in email. Our Sequential-CNN-LSTM model, which utilizes an LSTM to capture the temporal relations underlying per-email features, achieved 80.4% accuracy in predicting the direction of power between participant pairs in individual email threads, which is a 10.1% accuracy improvement over the state-of-the-art approach (Prabhakaran and Rambow, 2014). Our Separated-CNN model also obtains an accuracy of 83.0% in predicting power relations between individuals based on the entire set of messages exchanged between them, a significant boost over 70.0% accuracy obtained using traditional methods. We also present a qualitative error analysis that sheds light on the patterns that confuse the model.

To further our work, we plan to granularize the level at which features are learned. We hypothesize that by training a CNN on each *sentence* rather than email, the model will better capture mid-level indicators of power that occur between the word level and email level. We will also investigate ways to better incorporate structural features by accounting for their relevance to a holistic judgment of power; for example, features like gender and temporal position in a thread are more suited to merge with a higher level of the architecture like the per-individual LSTMs while features like number of email tokens are more suited to merge at the low level of the per-email CNNs. Lastly, we plan to incorporate additional datasets such as the Avocado Research Email Collection (Oard et al., 2015) to study cross-corpora performance.

6   Acknowledgements

We would like to thank Christopher Manning, Richard Socher, and Arun Chaganty, who served as course instructors for CS 224N (Natural Language Processing with Deep Learning, the course in which M. Lam, C. Xu and A. Kong developed the first iteration of this work) for their feedback on the project. V. Prabhakaran was supported by a John D. and Catherine T. MacArthur Foundation award granted to Jennifer Eberhardt and Dan Jurafsky. We also thank anonymous reviewers for their useful feedback.

References

Apoorv Agarwal, Adinoyi Omuya, Aaron Harnly, and Owen Rambow. 2012. A Comprehensive Gold Standard for the Enron Organizational Hierarchy. In *Proceedings of the 50th Annual Meeting of the Association for Computational Linguistics (Volume 2: Short Papers)*, pages 161–165, Jeju Island, Korea, July. ACL.

Philip Bramsen, Martha Escobar-Molano, Ami Patel, and Rafael Alonso. 2011. Extracting Social Power Relationships from Natural Language. In *Proceedings of the 49th Annual Meeting of the Association for Computational Linguistics: Human Language Technologies*, pages 773–782, Portland, Oregon, USA, June. ACL.

Lilia M Cortina, Vicki J Magley, Jill Hunter Williams, and Regina Day Langhout. 2001. Incivility in the Workplace: Incidence and Impact. *Journal of Occupational Health Psychology*, 6(1):64.

Cristian Danescu-Niculescu-Mizil, Lillian Lee, Bo Pang, and Jon Kleinberg. 2012. Echoes of Power: Language Effects and Power Differences in Social Interaction. In *Proceedings of the 21st International Conference on World Wide Web*, WWW '12, New York, NY, USA. ACM.

Jana Diesner, Terrill L Frantz, and Kathleen M Carley. 2005. Communication Networks from the Enron Email Corpus It's Always About the People. Enron is no Different. *Computational & Mathematical Organization Theory*, 11(3):201–228.

Eric Gilbert. 2012. Phrases That Signal Workplace Hierarchy. *CSCW '12 Proceedings of the ACM 2012 conference on Computer Supported Cooperative Work*, pages 1037–1046.

Crystal M Harold and Brian C Holtz. 2015. The Effects of Passive Leadership on Workplace Incivility. *Journal of Organizational Behavior*, 36(1):16–38.

Kathi N Miner, Isis H Settles, Jennifer S Pratt-Hyatt, and Christopher C Brady. 2012. Experiencing Incivility in Organizations: The Buffering Effects of Emotional and Organizational Support. *Journal of Applied Social Psychology*, 42(2):340–372.

Douglas Oard, William Webber, David Kirsch, and Sergey Golitsynskiy. 2015. Avocado Research Email Collection. *Philadelphia: Linguistic Data Consortium.*

Jeffrey Pennington, Richard Socher, and Christopher D. Manning. 2014. GloVe: Global Vectors for Word Representation. *Proceedings of the 2014 Conference on Empirical Methods in Natural Language Processing (EMNLP)*, pages 1532–1543.

Vinodkumar Prabhakaran and Owen Rambow. 2013. Written Dialog and Social Power: Manifestations of Different Types of Power in Dialog Behavior. In *Proceedings of the Sixth International Joint Conference on Natural Language Processing*, pages 216–224, Nagoya, Japan, October. Asian Federation of NLP.

Vinodkumar Prabhakaran and Owen Rambow. 2014. Predicting Power Relations between Participants in Written Dialog from a Single Thread. *Proceedings of the 52nd Annual Meeting of the Association for Computational Linguistics*, pages 339–344.

Vinodkumar Prabhakaran, Owen Rambow, and Mona Diab. 2012. Who's (Really) the Boss? Perception of Situational Power in Written Interactions. In *Proceedings of COLING 2012*, pages 2259–2274, Mumbai, India, December. The COLING 2012 Organizing Committee.

Vinodkumar Prabhakaran. 2015. *Social Power in Interactions: Computational Analysis and Detection of Power Relations*. Ph.D. thesis, Columbia University.

Sara Rosenthal. 2014. Detecting Influencers in Social Media Discussions. *XRDS: Crossroads, The ACM Magazine for Students*, 21(1):40–45.

Tomek Strzalkowski, George Aaron Broadwell, Jennifer Stromer-Galley, Samira Shaikh, Sarah Taylor, and Nick Webb. 2010. Modeling Socio-Cultural Phenomena in Discourse. In *Proceedings of the 23rd International Conference on COLING 2010*, Beijing, China, August. Coling 2010 Organizing Committee.

Swabha Swayamdipta and Owen Rambow. 2012. The Pursuit of Power and Its Manifestation in Written Dialog. *2012 IEEE Sixth International Conference on Semantic Computing*, 0:22–29.

Sarah M. Taylor, Ting Liu, Samira Shaikh, Tomek Strzalkowski, George Aaron Broadwell, Jennifer Stromer-Galley, Umit Boz, Xiaoai Ren, Jingsi Wu, and Feifei Zhang. 2012. Chinese and American Leadership Characteristics: Discovery and Comparison in Multi-party On-Line Dialogues. In *ICSC*, pages 17–21.

J.Y. Yeh and A. Harnly. 2006. Email Thread Reassembly Using Similarity Matching. In *Third Conference on Email and Anti-Spam (CEAS)*, pages 27–28.

Automated Acquisition of Patterns for Coding Political Event Data:
Two Case Studies

Peter Makarov
Institute of Computational Linguistics
University of Zurich, Switzerland
`makarov@cl.uzh.ch`

Abstract

We present a simple approach to the generation and labeling of extraction patterns for coding political event data, an important task in computational social science. We use weak supervision to identify pattern candidates and learn distributed representations for them. Given seed extraction patterns from existing pattern dictionaries, we use label propagation to label pattern candidates. We present two case studies. i) We derive patterns of acceptable quality for a number of international relations & conflicts categories using pattern candidates of O'Connor et al. (2013). ii) We derive patterns for coding protest events that outperform an established set of TABARI / PETRARCH hand-crafted patterns.

1 Introduction

Social scientists work with datasets of interactions between political actors (*political events*), which they extract manually or automatically (*code*) from large quantities of news text (Figure 1). The automated coding of political events, which dates back to the early 1990s (Gerner et al., 1994), is commonly performed using pattern matching with large manually compiled dictionaries of actor names and event patterns. Syntactic parsing is widely used to guide the application of patterns.

Example	U.S. military chief General Colin Powell said on Wednesday NATO would need to remain strong.
Event type	MAKE STATEMENT, GENERIC (010)
Example	Kenyan President Daniel Arap Moi on Monday urged Uganda to repatriate "all Kenyan criminals hiding there" to face trial, accusing them of killing Kenyan policemen in cross-border raids recently.
Event type	APPEAL FOR MATERIAL COOPERATION (021)

Example	Austrian unions blocked three motorways into the capital Vienna on Monday to protest government plans to reform the country's pension system.
Event type	OBSTRUCT PASSAGE, BLOCK (144)
Example	A small eastern German company on Wednesday became the first to announce a boycott by an American company over Berlin's refusal to back the U.S. administration's moves to disarm Iraq militarily.
Event type	CONDUCT STRIKE OR BOYCOTT (143)

Figure 1: Examples of political events and their CAMEO event categories (§ 2): IR events above and protest events below. The IR examples are from the CAMEO codebook (Schrodt, 2012). In the examples, the source actor is in red, the event in green, and the target actor in blue.

Despite their simplicity, pattern-based coding systems are as good as trained human coders at predicting event types (King and Lowe, 2003) and have been found sufficiently accurate for near real-time event monitoring (O'Brien, 2010). Compared to statistical systems for event extraction common in NLP (Ahn, 2006), one advantage of pattern-based event coding is that coding decisions are transparent and readily examinable, being triggered by the matching of specific patterns. Yet, manual pattern construction is

Proceedings of Workshop on Computational Linguistics for Cultural Heritage, Social Sciences, Humanities and Literature, pages 103–112
Santa Fe, New Mexico, USA, August 25, 2018.

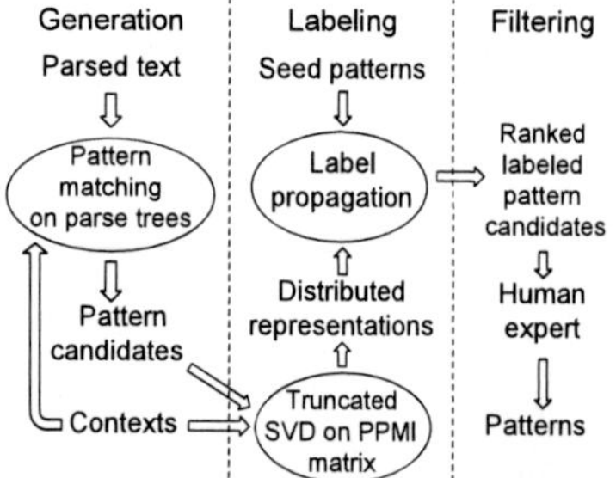

$$reject \xrightarrow{dobj} criticism \xrightarrow{prep\_of} blacklist \xrightarrow{dobj}$$
$$postpone \xrightarrow{dobj} visit \xrightarrow{poss} kill \xrightarrow{prep\_as}$$
$$pelt \xrightarrow{dobj} stones \qquad pelt \xrightarrow{prep\_at} police$$
$$attack \xrightarrow{nsubjpass} office \qquad remain \xrightarrow{prep\_despite} change$$
$$receive \xrightarrow{dobj} dobj \qquad protect \xrightarrow{prep\_from} violence$$

Figure 2: Overview of proposed pipeline: automated pattern acquisition and subsequent filtering of pattern candidates by a human expert.

Figure 3: Examples of pattern candidates: IR domain above (O'Connor et al., 2013), protest below.

prohibitively costly (Schrodt, 2006). Patterns are not easily portable across domains, and any adaptation to a new domain requires extensive human effort.

In this paper, we show how the automated acquisition, that is generation and labeling, of extraction patterns can be applied to the problem of the machine coding of political events. The goal is, on the one hand, to reduce human effort associated with pattern construction and, on the other, to show how to increase recall, which is often low in rule-based systems. By automatically generating pattern candidates and labeling them in a semi-supervised way, we produce many noisy patterns. Before any of them gets added to a pattern-based coder, they should be inspected by a human expert.

Our contribution is as follows: We combine ideas from traditional pattern acquisition by bootstrapping (Huang and Riloff, 2013), the more recent approaches to the grouping of semantically related patterns based on distributed representations (Krause et al., 2015; Batista et al., 2015), and semi-supervised labeling for lexicon induction (Hamilton et al., 2016; Rao and Ravichandran, 2009; Takamura et al., 2007) into a simple recipe for pattern construction, of practical interest to social scientists (Figure 2). We demonstrate the effectiveness of the approach by applying it to the important domains of international relations and conflicts (IR) and of protest events.

2   Related Work

There exists a whole family of political event coding systems that rely on dictionaries of patterns: TABARI, PETRARCH, PETRARCH2[1] (Norris et al., 2017), and VRA-Reader[2] (King and Lowe, 2003). One popular ontology of political events, primarily in the IR domain, is CAMEO (Gerner et al., 2002). It defines twenty broad categories, e.g. Reduce Diplomatic Relations or Investigate. Each topmost category is further divided into more specific subtypes, e.g. Investigate War Crimes. TABARI, PETRARCH, and PETRARCH2 come with extensive dictionaries of patterns that map verb phrases to CAMEO categories. Recently, there has been lot of interest in applying statistical learning to the coding of political events (Beieler, 2016; Hanna, 2017; Nardulli et al., 2015). O'Connor et al. (2013) present an unsupervised Bayesian coder, which models the gradual change in the types of events between actors over time.

Automated pattern acquisition has been a central topic in information extraction by pattern matching (Yangarber et al., 2000; Riloff and Jones, 1999) and is primarily associated with bootstrapping, a set of heuristic methods that establish similarity between patterns based on their occurrence in a small number of contexts. Huang and Riloff (2013) bootstrap verb-phrase patterns for protest event extraction by exploiting their co-occurrence with collective terms like "workers", "activists". Krause et al. (2015) explore the occurrence of event patterns in all contexts and train a feedforward neural network to produce event pattern embeddings.

The semi-supervised method of label propagation in a lexical similarity graph whose edge weights are computed from rich distributed representations has been used extensively for the derivation of large-scale polarity lexica (Hamilton et al., 2016; Velikovich et al., 2010). Various efficient techniques have become

---

[1] https://github.com/openeventdata/petrarch2
[2] http://vranet.com

available for obtaining powerful distributed representations of linguistic entities (Mikolov et al., 2013; Pennington et al., 2014; Cotterell et al., 2017). Levy et al. (2015) repopularize truncated singular value decomposition (SVD) in the context of word embeddings.

3 Method

This and the next section present the method. First, we generate pattern candidates from dependency parses (§ 3.1), then compute their distributed representations and label using label propagation (§ 3.2).

3.1 Generation of pattern candidates

A *pattern* is a most simple classifier (r, t) that consists of a regular expression r and a type t. If r matches some substring v of input text x, then x gets classified with t and v is the textual evidence of t in x. A *pattern candidate* is a regular expression. Given a set of types $\{t_1, \ldots, t_m\}$, an automated pattern acquisition method identifies sets of pattern candidates $\{P_1, \ldots, P_m\}$ such that P_i are likely correct classifiers for type t_i. To apply P_i to coding, one can either simply use all P_i as patterns for t_i (i.e. $\{(p, t_i) : p \in P_i\}$) or have a human expert examine P_i and build patterns from reliable pattern candidates only.

We follow the standard practice of using dependency paths as pattern candidates (Stevenson and Greenwood, 2006). A *dependency path* is a path through a syntactic dependency structure, i.e. an alternating sequence of labeled edges and nodes $(n_0, e_0, n_1, e_1, \ldots)$ such that each e_i connects n_{i-1} and n_i and e_i can be either left-to-right or right-to-left. A path can end with either a node or an edge. For example, $protester \xleftarrow{\text{subj}} pelt \xrightarrow{\text{dobj}} stone$ is a dependency path. We shall assume that dependency paths use lemmas instead of tokens. Whenever this is not the case we shall explicitly state it.

Being in a specific dependency relation with likely actor expressions is what makes an arbitrary dependency path a pattern candidate for some type. The exact nature of pattern candidates is dictated by weak supervision, which is specific to a domain.

We shall now detail the generation of pattern candidates for the protest and IR domains. IR pattern candidates are due to O'Connor et al. (2013) and are generated from paths connecting source and target actor expressions. Protest pattern candidates are predicates of collective actor expressions, an idea for pattern bootstrapping due to Huang and Riloff (2013).

Protest events. We work with 1.8M newswire documents[3] downloaded from the LexisNexis data service[4] using a search query with common protest-related keywords.[5] We process the documents with the Stanford CoreNLP toolkit (Manning et al., 2014). We build pattern candidate generation on the following observation (Huang and Riloff, 2013): Protest events are typically collective actions, and therefore, when they are expressed as verbs, their semantic agent will likely be a plural noun, e.g. "Workers took to the streets", "A group of students clashed with the police". This suggests a simple procedure: We find all plural nouns and traverse dependency trees collecting all predicates of which the plural nouns are agents.[6]

We identify all plural common nouns (i.e. NNS-tagged tokens)[7] and then traverse collapsed and

---

[3]Agence France Press, Deutsche Presse-Agentur (German Press Agency), BBC World from 2000-2014.

[4]`https://www.lexisnexis.com`

[5]initiative OR referendum OR petition! OR signature! OR campaign! OR protest! OR demonstrat! OR manifest! OR marche! OR marchi! OR parade OR rall! OR picket! OR (human chain) OR riot! OR affray OR festival OR ceremony OR (street theatre) OR (road show) OR vigil OR strike! OR boycott! OR block! OR sit-in OR squat! OR mutin! OR bomb! OR firebomb! OR molotov OR graffiti OR assault OR attack OR arson OR incendiar! OR (fire I/1 raising) OR (set AND ablaze) OR landmine OR sabot! OR hostage! OR assassinat! OR shot OR murdered OR killed (Kriesi et al., 2012)

[6]Our procedure is different in many important ways from that of Huang and Riloff (2013). We identify a larger set of syntactic constructions that contribute pattern candidates, including passives, relative clauses, and more types of verbal adjuncts. Unlike Huang and Riloff (2013), we do not distinguish between event phrases and purpose phrases (e.g. in the sentence "Workers took to the streets to demand better working conditions.", "took to the streets" would be an event phrase and "to demand better working conditions" a purpose phrase). We consider purpose phrases a subset of event phrases, partly because often the same predicate occurs as both. Further, the original proposal tries to identify purpose phrases, like in the example sentence above, with the help of the *xcomp* relation, which is in fact a parser error: Purpose phrases are not arguments but *advcl* dependents.

[7]In fact, we could have also included plural proper nouns (NNPS-tagged tokens).

CCprocessed dependencies (De Marneffe and Manning, 2008). A pattern candidate is a path from a verb to its (direct or prepositional) object or prepositional adjunct (i.e. a dependent in any relation matching $dobj|prep\_.*$). However, if the object or adjunct is an named entity (NE), we store the NE tag and discard the lemma. If a sentence matches one or more of the following cases, we extract pattern candidates and update the statistics of co-occurrence of plural common nouns and pattern candidates:

1. A plural common noun is a *nsubj* dependent (i.e. a subject of an active verb). E.g. in the sentence

   Protesters pelted stones at the police.

   we identify candidates $pelt \xrightarrow{dobj} stone$ and $pelt \xrightarrow{prep\_at} police$.

2. The main verb has a plural common noun subject and a *xcomp* or *vmod* dependent (i.e. a non-finite verbal complement or adjunct).[8] The non-finite dependent produces pattern candidates, e.g. $chant \xrightarrow{dobj} slogan$ from

   Protesters gathered on the street chanting slogans.

3. A plural common noun is an *agent* dependent. The verb that governs it produces a pattern candidate together with its *nsubjpass* dependent, or *rcmod* or *vmod* head. The former accounts for passives, the latter for finite and non-finite relative clauses, e.g.

   The office was attacked by angry protesters.

After excluding infrequent pattern candidates ($count < 15$) and nouns ($count < 5$), we obtain 72K unique pattern candidates and 11K plural common nouns. Together, they produce 3.6M pattern-noun samples (Figure 3).

International relations. Here, we re-use pattern candidates derived by O'Connor et al. (2013) from the English Gigaword corpus of newswire documents (Parker et al., 2009). A pattern candidate is a dependency path connecting source and target actor expressions. Actor expressions are identified with the help of the TABARI actor dictionaries. An actor expression is the minimal noun phrase containing a TABARI actor expression: a proper noun or adjective. Pattern candidates contain at most four notional words. The source actor must be a *nsubj* or *agent* dependent. Some dependency relations are not allowed in the patterns, e.g. *det* or *conj*. For further details, we refer the reader to the paper. Each pattern candidate is associated with a source-target actor pair (*dyad*) and the publication date of the news report. After filtering low-frequency pattern candidates and dyads, O'Connor et al. obtain 366K data samples featuring 421 dyads and 10K unique pattern candidates.

3.2 Labeling of pattern candidates

The semi-supervised labeling of pattern candidates requires a semantic similarity metric on the set of pattern candidates. Cosine similarity between vectors in some vector space, which somehow capture the semantics of the corresponding linguistic entities (e.g. words or patterns), is one very common similarity metric. The derivation of vector representations leverages the counts of how many times the linguistic entities occur in some specific *contexts* in the data. For example, in the derivation of word vectors, the contexts are simply neighboring words.

---

[8]We do not include *advcl* for simplicity: *advcl* dependents can have their own subjects different from the subject of the main verb.

Step 1: PPMI matrix Define matrix $\mathbf{M} \in \mathbb{R}^{m \times k}$ of PPMI scores, where m is the number of pattern candidates and k is the number of contexts, as

$$m_{qc} = \max\left(\log \frac{\hat{p}(q,c)}{\hat{p}(q)\,\hat{p}_\alpha(c)},\ 0 \right),$$

for pattern candidate q and context c. $\hat{p}(q,c)$ and $\hat{p}(q)$ are empirical distributions, $\hat{p}_\alpha(c)$ is a smoothed context distribution defined as $\hat{p}_\alpha(c) = \frac{\#(c)^\alpha}{\sum_c \#(c)^\alpha}$, where $\alpha \in \mathbb{R}$ and $\#(c)$ is the count of c in the data.

Step 2: Dimensionality reduction Perform singular value decomposition

$$\mathbf{M} = \mathbf{U} \cdot \mathbf{\Sigma} \cdot \mathbf{V}^\top$$

Rows vectors of matrix $\mathbf{U}^{\mathrm{tr}}$ truncated at the first l columns are distributed representations of pattern candidates.

Procedure 1: Derivation of distributed representations for pattern candidates.

Contexts. For event patterns, contexts can be actor expressions or other patterns that occur with the same actor expressions. For protest patterns, we use plural common nouns as contexts.

For IR patterns, similar to O'Connor et al. (2013) and Krause et al. (2015), we assume that a dyad and a time span induce a context: Patterns that occur with the same dyad in the texts from the same time span become contexts for one another. In our experiments, we take the time span to be a single day—the publication date. Thus, given a (dyad, publication date) tuple t, pattern candidates p and q that occur with t, $p \neq q$, are counted once as p being a pattern and q its context and once as q being a pattern and p its context. This is identical to Krause et al. (2015).

Distributed representations. We choose to derive distributed representations for pattern candidates by first constructing a pattern-context matrix $\mathbf{M}$ of positive pointwise mutual information (PPMI) scores (Step 1 of Procedure 1) and then performing SVD on $\mathbf{M}$ (Step 2 of Procedure 1). To this end, we use the `Hyperwords`[9] package. We apply context distribution smoothing with $\alpha = 0.75$ and retain only the pattern-to-latent-factors matrix $\mathbf{U}^{\mathrm{tr}}$ (Levy et al., 2015) truncated at 500 columns.

At this point, we can already cluster pattern candidates by e.g. exploring pattern frequencies (Krause et al., 2015). Fortunately, we have at our disposal the TABARI dictionary of labeled event patterns, which we can use in a semi-supervised learning procedure to label new patterns. This follows closely the approach of Hamilton et al. (2016), and we re-use much of their code.[10]

Similarity graph. First, we construct a weighted undirected graph of pattern similarity. Pattern candidates are nodes, and the weights of the edges $\mathbf{W}$ are computed using angular similarity, which turns cosine similarity into a distance metric. Self-loops are disallowed (Step 1 of Procedure 2). For efficiency, for each pattern candidate, we keep connections to only twenty five most similar nodes; all other edge weights are set to zero.

Label propagation. We apply the semi-supervised label propagation algorithm of Zhou et al. (2004) (Step 2 of Procedure 2) and use the TABARI verb pattern dictionary to identify seed patterns. For experiments with IR patterns, we find seeds for all but one of the topmost CAMEO categories (Mass Violence), with the number of seeds per category ranging from one to seventy-four. We identify thirty four seeds among protest event pattern candidates.

4 Experiments

We next evaluate the quality of the labeled pattern candidates. Event patterns are intended as high-precision classifiers: The words making a pattern are chosen carefully to generate as few false positives as possible. Pattern-based classifiers are typically weak in recall as it may be difficult to construct sufficiently many unambiguous patterns. Thus, any good new pattern potentially contributes to higher recall. Does our automated approach produce good new patterns? An evaluation that we conduct for IR patterns

---

[9] https://bitbucket.org/omerlevy/hyperwords
[10] https://github.com/williamleif/socialsent

Step 1: Edge weight matrix Define edge weight matrix $\mathbf{W} \in \mathbb{R}^{m \times m}$ as

$$w_{pq} = \begin{cases} \arccos\left(-\cos\theta\right) & \text{if } p \neq q, \\ 0 & \text{otherwise} \end{cases}$$

where $\cos\theta$ is the cosine similarity between row vectors $\mathbf{u}^{\text{tr}}_{p,*}$ and $\mathbf{u}^{\text{tr}}_{q,*}$ of $\mathbf{U}^{\text{tr}}$, the distributed representations of patterns p and q.

Step 2: Label propagation (After Zhou et al. (2004)) Given some seed patterns, define matrix $\mathbf{F}^{(0)} \in \mathbb{R}^{m \times c}$, where m is the number of patterns and c is the number of categories, as

$$f^{(0)}_{pk} = \begin{cases} 1 & \text{if } p \text{ is a seed pattern for category } k, \\ 0 & \text{otherwise} \end{cases} \tag{1}$$

Define transition matrix $\mathbf{T} \in \mathbb{R}^{m \times m}$ as

$$t_{pq} = \frac{w_{pq}}{\sum_{r=0}^{m} w_{rq}} \tag{2}$$

Set $\beta \in [0, 1]$. Until convergence, iterate

$$\mathbf{F}^{(t+1)} = \beta \mathbf{T}\, \mathbf{F}^{(t)} + (1 - \beta)\mathbf{F}^{(0)} \tag{3}$$

Let $\mathbf{F}^{(\infty)}$ be the label matrix after convergence is reached. Label unlabeled patterns q with $\hat{k} = \arg\max_k f^{(\infty)}_{qk}$.

Procedure 2: Labeling of pattern candidates by label propagation through pattern similarity graph.

aims at estimating the proportion of correct new patterns at various ranks, when ordered by label score $f^{(\infty)}_{qk}$. For protest events, we measure precision and recall on an annotated corpus.

International relations. We use IR patterns to code newswire documents from the LexisNexis data service. Out of twenty CAMEO categories, we randomly sample eight:

(A) four categories with the number of seed patterns greater than thirty: Engage in Diplomatic Cooperation, Fight/Assault,[11] Consult, Disapprove,

(B) two categories with ten to thirty seed patterns: Coerce, Reduce Relations, and

(C) two categories with fewer than ten seeds: Investigate, Exhibit Military Posture.

For each category k, we order the pattern candidates for k by label score $f^{(\infty)}_{qk}$ in descending order and randomly sample fifteen pattern candidates from among the first 50, 50-100, and 100-150 pattern candidates. We pair the sampled candidates with category labels and turn the resulting patterns to the TABARI / PETRARCH dictionary format.[12] We use PETRARCH to code actors and events with the help of these patterns. We also check that each event match respects the dependency path of the pattern. For each pattern, we randomly sample up to two sentences that it matches. This gives us a total of 551 sentences. To this, we add 130 sentences matched by thirteen patterns randomly sampled from the seeds of each category, with up to two sentences per pattern.

To estimate the proportion of correct new patterns, the author and one political science doctoral student check the predicted categories of all the sentences. The human coders try to indicate, whenever possible, whether the predicted category is incorrect for a reason other than the pattern assigning a wrong code. We exclude such cases from calculations. With this strategy, we aim to evaluate the (average stratified) precision of the patterns (i.e. their intended property as high-precision classifiers) irrespective of their frequency.[13] This is in contrast with estimating the precision of the entire pattern-based classifier, which would inevitably be dominated by high-frequency patterns.

---

[11] Here, we follow Boschee et al. (2013) and Boschee et al. (2015) in considering Fight and Assult a single topmost category.

[12] Somewhat surprisingly, above five percent of the patterns cannot be faithfully converted to PETRARCH format as they are headed by a noun and not a verb.

[13] An alternative strategy would be to manually inspect a list of patterns, which has a downside that we may overlook ambiguities that become apparent when we see a pattern in a sentence that it matches.

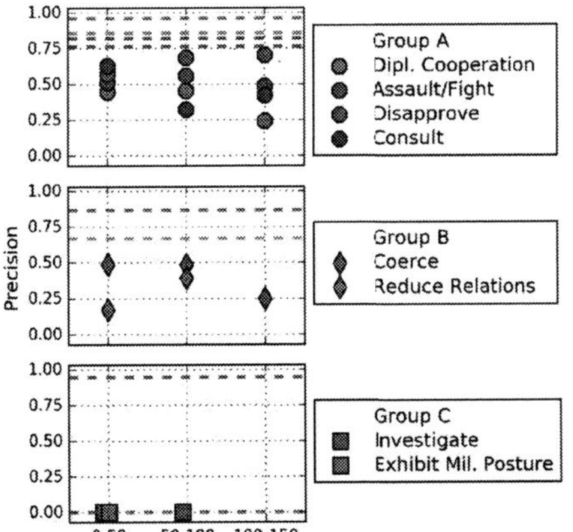
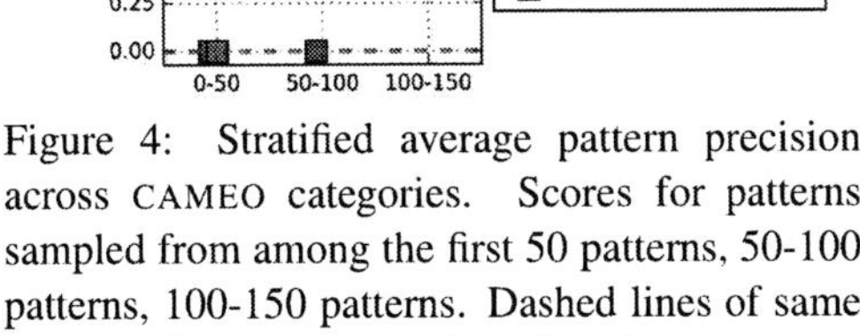

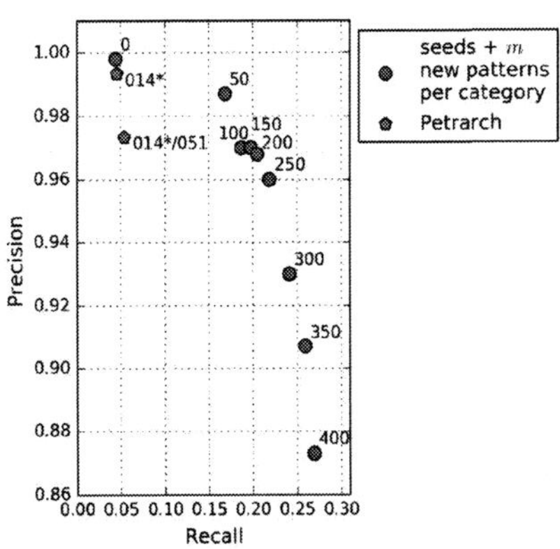

Figure 4: Stratified average pattern precision across CAMEO categories. Scores for patterns sampled from among the first 50 patterns, 50-100 patterns, 100-150 patterns. Dashed lines of same color mark average precision of seed patterns.

Figure 5: Precision and recall of seeds + m new patterns per protest subcategory and PE-TRARCH with default verb patterns and without actor coding. PETRARCH: 014* counting only protest events, 014*/051 counting protest events and events of subcategory (051) Rally Support For.

Figure 4 shows the results. The patterns for the categories with many seeds (groups **A** and **B**) perform well and compare favorably to seed patterns. Group **C** produce very few coded sentences, and no sentence is correctly coded. About eleven percent of all the sentences have been excluded. The most common causes for that are sentences from sports news (34%), hypothetical constructions (23%), negation (22%), and wrongly coded actors (12%). These sources of error are clearly failures not of the automatically generated patterns but the automated coder, e.g. its inability to take into account negation or check whether a pattern match is embedded under a modal verb. The inter-coder agreement for this evaluation is modest, with a Cohen's kappa of 0.64.

Protest events. We use the corpus of Makarov et al. (2016) of English Gigaword documents annotated with protest events and resembling standard benchmark datasets for event extraction, e.g. the ACE 2005 corpus (ACE, 2005). Unlike the IR patterns for which we resort to a complex evaluation strategy, with this corpus, we can directly and fully automatically estimate both precision and recall. We select sentences for which at least two of the coders code the same event. We only use sentences which feature event types that correspond to the five CAMEO protest codes.[14] We obtain a total of 572 labeled sentences. We randomly sample another 600 sentences of newswire text not from the corpus and use them to approximate the negative class, i.e. sentences without protest events.

Collective actions often do not mention a target actor directly (as in e.g. "protest against the anti-gay law"). Since an automated coder codes an event only if both source and target actors are matched, we choose to evaluate protest patterns without actor coding (otherwise, only very few events would be coded).

We note that some positive-class sentences cannot be coded without the knowledge of the context of the document. Another complication is that protest events are often referred to with standalone nouns like "demonstration" or "rally" and not verb phrases denoting protest actions, e.g. "the Florence demonstration was expected to be the biggest in the country" or "a group of rowdy youths broke away from the peaceful demonstration". Such cases, therefore, cannot be coded by a pattern-based coder that associates events with verb phrases. This suggests that the upper bound on recall in this evaluation is much below 100%.

---

[14]Subcategories of Protest (14*): Uncategorized Protest (140), Demonstration (141), Hunger Strike (142), Strike/Boycott (143), Obstruction of Passage (144), and Riots (145)

We compare the following conditions:

i) We code with seed patterns plus, for each of the five protest subcategories, the first m new patterns, when ranked by label score in descending order. We let m range from 0 to 400. We apply patterns by matching their dependency paths.

ii) As our baseline, we run PETRARCH with its default pattern dictionary (of a few hundreds of protest event patterns) and the actor coding function switched off. Additionally, we test a condition in which we consider category (051) Rally Support For as another protest category: Many protest events with a positive stance on an issue (as in "rallied for immigrant rights") end up being coded this code.

We manually check the events that either system finds in the negative-class sentences. We find eight sentences with protest events, which we then count as instances of the positive class.

The results indicate (Figure 5) that new patterns dramatically increase recall and precision remains high. Most matches by PETRARCH come from matching single verbs: "demonstrate", "protest", "rally". The new patterns, on the other hand, are more lexically diverse: Patterns that fire feature forty seven (at $m = 50$) to fifty five (at $m = 400$) different verbs.

5   Discussion

How do we justify the choices of the techniques in the pipeline? One finds various strategies in the literature for the generation of event and relation extraction patterns that typically employ as contexts nouns, especially proper nouns (Riloff and Jones, 1999; Carlson et al., 2010), although other kind of expressions also appear, e.g. verb phrases (Huang and Riloff, 2013). Although one can build patterns over words (Du and Yangarber, 2015), patterns over parse trees have been found useful abstractions (Sudo et al., 2003; Bunescu and Mooney, 2005; Stevenson and Greenwood, 2005). Likewise, other strategies for factorizing a pattern-context co-occurrence matrix can be employed. However, truncated SVD of a PPMI matrix provides competitive representations (Levy et al., 2015; Hamilton et al., 2016) and does not build in any assumptions about the nature of entities and contexts.

Pattern-based coding suffers from the simple logic of pattern application and errors in linguistic analyses. A more flexible and better performing approach is based on statistical learning (Boschee et al., 2013; Boschee et al., 2015). Syntactic patterns can be used as features in such a statistical event coding system. Syntactic information is important to systems solving a related task of semantic role labeling (Marcheggiani and Titov, 2017; Roth and Lapata, 2016; FitzGerald et al., 2015).

6   Conclusion

We present an approach for learning dictionaries of verb patterns for the coding of political events. The method uses pattern matching over dependency parse trees to identify pattern candidates, then computes distributed representations for them that define weights in a similarity graph. The labels of unlabeled pattern candidates are learned with a semi-supervised algorithm of label propagation through the resulting graph. New patterns evaluate favorably on two important domains of political interactions.

Acknowledgements

We would like to thank Simon Clematide and the anonymous reviewers. This work has been supported by European Research Council Grant No. 338875.

References

2005. The Automated Content Extraction 2005 (ACE 05) challenge. `https://www.ldc.upenn.edu/collaborations/past-projects/ace/annotation-tasks-and-specifications`.

David Ahn. 2006. The stages of event extraction. In *Proceedings of the Workshop on Annotating and Reasoning about Time and Events*, pages 1–8. ACL.

David S Batista, Bruno Martins, and Mário J Silva. 2015. Semi-supervised bootstrapping of relationship extractors with distributional semantics. In *Proceedings of the 2015 Conference on Empirical Methods in Natural Language Processing, Association for Computational Linguistics, Lisbon, Portugal*, pages 499–504.

John Beieler. 2016. Generating politically-relevant event data. *NLP+CSS 2016*.

Elizabeth Boschee, Premkumar Natarajan, and Ralph Weischedel. 2013. Automatic extraction of events from open source text for predictive forecasting. In *Handbook of Computational Approaches to Counterterrorism*, pages 51–67. Springer.

Elizabeth Boschee, Jennifer Lautenschlager, Sean O'Brien, Steve Shellman, James Starz, and Michael Ward. 2015. BBN ACCENT Event Coding Evaluation.updated v01.pdf (ICEWS Coded Event Data). `http://dx.doi.org/10.7910/DVN/28075`.

Razvan C Bunescu and Raymond J Mooney. 2005. A shortest path dependency kernel for relation extraction. *HLT/EMNLP*, pages 724–731.

Andrew Carlson, Justin Betteridge, Richard C Wang, Estevam R Hruschka Jr, and Tom M Mitchell. 2010. Coupled semi-supervised learning for information extraction. In *Proceedings of the third ACM international conference on Web search and data mining*, pages 101–110. ACM.

Ryan Cotterell, Adam Poliak, Benjamin Van Durme, and Jason Eisner. 2017. Explaining and generalizing skipgram through exponential family principal component analysis. *EACL 2017*, 175.

Marie-Catherine De Marneffe and Christopher D Manning. 2008. Stanford typed dependencies manual. Technical report, Technical report, Stanford University.

Mian Du and Roman Yangarber. 2015. Acquisition of domain-specific patterns for single document summarization and information extraction. In *The Second International Conference on Artificial Intelligence and Pattern Recognition (AIPR2015)*, page 30.

Nicholas FitzGerald, Oscar Täckström, Kuzman Ganchev, and Dipanjan Das. 2015. Semantic role labeling with neural network factors. In *EMNLP*, pages 960–970.

Deborah J Gerner, Philip A Schrodt, Ronald A Francisco, and Judith L Weddle. 1994. Machine coding of event data using regional and international sources. *International Studies Quarterly*, pages 91–119.

Deborah J Gerner, Philip A Schrodt, Omür Yilmaz, and Rajaa Abu-Jabr. 2002. Conflict and mediation event observations (CAMEO): A new event data framework for the analysis of foreign policy interactions. *International Studies Association, New Orleans*.

William L Hamilton, Kevin Clark, Jure Leskovec, and Dan Jurafsky. 2016. Inducing domain-specific sentiment lexicons from unlabeled corpora. *arXiv preprint arXiv:1606.02820*.

Alex Hanna. 2017. MPEDS: Automating the Generation of Protest Event Data. Available at SSRN: `https://osf.io/preprints/socarxiv/xuqmv`.

Ruihong Huang and Ellen Riloff. 2013. Multi-faceted event recognition with bootstrapped dictionaries. In *HLT-NAACL*, pages 41–51.

Gary King and Will Lowe. 2003. An automated information extraction tool for international conflict data with performance as good as human coders: A rare events evaluation design. *International Organization*, 57(03):617–642.

Sebastian Krause, Enrique Alfonseca, Katja Filippova, and Daniele Pighin. 2015. Idest: Learning a distributed representation for event patterns. In *Proceedings of the 2015 Conference of the North American Chapter of the Association for Computational Linguistics: Human Language Technologies (NAACL'15)*, pages 1140–1149.

Hanspeter Kriesi, Edgar Grande, Martin Dolezal, Marc Helbling, Dominic Höglinger, Swen Hutter, and Bruno Wüest. 2012. *Political conflict in western Europe*. Cambridge University Press.

Omer Levy, Yoav Goldberg, and Ido Dagan. 2015. Improving distributional similarity with lessons learned from word embeddings. *Transactions of the Association for Computational Linguistics*, 3:211–225.

Peter Makarov, Jasmine Lorenzini, and Hanspeter Kriesi. 2016. Constructing an annotated corpus for protest event mining. *NLP+CSS 2016*, page 102.

Christopher D Manning, Mihai Surdeanu, John Bauer, Jenny Finkel, Steven J Bethard, and David McClosky. 2014. The Stanford CoreNLP Natural Language Processing Toolkit. In *Proceedings of 52nd Annual Meeting of the Association for Computational Linguistics: System Demonstrations*, pages 55–60.

Diego Marcheggiani and Ivan Titov. 2017. Encoding sentences with graph convolutional networks for semantic role labeling. *EMNLP*.

Tomas Mikolov, Ilya Sutskever, Kai Chen, Greg S Corrado, and Jeff Dean. 2013. Distributed representations of words and phrases and their compositionality. In *Advances in neural information processing systems*, pages 3111–3119.

Peter F Nardulli, Scott L Althaus, and Matthew Hayes. 2015. A progressive supervised-learning approach to generating rich civil strife data. *Sociological Methodology*.

Clayton Norris, Philip Schrodt, and John Beieler. 2017. PETRARCH2: Another event coding program. *The Journal of Open Source Software*, 2(9), jan.

Sean P O'Brien. 2010. Crisis early warning and decision support: Contemporary approaches and thoughts on future research. *International Studies Review*, 12(1):87–104.

Brendan O'Connor, Brandon M Stewart, and Noah A Smith. 2013. Learning to extract international relations from political context. In *ACL (1)*, pages 1094–1104.

Robert Parker, Linguistic Data Consortium, et al. 2009. *English Gigaword Fourth Edition LDC2009T13*. Linguistic Data Consortium.

Jeffrey Pennington, Richard Socher, and Christopher D Manning. 2014. Glove: Global vectors for word representation. In *EMNLP*, volume 14, pages 1532–1543.

Delip Rao and Deepak Ravichandran. 2009. Semi-supervised polarity lexicon induction. In *Proceedings of the 12th Conference of the European Chapter of the Association for Computational Linguistics*, pages 675–682. Association for Computational Linguistics.

Ellen Riloff and Rosie Jones. 1999. Learning dictionaries for information extraction by multi-level bootstrapping. In *AAAI/IAAI*, pages 474–479.

Michael Roth and Mirella Lapata. 2016. Neural semantic role labeling with dependency path embeddings. *arXiv preprint arXiv:1605.07515*.

Philip A Schrodt. 2006. Twenty years of the Kansas event data system project. *The political methodologist*, 14(1):2–8.

Philip A Schrodt. 2012. CAMEO: Conflict and mediation event observations event and actor codebook. Version: 1.1b3.

Mark Stevenson and Mark A Greenwood. 2005. A semantic approach to IE pattern induction. In *Proceedings of the 43rd Annual Meeting on Association for Computational Linguistics*, pages 379–386. Association for Computational Linguistics.

Mark Stevenson and Mark A Greenwood. 2006. Comparing information extraction pattern models. In *Proceedings of the Workshop on Information Extraction Beyond The Document*, pages 12–19. Association for Computational Linguistics.

Kiyoshi Sudo, Satoshi Sekine, and Ralph Grishman. 2003. An improved extraction pattern representation model for automatic IE pattern acquisition. *ACL*, pages 224–231.

Hiroya Takamura, Takashi Inui, and Manabu Okumura. 2007. Extracting semantic orientations of phrases from dictionary. In *HLT-NAACL*, volume 2007, pages 292–299.

Leonid Velikovich, Sasha Blair-Goldensohn, Kerry Hannan, and Ryan McDonald. 2010. The viability of web-derived polarity lexicons. In *Human Language Technologies: The 2010 Annual Conference of the North American Chapter of the Association for Computational Linguistics*, pages 777–785. Association for Computational Linguistics.

Roman Yangarber, Ralph Grishman, Pasi Tapanainen, and Silja Huttunen. 2000. Automatic acquisition of domain knowledge for information extraction. In *Proceedings of the 18th conference on Computational linguistics-Volume 2*, pages 940–946. Association for Computational Linguistics.

Dengyong Zhou, Olivier Bousquet, Thomas Navin Lal, Jason Weston, and Bernhard Schölkopf. 2004. Learning with local and global consistency. In *NIPS*, volume 16, pages 321–328.

A Method for Human-Interpretable Paraphrasticality Prediction

Maria Moritz[1], Johannes Hellrich[2,3], and Sven Buechel[3]
[1]Institute of Computer Science, University of Göttingen, Germany
[2]Graduate School "The Romantic Model", Friedrich-Schiller-Universität Jena, Germany
[3]JULIE Lab, Friedrich-Schiller-Universität Jena, Germany
`mmoritz@gwdg.de`

Abstract

The detection of reused text is important in a wide range of disciplines. However, even as research in the field of plagiarism detection is constantly improving, heavily modified or paraphrased text is still challenging for current methodologies. For historical texts, these problems are even more severe, since text sources were often subject to stronger and more frequent modifications. Despite the need for tools to automate text criticism, e.g., tracing modifications in historical text, algorithmic support is still limited. While current techniques can tell if and how frequently a text has been modified, very little work has been done on determining the degree and kind of paraphrastic modification—despite such information being of substantial interest to scholars. We present a human-interpretable, feature-based method to measure paraphrastic modification. Evaluating our technique on three data sets, we find that our approach performs competitive to text similarity scores borrowed from machine translation evaluation, being much harder to interpret.

1 Introduction

Why is Text Reuse important? The term text reuse refers to the repetition of a text within a new context. Examples are citations, paraphrases of a text, allusions, or even cases of cross-linguistic reuse in the form of translations. In the humanities context, the detection of text reuse helps tracing down lines of transmission, which is essential to the field of textual criticism (Büchler et al., 2012). Text reuse detection can also help consolidating today's digital libraries by assuring the consistency of content by inter-linking related documents (Schilling, 2012).

Background: To this date, a lot of effort has been put into the investigation of detecting *plagiarism*, a special kind of text reuse. However, while constantly improving (see Ferrero et al. (2017)), contemporary detection techniques are still quite unreliable when text is heavily modified. Historical text is even more challenging through incompleteness, copying errors, and evolution of language. Thus, only limited algorithmic support exists for the identification and analysis of (especially paraphrastic) repetition in such documents.

While existing reuse detection techniques are able to tell *if* and *how frequently* a text has been modified, it is important to also determine the degree and characteristics of paraphrastic modification, i.e., the "features" that constitute a given modification. As such, understanding type and degree of reuse is an important prerequisite for enhancing reuse detection techniques for historical texts as well as giving scholars hints for deeper investigation. In this work, we present a technique to measure paraphrastic modification which is both human-interpretable and semantically informed. This interpretability sets our method apart from recent approaches based on distributional semantics which do not allow for easy manual inspection of individual model decisions (Wieting et al., 2015).

We already investigated descriptive characteristics of paraphrasing in a specific humanities use case (Moritz et al., 2018). We found changes in inflection, synonym replacement and co-hyponym replacement to be the most frequent paraphrastic modifications, thus supporting the feasibility of feature-based approaches to this problem.

Method and Questions: We measure the degree of modification based on a list of *modification operations* that we count in a prioritized order based on relations between aligned, parallel sentences. These

Proceedings of Workshop on Computational Linguistics for Cultural Heritage, Social Sciences, Humanities and Literature, pages 113–118
Santa Fe, New Mexico, USA, August 25, 2018.

relationships between two words can range from exact copy (no operation necessary) to co-hyponymy, see Table 1. Compared to scores such as Meteor that make use of synonymy, but do not model other relationships, our score also includes information on hypernymy, hyponymy, and co-hyponymy. This is especially useful in historical text, since meaning and, therefore, relationships change over time. The order in which these operations are counted is intuitive and follows the usual prepossessing steps that one would perform to reduce variance in a text corpus. Table 2 shows an example of the alignment output, thus illustrating our method. The relative frequencies of the operations then serve as input features for a binary classifier.

In this contribution we investigate, how our human-interpretable method compares against text similarity metrics borrowed from machine translation evaluation (also serving as input for a classifier). In particular, we examine the performance of those approaches for semantic equivalency in: (**RQ1**) a modern English paraphrase corpus; (**RQ2**) a parallel Bible corpus; and (**RQ3**) a medieval Latin text reuse dataset.

Operation	Example Pair
no operation necessary	*above, above*
lower-casing match	*LORD, Lord*
normalizing match	*desireth, desires*
lemmatizing match	*mine, my*
derivation match	*help, helper*
short edit distance match	*Phinehas, Phinees*
words are synonyms	*went, departed*
word1 is hypernym of word2	*coat, doublet*
word1 is hyponym of word2	*spears, arms*
words are co-hyponyms	*steps, feet*
other	—

Table 1: Overview of transformation operations.[2]

2   Related Work

Surface Feature Approaches: Levenshtein's (1966) edit distance, which is based on character-level removal, insertion, and replacement operations, can be considered as one of the earliest works to measure text similarity. Büchler et al. (2012) use overlapping bi-grams to maximize recall in a reuse detection task of Homeric quotations, showing a good precision of more than 70% at the same time. Those techniques rely on surface features (token and character-level) only. Thus, our proposed method differs by also incorporating semantic information (lexico-semantic relationships between aligned word pairs).

Semantic Approaches: Computing the semantic similarity between two sentences is a popular task in NLP (Xu et al., 2015). Osman et al. (2012) present a plagiarism detection technique based on semantic role labeling. They analyze text by identifying the semantic space of each term in a sentence and find semantic arguments for each sentence. They also assign weights to the arguments and find that not all of them affect plagiarism detection. Techniques from the field of paraphrase detection can be used for e.g., sentence similarity, entailment, and sentiment classification. Wieting et al. (2015) use embedding models to identify paraphrastic sentences in such a mixed NLP task employing a large corpus of short phrases associated with paraphrastic relatives. Their simplest model represents a sentence embedding by the averaged vectors of its tokens, the most complex model is a long short-term memory (LSTM) recurrent neural network. They find that the word averaging model performs best on sentence similarity and entailment, and the LSTM performs best on sentiment classification. Although these methods generally show good results, they typically allow no manual inspection of why a specific judgment is made and are thus ill-suited for applications in the humanities.

Approaches Based on Machine Translation (MT) Evaluation Metrics: Madnani et al. (2012) conduct a study on the usefulness of automated MT evaluation metrics (e.g., BLEU, NIST and Meteor) for the task of paraphrase identification. They train an ensemble of different classifiers using scores of MT metrics as features. They evaluate their model on two corpora for paraphrase and plagiarism detection, respectively, finding that it performs very satisfyingly. This approach to paraphrase and plagiarism detection based on MT metrics combines surface and semantic features since Meteor incorporates synonymy information (see below). Yet, the number of semantic features used is limited and so is also the interpretability of this approach.

---

[2]Note that we distinguish operations with and without changes in part-of-speech, hence in total we work with twenty one different operations.

OP	NOP	NOP	cohypo	NOP	syn	NOP	fallback	NOP	NOP	NOP	NOP	NOP	syn	fallback
token s1	It	is	unlawful	he	contends	to	co-operate	with	any	one	who	is	doing	wrong
token s2	It	is	law	he	argues	to	-	with	any	one	who	is	performing	-

Table 2: Example of operation (feature) based alignment. Features here are no operation =9/14 (NOP), cohyponym =1/14 (cohypo), synonym=1/14 (syn), and fallback =2/14.

3 External Resources

Tools: We use BabelNet (Navigli and Ponzetto, 2012) as a resource for retrieving relationships between *English* words, namely synonym, hypernym, hyponym and co-hyponyms. For the *Latin* evaluation dataset we use the Latin WordNet by Minozzi (2009).[3] To normalize, lemmatize, and part-of-speech (POS) tag the text data, we use MorphAdorner,[4] a tool for lemmatizing Early Modern English text which is also applicable to contemporary English. For the *Latin* dataset, we use the respective TreeTagger model (Schmid, 1994). To align sentences from a given parallel corpus on the token level we use the Berkeley Word Aligner (DeNero and Klein, 2007), a statistical, unsupervised word aligner originally designed for machine translation.

Contemporary Paraphrase Detection: As a gold dataset for paraphrase prediction, we use an English corpus of semantically equivalent sentences that originates from the PAN 2010 plagiarism detection challenge. Starting from text that was aligned on the *paragraph* level, Madnani et al. (2012) generated a set of aligned *sentences* using heuristics. Negative pairings were created by sampling non-aligned sentences with an overlap of four words. The training and test set comprise 10,000 and 3,000 sentence pairs, respectively. Both sets are balanced regarding positive and negative labels.

Bible Translation Class Prediction: We use a parallel corpus of eight English Bible translations that we gathered from three sources.[5] We split them in two classes: literal translations— those being directly translated from the primary languages Hebrew and Ancient Greek coming with rich linguistic diversity—and translations that mainly follow the translation tradition of the Anglican Church (standard). Table 3 lists the detailed edition names accompanied by its publishing date and its class.

Bible	Published	Class
Douay-Rheims Challoner Rev. (DRC)	1749-1752	standard
King James Version (KJV)	1769	standard
The Webster Bible (WBT)	1833	standard
Darby Bible (DBY)	1867-1890	standard
English Revised Version (ERV)	1881-1894	standard
English Septuagint (LXXE)	1851	literal
Young's Literal Translation (YLT)	1862	literal
Smith's Literal Translation (SLT)	1876	literal

Table 3: Overview of English Bible translations used.

For the experiments we extract parallel verses from two different editions and try to predict if they come from the same or different translation classes (literal vs. standard).

Latin Reuse Detection: Excerpts from a total of twelve works and two work collections from the 12th century Latin writer Bernard of Clairvaux constitute our third dataset. The team behind the Biblindex project (Mellerin, 2014)[6] manually identified 1,100 instances of text reuse in these writings and bundled them into a corpus. Every instance of reuse relates to a Bible verse from the Biblia Sacra Juxta Vulgatam Versionem and is typically half as long as the original verse. Negative training data of equal size were obtained by randomly shuffling the initial dataset.

---

[3] http://multiwordnet.fbk.eu/english/home.php
[4] http://morphadorner.northwestern.edu/
[5] http://www.biblestudytools.com/, www.mysword.info/, Parallel Text Project (Mayer and Cysouw, 2014).
[6] http://www.biblindex.mom.fr/

4   Methods

Our method relies on the relative frequencies of modification operations (see Table 1) in an aligned sentence pair which later serve as features for a classifier:

$$x_i = \frac{\#o_i}{\sum_{j=0}^{m} \#o_j} \tag{1}$$

where x_i is the relative frequency of a modification operation i in an aligned sentence pair, m is the number of features, and o_i is the absolute frequency of operation i.[7] Our method, hence, can be understood as a collection of features that are represented as relative frequencies of edits obtained from empirical values. These features are used as input to a maximum entropy classifier to predict if two sentences are paraphrases of each other. MaxEnt was chosen due to its simplicity, relying on a linear combination of features. Thus feature weights can be roughly interpreted as importance of the respective modification operation after fitting the model. Recall the example alignment presented in Table 2 illustrating the high interpretability of our approach. Our method will be denoted "multi_f" (multiple features) for the remainder of this paper.

We evaluate our method by comparing it to several reference methods based on machine-translation evaluation metrics.[8] To adapt these to our different paraphrase detection tasks, the source Bible provides the reference sentence (ref) and the target Bible (and Bernard's reuse respectively) provides the system output (sys). From the Gold corpus, also the source text (numbered in the repository with 1, see Madnani et al. (2012)) serves as reference, and the paraphrastic reuse of it (numbered with 2), provides the system output.

Reference Methods: Often, machine translation metrics are based on simple edit distance measures. Unlike simple word error rate (WER; Su et al. (1992)), which depends on a strict word order, the position-independent error rate (**PER**; Tillmann et al. (1997)) uses a bag-of-words approach. Popović and Ney (2007) define PER based on counts of independent words that system output and reference sentence have in common. We adapt their document-wide score to the sentence level:

$$PER = \frac{1}{2 \cdot N_{ref}} (|N_{ref} - N_{sys}| + \sum_e |n(e, ref) - n(e, sys)|), \tag{2}$$

where N_{sys} is the length (in words) of the target reuse text—in MT a.k.a. *the system output* version of a text—and N_{ref} is the length of the source text—in MT a.k.a. *the reference sentence* for a system output—, and $n(e, ref)$ is the frequency of a given word e in the reference sentence.

The translation edit rate (**TER**; Snover et al. (2006)) is the number of edits that a system output should undergo so that it matches a reference sentence. TER[9] is normalized by the length of the reference input. Following Papineni et al. (2002), we define a sentence-based **BLEU** score:

$$BLEU = BP \times \exp(\sum_{n=1}^{N} \frac{1}{N} \log p_n) \tag{3}$$

where N is the maximum n-gram size, which we set to 2. p_n is a precision score that is calculated based on n-grams in both, source and target texts (see Papineni et al. (2002)). We omit BLEU's brevity penalty which would otherwise dominate our sentence level analysis.

The last measure we consider is **Meteor** 1.5 (Denkowski and Lavie, 2014). Meteor especially differs from other scores by considering not only precision, but also recall. It further takes synonymy and paraphrases into account. Meteor introduces so called matchers that are represented by exact match, stem match, synonym match or paraphrase match. The hypothesis (system) and reference texts h and r are split into content words h_c and r_c, and function words h_f and r_f. Precision and recall measures are then used to

---

[7] $m = 18$ because we dropped three features after development experiments, i.e., no operation necessary, lemmatization match and hypernym match.

[8] We had to change some of the metrics to capture distance (instead of a similarity) by using their complement.

[9] We use the implementation from: `www.cs.umd.edu/\%7Esnover/tercom/`, acc. May '18

determine the harmonic mean F_{mean}. Together with a fragmentation penalty that measures the degree of chunks, the Meteor score is calculated by $Meteor = (1 - penalty) \times F_{mean}$.

Similar to Madnani et al. (2012) we use these MT scores separately in a classification task to predict paraphrasticality where the respective MT score is fed into a MaxEnt classifier as only feature.

5 Results

Detecting Paraphrases (RQ1): Using the relative operation count from the alignment as features in a classification task, we determine the classification accuracy of our approach on the gold corpus. We run a maximum entropy classifier on our operation features. The results in Table 4 show that Meteor performs best on that task, followed by our approach.

name	RQ1	RQ2	RQ3
multi_f only WN	87.6	67.2	-
multi_f synonyms only	87.7	67.1	88.9
multi_f w/o cohyponyms	87.9	67.3	89.8
multi_f (all features)	87.6	67.3	**90.7**
TER	85.8	67.0	61.9
PER	85.4	67.4	87.6
BLEU	83.9	**68.1**	83.6
Meteor	**89.5**	67.8	88.9

Table 4: Accuracy in solving our three tasks.

Predicting Translation Classes (RQ2): Here we want to determine if two aligned Bible editions are of the same translation class (labeled with 0), or of different classes (labeled with 1); we distinguish between standard vs. literal translations. We use the operation counts based on two aligned verses as features in this binary classification task. Our operations equip us with a fine-grained description of the degree of modification of two text excerpts. The Bible corpus is a suitable source for measuring the degree of modification, since it holds a broad variety of paraphrastic reuses. To estimate a human judgment of deviation, we assume that standard translations are more homogeneous to each other (based on their evolution history) than literal translations that demand for more creative language use (Moritz et al., 2018). We use 10-fold-cross validation on the shuffled dataset. The results in Table 4 show that all methods under consideration perform comparably well. We also find that our proposed method suffers from a drop of accuracy when semantic features are ablated. When only WordNet, not BabelNet, is used for identifying lexico-semantic relations, performance increases slightly, which we attribute to noise that comes with using BabelNet.

Detecting Latin Reuse (RQ3): Finally, we predict reuse in the medieval Latin dataset. Moritz et al. (2016) found out that co-hyponymy (besides synonymy) can be a common means of substitution in reuse, especially in medieval texts. Consequently, our method is well suited for this task, because it considers semantic relations beyond synonymy.[10] Again, we use 10-fold cross-validation on the shuffled dataset. Table 4 shows that dropping features such as co-hyponyms indeed worsens the accuracy. The low score of TER may be explained by the fact that this metric's normalization term is based on the length of the *reference* version of a sentence. In our setup the Bible verse is the reference and the system output is the reuse. The reuse however, is often shorter than the Bible verse (see above).

6 Discussion and Conclusion

We presented a method for paraphrase detection that describes reuse based on the frequency of specific modification operations and is thus easily interpretable for humans. We showed that modeling reuse in historical text using semantic relations beyond synonyms achieves results comparable to using features derived from machine translation metrics. Moreover, our method is especially useful for applications in the humanities as operation frequencies, their respective feature weights, and, by extensions, individual model decisions are open to manual inspection. In future work, we plan to tune parameters and to qualitatively analyze weaknesses of our method (e.g., due to the tools used for pre-processing and alignment).

Acknowledgements

This research was partially funded by the German Federal Ministry of Education and Research (grant 01UG1509) and the Deutsche Forschungsgemeinschaft (grant GRK 2041/1).

---

[10] Note that Meteor only contains synonym data in English, which can also influence its accuracy.

References

Marco Büchler, Gregory Crane, Maria Moritz, and Alison Babeu. 2012. Increasing recall for text re-use in historical documents to support research in the humanities. In *Theory and Practice of Digital Libraries*, pages 95–100.

John DeNero and Dan Klein. 2007. Tailoring word alignments to syntactic machine translation. In *ACL 2007*, pages 17–24.

Michael Denkowski and Alon Lavie. 2014. Meteor universal: Language specific translation evaluation for any target language. In *Proceedings of the ninth workshop on statistical machine translation*, pages 376–380.

Jérémy Ferrero, Laurent Besacier, Didier Schwab, and Frédéric Agnès. 2017. Using word embedding for cross-language plagiarism detection. In *EACL: Volume 2, Short Papers*, pages 415–421.

Vladimir I Levenshtein. 1966. Binary codes capable of correcting deletions, insertions, and reversals. In *Soviet physics doklady*, pages 707–710.

Nitin Madnani, Joel Tetreault, and Martin Chodorow. 2012. Re-examining machine translation metrics for paraphrase identification. In *NAACL 2012*, pages 182–190.

Thomas Mayer and Michael Cysouw. 2014. Creating a massively parallel bible corpus. In *LREC 2014*.

Laurence Mellerin. 2014. New ways of searching with biblindex, the online index of biblical quotations in early christian literature. In *Digital Humanities in Biblical, Early Jewish and Early Christian Studies*. Brill, Leiden.

Stefano Minozzi. 2009. The latin wordnet project. In Peter Anreiter and Manfred Kienpointner, editors, *Innsbrucker Beitrge zur Sprachwissenschaft*, pages 707–716.

Maria Moritz, Andreas Wiederhold, Barbara Pavlek, Yuri Bizzoni, and Marco Büchler. 2016. Non-literal text reuse in historical texts: An approach to identify reuse transformations and its application to bible reuse. In *EMNLP 2016*, pages 1849–1859.

Maria Moritz, Johannes Hellrich, and Sven Buechel. 2018. Towards a metric for paraphrastic modification. In *Digital Humanities 2018*, pages 457–460.

Roberto Navigli and Simone Paolo Ponzetto. 2012. Babelnet: The automatic construction, evaluation and application of a wide-coverage multilingual semantic network. *Artificial Intelligence*, 193:217–250.

Ahmed Hamza Osman, Naomie Salim, Mohammed Salem Binwahlan, Rihab Alteeb, and Albaraa Abuobieda. 2012. An improved plagiarism detection scheme based on semantic role labeling. *Applied Soft Computing*, 12(5):1493–1502.

Kishore Papineni, Salim Roukos, Todd Ward, and Wei-Jing Zhu. 2002. BLEU: a method for automatic evaluation of machine translation. In *ACL 2002*, pages 311–318.

Maja Popović and Hermann Ney. 2007. Word error rates: Decomposition over pos classes and applications for error analysis. In *Proceedings of the Second Workshop on Statistical Machine Translation*, pages 48–55.

Virginia Schilling. 2012. Introduction and Review of Linked Data for the Library Community, 20032011. `http://www.ala.org/alcts/resources/org/cat/research/linked-data`.

Helmut Schmid. 1994. Probabilistic part-of-speech tagging using decision trees. In *Proceedings of International Conference on New Methods in Language Processing*, pages 44–49.

Matthew Snover, Bonnie Dorr, Richard Schwartz, Linnea Micciulla, and John Makhoul. 2006. A study of translation edit rate with targeted human annotation. In *Proceedings of the 7th Conference of the Association for Machine Translation in the Americas*, pages 223–231.

Keh-Yih Su, Ming-Wen Wu, and Jing-Shin Chang. 1992. A new quantitative quality measure for machine translation systems. In *COLING 1992: Volume 2*, pages 433–439.

Christoph Tillmann, Stephan Vogel, Hermann Ney, Arkaitz Zubiaga, and Hassan Sawaf. 1997. Accelerated dp based search for statistical translation. In *Proceedings of the fifth European Conference on Speech Communication and Technology*.

John Wieting, Mohit Bansal, Kevin Gimpel, and Karen Livescu. 2015. Towards universal paraphrastic sentence embeddings. *arXiv preprint arXiv:1511.08198*.

Wei Xu, Chris Callison-Burch, and Bill Dolan. 2015. Semeval-2015 task 1: Paraphrase and semantic similarity in twitter (pit). In *SemEval 2015*, pages 1–11.

Exploring word embeddings and phonological similarity for the unsupervised correction of language learner errors

Ildikó Pilán
Språkbanken, University of Gothenburg
Sweden
ildiko.pilan@gu.se

Elena Volodina
Språkbanken, University of Gothenburg
Sweden
elena.volodina@gu.se

Abstract

The presence of misspellings and other errors or non-standard word forms poses a considerable challenge for NLP systems. Although several supervised approaches have been proposed previously to normalize these, annotated training data is scarce for many languages. We investigate, therefore, an unsupervised method where correction candidates for Swedish language learners' errors are retrieved from word embeddings. Furthermore, we compare the usefulness of combining cosine similarity with orthographic and phonological similarity based on a neural grapheme-to-phoneme conversion system we train for this purpose. Although combinations of similarity measures have been explored for finding correction candidates, it remains unclear how these measures relate to each other and how much they contribute individually to identifying the correct alternative. We experiment with different combinations of these and find that integrating phonological information is especially useful when the majority of learner errors are related to misspellings, but less so when errors are of a variety of types including, e.g. grammatical errors.

1 Introduction

During the language acquisition process, learners often use word forms which deviate, in one way or another, from a standard that native (L1) speakers usually adhere to. These deviations, also referred to as *errors* or *non-normative* forms, result often in differences in spelling which can lead to forms that might not exist in a language (*non-word* errors). Inferring the intended meaning and the correct word form for such errors can be challenging both for humans and for machines.

In previous work, a number of approaches have been tested for the automatic correction of language learner errors, which rely often on annotated data (Ng et al., 2014; Mishra and Kaur, 2013). For normalizing native speakers' non-standard use of spelling, however, a recent direction being explored is the use of word embeddings as an unsupervised solution (Bertaglia and Nunes, 2016; Fivez et al., 2017). A major advantage of this approach is that it does not require annotated training data. Such methods rely on the intuition that semantically similar words are grouped close to each other in the vector space. Incorporating character n-grams when building word representations completes this type of similarity with orthographic and morphological relatedness (Bojanowski et al., 2016). This can be useful for detecting correction candidates for those types of errors that involve only a slight variation of word forms, such as spelling and inflectional errors. Cosine similarity is often combined with other lexical similarity measures (Bertaglia and Nunes, 2016), their individual contribution and interaction, however, remains less explored. The research questions that we address in this article are:

- RQ1: How useful are word embeddings based on character n-grams for retrieving correction candidates for language learners' errors?

- RQ2: Does capturing phonological similarities between sounds provide helpful additional information for identifying corrections?

Proceedings of Workshop on Computational Linguistics for Cultural Heritage, Social Sciences, Humanities and Literature, pages 119–128
Santa Fe, New Mexico, USA, August 25, 2018.

- RQ3: What combination of different similarity measures is most efficient in this context?

The usefulness of word embeddings with character n-grams has not been previously explored specifically for correcting errors made by second or foreign language (L2) learners. While there might be similarities between the type of spelling errors that L1 and L2 speakers make (e.g. based on the position of keys while typing), in the case of the latter category grammatical errors may also occur. Moreover, L2 spelling errors may be often induced also by sound similarity or orthographic differences between L1 and L2.

Since data annotated with information about L2 errors and their correction is scarce for most languages, exploring unsupervised methods in this context is particularly valuable. This is the case also for Swedish, the target language of our experiments. As an unsupervised solution, we evaluate embeddings where words are represented as the sum of their character n-grams for L2 error correction by inspecting how often correction candidates occur among the most similar words based on cosine similarity. We compare embeddings created using a large collection of Wikipedia articles with embeddings trained on a smaller amount of *specialized* corpora related to L2 learning combined with blog texts. We find that the latter alternative provides twice more often the correction among the set of most similar words than the former.

One of the obstacles of spelling words correctly is that different graphemes can be used to encode the same sound in a certain language. This similarly in pronunciation, however goes beyond the type of information that a similarity measure based on character n-grams and orthography could provide. Therefore, we propose a phonological similarity measure for capturing this aspect. To address RQ2, we train a grapheme-to-phoneme conversion system based on neural networks to be able to map even out-of-vocabulary (OOV) words, such as non-word errors, to a phonological representation. We show that this system improves on the results of a previous rule-based attempt at solving this task for Swedish. We then compute the similarity based on a Levenshtein distance discounted for phonological relatedness between the phonological representation of each non-word error and that of the intended word. Furthermore, we investigate the correlation between different similarity measures and find that phonological similarity correlates less with cosine and orthographic similarity than these two with each other.

In relation to RQ3, we compare cosine, orthographic and phonological similarity and investigate their interaction for finding the intended word for an L2 error. We aggregate cosine similarity and the other two similarity measures individually and in combination and observe how the ranking of the correct word changes compared to other most similar words retrieved from word embeddings. Our results indicate that combining cosine and orthographic similarity worked best for the variety of errors found in learner essays, whist for errors collected from spelling exercises summing all three measures, or combining cosine and phonological similarity was more efficient.

This work has also a number of engineering contributions, which are being made freely available.[1] This includes (i) a word embedding incorporating character n-grams, trained on a combination of L2 relevant corpora and blog texts; (ii) a grapheme-to-phoneme conversion system for Swedish based on a large lexical database and deep learning methods; (iii) the implementation of a phonological similarity measure based on binary phonological features rooted in linguistic theory.

This article is structured as follows. In section 2, we present previous work related to error correction, which is followed by the description of a small evaluation dataset (Section 3) used to measure the usefulness of the proposed techniques. We then describe the word embeddings (Section 4) and the grapheme-to-phoneme conversion system (Section 5) created, which are at the basis of the similarity measures used for finding optimal correction candidates. Section 6 details the results of our experiments on the usefulness of the similarity measures. Finally, we conclude our paper in Section 7.

2   Related work

In this section, we first summarize previous literature on error correction with the use of NLP in the educational domain. Then, we focus specifically on the use of word embeddings for spelling normalization and previous attempts at solving this task with different methods for Swedish.

---

[1]The resources are available at https://github.com/IldikoPilan/swell-norm

2.1 Error correction in educational NLP applications

Throughout the language learning process, learners produce a range of written responses which vary in size and quality depending on the specific task and learners' proficiency level. A common scale of proficiency levels is the CEFR, the Common European Framework of Reference for Languages (Council of Europe, 2001). The CEFR proposes a six-point scale of proficiency levels which ranges from A1 (beginner) to C2 (advanced) level.

Learner-written texts are challenging to process automatically since, unlike the standard language texts used for training most NLP tools, they often contain errors. This is especially problematic for texts written by lower proficiency learners where the amount of such errors can have a substantial impact on the accuracy of automatic analyses. Both rule-based and statistical methods have been explored for the automatic detection and correction of errors, including finite state transducers (Antonsen, 2012) and different hybrid systems proposed in connection with the CoNLL Shared Task on grammatical error correction for L2 English (Ng et al., 2014). Most of the competing systems of this Shared Task re-used existing spell checking systems in their L2 error correction pipeline. Solutions for dealing specifically with L2 misspelling remained, however, less explored.

Language learning errors provide useful insights into L2 learners' development and have therefore been used for assessing writing quality. Yannakoudakis et al. (2011) present experiments for automatically predicting overall, human-assigned scores for texts written by L2 English test takers at upper-intermediate level. Error-rate features showed a high correlation with these scores. E-rater (Burstein, 2003) is a commercial essay scoring system that measures writing quality based on a variety of linguistic features. Also in this system, grammatical accuracy is used as an indicator of quality alongside the topical relevance of the vocabulary used and features based on discourse analysis.

2.2 Spelling error correction with word embeddings

Word embeddings represent words in a vector space by grouping semantically similar words near each other based on the idea that words that share similar contexts are semantically related (Baroni et al., 2014). We can measure how closely related two or more words are based on cosine similarity from these representations. Word embeddings are useful for a number of lexical semantic tasks such as detecting synonyms and disambiguating word senses, see e.g. in Iacobacci et al. (2016). Recently, the usefulness of these models has been also explored for spelling error correction. Bertaglia and Nunes (2016) explore word embeddings for normalizing noisy user-generated content for Brazilian Portuguese. The authors collect correction candidates from the embeddings based on cosine similarity and rank them by computing a combined similarity score. This includes, besides cosine similarity, a lexical similarity measure consisting of edit distance, longest common sub-sequence and diacritical similarity. Fivez et al. (2017) present a similar method for spelling error correction in English clinical text based on character n-gram embeddings. Correction candidates are collected from a lexicon based on both graphical and phonological distance and the candidate maximizing cosine similarity with the context words appearing around the error is chosen as correction. The authors find that this approach outperformed existing off-the-shelf systems.

2.3 Spelling error correction for Swedish

Grigonyte and Hammarberg (2014) present a method for automatically identifying those misspellings made by L2 Swedish learners which are induced by a similarity in pronunciation. In the data[2] analyzed by the authors, 21% of L2 misspellings were related to pronunciation similarities. They propose a model based on a small dataset of errors and their corrections as well as a language model for distinguishing pronunciation-related misspellings and find that incorporating additional information in their model would be required for an improved performance.

Stymne et al. (2017) propose an annotation layer incorporating error correction for a corpus of L1 and L2 Swedish student writings. In their pilot experiment, correction candidates are collected from a smaller amount of annotated data and a lexical resource using a Levenshtein distance with discounted weights

---

[2]We investigated the availability of this data, but did not receive access to it up to the time of writing.

for frequently occurring errors. When several candidates are available, the most frequent correction candidate is chosen as correction. The authors report an accuracy of 71% without the use of annotated training data for the whole corpus and 73% for texts written by L2 learners with a model using training data.

3   Evaluation data for L2 Swedish error correction

To evaluate the usefulness of word embeddings and similarity measures, we combined L2 Swedish learner error data from two different sources: a corpus of learner essays and logged spelling exercises. From the SweLL learner corpus (Volodina et al., 2016), we collected errors from 24 randomly sampled essays between CEFR levels A1 – B1 from the SpIn sub-corpus. Learners' native languages included Romanian, Vietnamese, Somali, Tigrinya, Dari, Latvian, Thai, Mandarin Chinese, Kurdish, Swahili, Albanian and Arabic. During the manual error correction, each non-lemmatized token was analyzed and, if they were errors, they were manually corrected. Only errors for which the intended token could be unambiguously determined were included. Errors with capitalization, foreign words and containing @, signaling unintelligible handwritten characters, were excluded.

Besides essays, we collected errors also from spelling exercise logs (SpellEx) from a Swedish language learning platform, *Lärka*[3]. We collected non-word errors from the responses of the 10 language learners (ranging from beginner to advanced level) who participated in a previous evaluation of the platform (Pijetlovic, 2013; Volodina and Pijetlovic, 2015). Word segmentation errors and other errors consisting of valid inflectional forms were not considered. The size of the dataset in terms of number of L2 errors and their distribution across data sources and CEFR levels is presented in Table 1. Digits in parenthesis for SpIn indicate the number of individual essays.

	A1	A2	B1	Sub-total	Total
SpIn	82 (8)	62 (9)	58 (7)	202	
SpellEx	NA	NA	NA	253	**455**

Table 1: The number of corrected non-word L2 errors in the dataset.

It is worth noting that, while the spelling exercise log part of the data consisted mainly of L2 spelling errors, the errors collected from the essays displayed a wider variety of error types including grammatical and vocabulary errors. Duplicate pairs of error and intended word have been removed from the dataset, thus the numbers in Table 1 refer to unique error types.

4   Word embeddings enhanced with character n-grams for learner error correction

In this work, we use FastText (Bojanowski et al., 2016) for training embeddings. FastText is a recently proposed approach that enhances traditional word-based vectors by representing each word as a bag of character n-grams. Incorporating this type of subword information, besides semantic relatedness, allows for capturing also orthographic and morphological similarity.

We compare pre-trained word vectors[4] using a large amount of Swedish Wikipedia articles with word vectors we trained specifically for the purpose of finding L2 error correction candidates, which can be an alternative (or a complement) to lexicon-based lookups. We base our embeddings on corpora which are more similar to what L2 learners produce in terms of topic or complexity. These include a small set of specialized corpora (*SpecC*) combining easy-to-read texts (Heimann Mühlenbock, 2013), L2 coursebook texts (Volodina et al., 2014) and L2 learner essays (Volodina et al., 2016) We combine these with a large amount of blog texts to ensure a sufficiently large lexical basis for our representations. The blog texts were collected via the corpus query system, *Korp*[5] (Borin et al., 2012). Compared to Wikipedia, the topic of these blog texts is more similar to that of learner texts dealing often with everyday topics, which is part

---

[3]https://spraakbanken.gu.se/larka/
[4]https://fasttext.cc/docs/en/pretrained-vectors.html
[5]https://spraakbanken.gu.se/korp/

of language learning curricula according to CEFR, especially between beginner (A1) and intermediate levels (B1) (Council of Europe, 2001). Moreover, blog texts might contain misspellings, which, although not necessarily produced by L2 speakers, can potentially increase the usefulness of this type of data for detecting correction candidates for L2 errors.

The total number of tokens in the combination of corpora used for our embeddings was 25 million tokens (8% being from SpecC), which resulted in a vocabulary size of 307,349 word forms. This is a considerably smaller vocabulary size than that of the pre-trained Wikipedia embeddings consisting of 1,143,273 word forms. The pre-trained embeddings were based on the skip-gram model and they used the default parameters and 300 dimensions. We train embeddings using Continuous Bag-of-Words model (CBOW) which can be used also to predict target words from the context (Mikolov et al., 2013). We preserve most parameters with their default values, except for four exceptions. We set the number of dimensions to 300 and we considered n-grams between 2 and 5 (instead of the default 3 and 6), in attempt to better handle short words, which are common at lower proficiency levels. We also reduce the minimum number of occurrences for a word to be included to 2 and add a duplicate copy of the small amount of learner-written texts in the training data.

5 Phonological similarity based on Levenshtein distance

Levenshtein (edit) distance is a common measure of the difference between strings in terms of the minimum number of single character edits required to map one string into another (Levenshtein, 1966). These edits can consist of deletions, additions and substitutions. The traditional version of this measure makes a binary decision about whether a pair of characters match. Some characters, however, are more likely to be misspelled as certain characters than others. This can be either due to the frequent omission of highly language-dependent diacritics or due to a similarity in the sound encoded by different graphemes. An example for the former case is: *traffas* instead of *träffas* 'meet'. To account for phonological differences, we first train a grapheme-to-phoneme conversion system that can map a string (even if it contains errors) to its phonological representation, which we describe in the next sub-section.

5.1 A neural grapheme-to-phone conversion for Swedish

Grapheme-to-phoneme (g2p) conversion is a task consisting of transforming the orthographical representation of words into their phonological equivalent. This is an important building block of, among others, text-to-speech (TTS) applications. A number of approaches have been explored in the past to tackle this conversion, which include both rule-based and data-driven methods. Torstensson (2002) presents a rule-based approach to g2p conversion for a Swedish TTS system and reports a rate of correctly transcribed words of 78% when testing on about 3700 unique words.

In this work, we train a g2p conversion system for Swedish based on a g2p toolkit[6] available within CMUSphinx (Yao and Zweig, 2015), an open source software mainly aiming at speech recognition. This g2p toolkit uses TensorFlow (Abadi et al., 2016) and a transformer model[7] relying on an attention mechanism. The toolkit has been successfully applied by a number of large companies (Yao and Zweig, 2015). The advantage of this g2p system is that, as opposed to other approaches, it does not require phoneme to grapheme alignments. Instead, mappings are learned directly from a list of words consisting of pairs of orthographic and phonemic representations for each word.

We use the Swedish lexical database of the Nordisk språkteknologi holding AS (NST)[8] to collect orthographic forms and their transcriptions encoded in Speech Assessment Methods Phonetic Alphabet (SAMPA). Before feeding the transcriptions to the g2p system, we automatically segment them as the example CMU dictionary for English. Length information is retained in the transcriptions, but we remove other non-phone related information (e.g. syllable and compound constituent boundaries). When collecting information from the dictionary, we select only base forms that were assigned a Swedish language code[9] and that were not tagged as garbage entries or as acronyms. All orthographic forms are

---

[6]https://github.com/cmusphinx/g2p-seq2seq
[7]https://ai.googleblog.com/2017/06/accelerating-deep-learning-research.html
[8]https://www.nb.no/sprakbanken/show?serial=sbr-22
[9]The NST dictionary contains some non-Swedish entries from other languages.

normalized to lower case and duplicates are removed, which results in a dataset consisting of 103,026 pairs of orthographic forms and their transcriptions.

We train a model with the default parameters using 90% of the extracted NST data and comparing two different sizes for the hidden units (64 and 512). We then measure the performance of the system on the held-out 10% (10,302) of the data in terms of accuracy and word error rate (WER). In Table 2, we compare our results with those presented for English using the same implementation. As a baseline (BL) for Swedish, we use the results reported in Torstensson (2002).

	Swedish-BL	Swedish		English	
# units	NA	64	512	64	512
Accuracy (%)	78.3	82.6	**86.6**	68.7	76.7
WER (%)	21.7	17.4	**13.4**	31.3	23.3

Table 2: The performance of the Swedish g2p conversion system.

Our system outperforms considerably the previously reported results for Swedish for this task. Moreover, our neural models for Swedish achieve a higher accuracy than those for English with both 64 and 512 units. Besides some differences in the underlying data, this may be due to the fact that Swedish orthography is closer to the pronounced forms of words.

5.2 Measuring distance between sounds based on binary phonological features

To be able to measure distance between sounds, we adopt the binary feature representation described in Hayes (2009), where each phoneme is characterized across 26 dimensions divided into three categories: manner, place and laryngeal features. For a detailed description of each feature and their value per phoneme, see Hayes (2009).

Some peculiar sounds in Swedish that occur less commonly in other languages include retroflex sounds (e.g. ʈ, ɖ) and the doubly articulated postalveolar-velar fricative (/ɧ/). Since the latter was missing from the phonemes listed in the feature charts from Hayes (2009), we deduced its values by combining the features of the two sounds it is composed of according to IPA,[10] namely /ʃ/ and /x/.

5.3 From Levenshtein distance to a phonological similarity measure

We employ a memory efficient version of the Levenshtein distance (LD) using two row matrices.[11] We replace the original *cost* of 1 for non-matching characters with a value that expresses a phonological similarity between two phonemes. The similarity is computed based on the phonological features of these sounds. The cost for this phonological distance (PH-LD) is computed as the ratio of features with matching values divided by the total number of features relevant for at least of the two sounds being compared. In section 6, we report results for both the traditional version of LD and the proposed phonological LD.

We transform both types of LD distances into a normalized similarity measure to make it more comparable with cosine similarity values. We compute orthographic similarity as $1 - \frac{LD}{N_{char}}$ and phonological similarity as $1 - \frac{PH-LD}{N_{phon}}$, where N_{char} and N_{phon} stand for the number of characters and phonemes in the word respectively.

6 Investigating the usefulness of similarity measures for L2 error correction

6.1 The efficiency of retrieving L2 error corrections based on cosine similarity

To start with, we evaluate the usefulness of word embeddings for retrieving the intended word for learner errors. Table 3 shows the percentage of errors for which the correction appeared among a varying number

[10]https://www.internationalphoneticassociation.org/content/full-ipa-chart
[11]We used Christopher P. Matthews' Python implementation available at https://en.wikibooks.org/wiki/Algorithm_Implementation/Strings/Levenshtein_distance#Python

of k most similar words.

	SpecC+Blogs			Wikipedia		
Top k	SpIn	SpellEx	Avg	SpIn	SpellEx	Avg
10	40.6	50.2	45.4	18.8	24.5	21.65
25	49.0	57.3	53.15	24.8	28.1	26.45
50	59.4	63.2	61.3	28.7	31.6	30.15
100	64.4	66.4	**65.4**	31.2	34.4	**32.8**

Table 3: Percentage of corrections occurring among the k most similar words.

The word embeddings created specifically for L2 error correction purposes (SpecC+Blogs) based on data relevant for the task proved to be considerably more useful for retrieving the intended word for learner errors than the pre-trained Wikipedia embeddings. This task-specific embedding contained approximately twice more often (or more) the intended word than its counterpart at all levels of k. Furthermore, word embeddings were more suitable for finding the correct alternative for the errors collected from the spelling exercises even though words from the essay corpus were used as part of the training data for the embeddings. This may be due to the fact that the errors in the essays include a higher percentage of grammatical errors besides spelling errors and embeddings enhanced with character n-grams may be more useful for the latter type.

6.2 Relationship between similarity measures

In the next step, we compare the average value of each similarity measure in the two different sources of L2 error data to investigate whether there is a difference in their usefulness.

	CosSim	OrthSim	PhonSim
SpIn	0.683 (0.181)	0.773 (0.115)	0.904 (0.100)
SpellEx	0.747 (0.184)	0.773 (0.142)	0.918 (0.107)

Table 4: Mean and standard deviation values (in parenthesis) for different similarity measures.

As Table 4 shows, the mean values of all three similarity measures are higher for the SpellEx data, containing mostly spelling errors. The similarity measures we investigate here seem therefore more efficient for capturing the similarity with an intended word for spelling errors rather than for a variety of different error types. Normalized phonological similarity values are, on average, higher than the values of the other two similarity measures, but it is hard to draw conclusions from comparing directly the average values per measure since they are computed differently.

To understand how much additional information the different similarity measures carry compared to each other, we measure also the Spearman's correlation (ρ) between them pairwise. We find that all three similarity measures positively correlate[12] with each other, but to a varying degree. Cosine similarity correlates more with orthographic ($\rho = 0.693$) than with phonological similarity ($\rho = 0.449$). Word embeddings do indeed incorporate character n-grams which rely on the same type of information as the one at the basis of orthographic similarity. Phonological similarity correlates less both with cosine and with orthographic similarity ($\rho = 0.449$ and $\rho = 0.472$ respectively). Some types of errors produce, in fact, an orthographic dissimilarity, but not a phonological one. These include errors with double consonants and different graphemes mapping to the same phoneme. In Table 5, we provide some examples for pairs of words with orthographic and phonological forms to illustrate these cases. (Phonological LD values, omitted from the table are 0 in all cases.)

---

[12] For all correlations $p = < 0.001$ holds.

Error		Correction		Translation	LD	Type of error
Orth	Phon	Orth	Phon			
bettre	b E t r e	*bättre*	b E t r e	'better'	1	wrong grapheme
tjeck	s' E k	*check*	s' E k	'check'	2	wrong grapheme
fortsäta	f U t' s' E: t a	fortsätta	f U t' s' E: t a	'continue'	1	consonant doubling

Table 5: Examples of errors producing orthographic, but not phonological distance.

As we showed in this section, phonological similarity has the potential to provide useful additional information when compared to the other two similarity measures. In the next sub-section, we investigate whether combining orthographic and phonological similarity improves the cosine similarity-based rank of an intended word for L2 errors.

6.3 The efficiency of the combination of different similarity measures

When using similarity measures for error correction purposes, a commonly adopted option is to choose the correction candidate that maximizes the different types of similarities, see e.g. Bertaglia and Nunes (2016). In this section, we investigate whether adding orthographic and phonological similarity can improve the initial, cosine similarity-based rank of an L2 error correction. We consider only those errors here for which the correction appeared among the 50 most similar words in the word embeddings trained on the combination of specialized corpora and blog texts. These errors were 280 in total from the two data sources. Table 6 presents the average ranks of the corrections and their standard deviation based on cosine similarity and their combination with the other measures. (A lower rank indicates a higher degree of similarity.)

	CosSim	CosSim+OrthSim	CosSim+PhonSim	CosSim+OrthSim+PhonSim
SpIn	6.91 (10.1)	**1.95 (1.71)**	2.32 (3.23)	2.61 (3.83)
SpellEx	10.83 (12.99)	2.82 (3.40)	3.54 (5.15)	**1.62 (1.54)**

Table 6: Average ranks per similarity measures.

On average, the best ranking was obtained by the combination of cosine and orthographic similarity for the essay errors from SpIn. For the spelling errors, however, incorporating also phonological information achieved the best results in terms of average ranks.

In the last set of experiments, we explore how often combining cosine similarity with orthographic and phonological similarity improved, worsened or had no impact on the cosine similarity-based ranking of the corrections. Table 7 presents the percentage of errors for each of these three types of effects per similarity measure combination. We find that combining cosine similarity with orthographic or phonological similarity boosts the ranking of the corrections in more that half of the cases. The results from Table 7 confirm the ones from Table 6: adding phonological similarity information boosts the ranks of corrections only for the spelling error data, but not for the mixed type of L2 errors from SpIn. Moreover, relying on more than one similarity measure seems to be more beneficial for the wider spectrum of errors occurring in learner essays (SpIn) where measure combinations yielded an improvement in ranking on average for ca. 10% more of the errors than for SpellEx.

7   Conclusion

In this paper, we explored different similarity measures and their interaction for the purposes of correcting errors made by language learners. We presented word vectors created for this purpose using task-relevant corpora which proved to be more efficient for retrieving corrections than pre-trained embeddings based on Wikipedia. Since almost 4 out of 10 times the correction did not appear among

		Improvement	No change	Drop
CosSim+OrthSim	SpIn	**64.86**	27.02	8.10
	SpellEx	48.99	44.96	6.04
CosSim+PhonSim	SpIn	61.26	22.52	16.21
	SpellEx	52.34	34.89	12.75
CosSim+OrthSim+PhonSim	SpIn	63.06	27.02	9.90
	SpellEx	**53.02**	39.59	7.38

Table 7: Effect of combining similarity measures.

the most similar words in the word embeddings, dictionary lookups for candidates within a certain edit distance would be a useful complement.

Furthermore, we trained a neural g2p system for computing phonological similarity between transcribed errors and their corrections which outperformed previously reported results targeting this task for Swedish. Although based on a similar type of information, complementing cosine similarity with orthographic similarity yielded considerable improvements for the ranking of corrections for a varied type of L2 errors found in essays. Adding phonological similarity information to cosine similarity, on the other hand, proved more useful for data containing spelling errors. The similarity measures described can be easily re-used for other languages with the availability of a lexicon with pairs of orthographic forms and their phonological transcription and by complementing the list of sounds and their phonological features with any potentially missing language-specific sound. The trained word embeddings, the Swedish g2p system and the implementation of the phonological similarity measure have been made publicly available to foster code reuse and replicability.

Future work could explore additional methods for both the retrieval of correction candidates for L2 errors and for ranking them. These could include, among others, language models, diacritical symmetry and a longest common subsequence measure. Moreover, the usefulness of the measures described could be investigated further with additional evaluation data both for Swedish and for other languages.

Acknowledgements

This work has been carried out within the "SweLL - research infrastructure for Swedish as a second language" project funded by the Swedish Foundation for Humanities and Social Sciences. We would also like to thank the Royal Swedish Academy of Letters, History and Antiquities for providing a travel grant to the first author via the Wallenberg Foundation.

References

Martín Abadi, Ashish Agarwal, Paul Barham, Eugene Brevdo, Zhifeng Chen, Craig Citro, Greg S Corrado, Andy Davis, Jeffrey Dean, Matthieu Devin, et al. 2016. TensorFlow: Large-scale machine learning on heterogeneous distributed systems. *arXiv preprint arXiv:1603.04467*.

Lene Antonsen. 2012. Improving feedback on L2 misspellings – an FST approach. In *Proceedings of the workshop on NLP for Computer-Assisted Language Learning*, pages 1–10. Linköping University Electronic Press.

Marco Baroni, Georgiana Dinu, and Germán Kruszewski. 2014. Don't count, predict! A systematic comparison of context-counting vs. context-predicting semantic vectors. In *Proceedings of the 52nd Annual Meeting of the Association for Computational Linguistics (Volume 1: Long Papers)*, volume 1, pages 238–247.

Thales Felipe Costa Bertaglia and Maria das Graças Volpe Nunes. 2016. Exploring word embeddings for unsupervised textual user-generated content normalization. In *Proceedings of the 2nd Workshop on Noisy User-generated Text*. COLING.

Piotr Bojanowski, Edouard Grave, Armand Joulin, and Tomas Mikolov. 2016. Enriching word vectors with subword information. *arXiv preprint arXiv:1607.04606*.

Lars Borin, Markus Forsberg, and Johan Roxendal. 2012. Korp – the corpus infrastructure of Språkbanken. In *LREC*, pages 474–478.

Jill Burstein. 2003. The e-rater Scoring Engine: Automated Essay Scoring with Natural Language Processing. *Lawrence Erlbaum Associates, Inc.*

Council of Europe. 2001. *Common European Framework of Reference for Languages: Learning, Teaching, Assessment.* Press Syndicate of the University of Cambridge.

Pieter Fivez, Simon Šuster, and Walter Daelemans. 2017. Unsupervised context-sensitive spelling correction of clinical free-text with word and character n-gram embedding. In *16th Workshop on Biomedical Natural Language Processing of the Association for Computational Linguistics*, pages 143–148.

Gintare Grigonyte and Björn Hammarberg. 2014. Pronunciation and spelling: the case of misspellings in Swedish l2 written essays. In *6th International Conference on Human Language Technologies-The Baltic Perspective (Baltic HLT), Kaunas, Lithuania, September 26-27, 2014*, pages 95–98. IOS Press.

Bruce Hayes. 2009. *Introductory Phonology*. John Wiley & Sons.

Katarina Heimann Mühlenbock. 2013. I see what you mean—assessing readability for specific target groups. *Data linguistica*, (24).

Ignacio Iacobacci, Mohammad Taher Pilehvar, and Roberto Navigli. 2016. Embeddings for word sense disambiguation: An evaluation study. In *Proceedings of the 54th Annual Meeting of the Association for Computational Linguistics (Volume 1: Long Papers)*, volume 1, pages 897–907.

Vladimir I Levenshtein. 1966. Binary codes capable of correcting deletions, insertions, and reversals. In *Soviet physics doklady*, volume 10, pages 707–710.

Tomas Mikolov, Kai Chen, Greg Corrado, and Jeffrey Dean. 2013. Efficient estimation of word representations in vector space. *arXiv preprint arXiv:1301.3781*.

Ritika Mishra and Navjot Kaur. 2013. A survey of spelling error detection and correction techniques. *International Journal of Computer Trends and Technology*, 4(3):372–374.

Hwee Tou Ng, Siew Mei Wu, Ted Briscoe, Christian Hadiwinoto, Raymond Hendy Susanto, and Christopher Bryant, editors. 2014. *Proceedings of the 18th Conference on Computational Natural Language Learning: Shared Task on grammatical error correction.* Association for Computational Linguistics, Baltimore, Maryland.

Dijana Pijetlovic. 2013. Swedish spelling game: Developing Swedish spelling exercises on the ICALL platform Lärka using Text-to-Speech technology. Master's thesis, University of Gothenburg.

Sara Stymne, Eva Pettersson, Beáta Megyesi, and Anne Palmér. 2017. Annotating errors in student texts: First experiences and experiments. In *Proceedings of the Joint 6th Workshop on NLP for Computer Assisted Language Learning and 2nd Workshop on NLP for Research on Language Acquisition at NoDaLiDa, Gothenburg, 22nd May 2017*, number 134, pages 47–60. Linköping University Electronic Press.

Niklas Torstensson. 2002. Grapheme-to-phoneme conversion, a knowledge-based approach. *Speech Music and Hearing TMH-QPSR-Fonetik*, 44:117–120.

Elena Volodina and Dijana Pijetlovic. 2015. Lark trills for language drills: Text-to-speech technology for language learners. In *Proceedings of the Tenth Workshop on Innovative Use of NLP for Building Educational Applications*, pages 107–117.

Elena Volodina, Ildikó Pilán, Stian Rødven Eide, and Hannes Heidarsson. 2014. You get what you annotate: a pedagogically annotated corpus of coursebooks for Swedish as a second language. In *Proceedings of the 3rd workshop on NLP for Computer Assisted Language Learning*, pages 128–144.

Elena Volodina, Ildikó Pilán, Ingegerd Enström, Lorena Llozhi, Peter Lundkvist, Gunlög Sundberg, and Monica Sandell. 2016. SweLL on the rise: Swedish learner language corpus for European Reference Level studies. In *Proceedings of the Tenth International Conference on Language Resources and Evaluation*.

Helen Yannakoudakis, Ted Briscoe, and Ben Medlock. 2011. A new dataset and method for automatically grading ESOL texts. In *Proceedings of the 49th Annual Meeting of the Association for Computational Linguistics: Human Language Technologies – Volume 1*, pages 180–189. Association for Computational Linguistics.

Kaisheng Yao and Geoffrey Zweig. 2015. Sequence-to-sequence neural net models for grapheme-to-phoneme conversion. *arXiv preprint arXiv:1506.00196*.

Towards Coreference for Literary Text:
Analyzing Domain-Specific Phenomena

Ina Rösiger, Sarah Schulz and Nils Reiter
Institute for Natural Language Processing
University of Stuttgart
{roesigia,schulzsh,nils.reiter}@ims.uni-stuttgart.de

Abstract

Coreference resolution is the task of grouping together references to the same discourse entity. Resolving coreference in literary texts could benefit a number of Digital Humanities (DH) tasks, such as analyzing the depiction of characters and/or their relations. Domain-dependent training data has shown to improve coreference resolution for many domains, e.g. the biomedical domain, as its properties differ significantly from news text or dialogue, on which automatic systems are typically trained. This also holds for literary texts. We therefore analyze the specific properties of coreference-related phenomena on a number of texts and give directions for the adaptation of annotation guidelines. As some of the adaptations have profound impact, we also present a new annotation tool for coreference, with a focus on enabling annotation of long texts with many discourse entities.

1 Introduction

Noun phrase (NP) coreference resolution is the task of determining which noun phrases in a text or dialogue refer to the same discourse entities (Ng, 2010). Resolving noun phrases can benefit downstream applications revolving around automatic text understanding, such as summarization and textual entailment. Furthermore, coreference resolution is an important stepping stone for analyzing narrative texts, as many such texts are built around characters – a frequently mentioned discourse entity. Coreference resolution therefore has applications within computational literary studies, which applies approaches such as network analysis, plot sentiment analysis, or distinguishing character types.

Corpora annotated with coreference information often consist of news texts or dialogues, with a few exceptions mostly in the biomedical and scientific domain. Literary texts differ from news texts and dialogues to a great extent, as their purpose is not to transfer information as it is the principle task of a newspaper, but rather to provide poetic descriptions and good storytelling. Literary texts have been shown to comprise sophisticated language, with a rich vocabulary, direct and indirect speech and a large set of syntactic constructions (van Cranenburgh and Bod, 2017). For this domain, annotated data are scarce: To the best of our knowledge, there are only a few corpora containing coreference annotations in literary texts (cf. Section 2), for which no domain-specific considerations have been described.

This paper aims at providing a theoretical yet empirically-tested basis for the annotation of coreference information in literary texts. We achieve this by a) analyzing the way coreference-related phenomena behave differently in literary texts and by b) uncovering new coreference-related phenomena that are specific to literary texts. To this end, we conduct an annotation study that uses existing annotation guidelines as a starting point, and refines them in an iterative process. Our focus here is to provide an analysis of the properties of literary texts that need to be considered when creating annotation guidelines and subsequently corpora. On a meta level, this study also gives insights into the dependency of annotation guidelines on the domain and/or text type.

The paper is structured as follows. Section 2 reviews existing corpora annotated with coreference. Section 3 presents the literary-specific considerations which are relevant for coreference annotations

Proceedings of Workshop on Computational Linguistics for Cultural Heritage, Social Sciences, Humanities and Literature, pages 129–138
Santa Fe, New Mexico, USA, August 25, 2018.

and Section 4 overviews how we propose to update existing annotation guidelines. Section 4 moreover describes a new annotation tool, which was designed to handle the properties we considered crucial for coreference annotation in our domain. Finally, we conclude in Section 5.

2   Existing Corpora

Coreference resolution is a highly active NLP area, with many previous annotation efforts, which enabled the creation of well-performing automatic resolvers, such as the state-of-the-art neural coreference resolver by Clark and Manning (2016). Automatic tools are typically trained on the benchmark dataset OntoNotes, which spans multiple genres (mostly newswire, broadcast news, broadcast conversation, web text, among others) across three languages – English, Chinese and Arabic (Weischedel et al., 2011). The English portion contains 1.6M words. Before OntoNotes, the (much smaller) benchmark datasets used were the MUC (Hirschman and Chinchor, 1998) and ACE (Doddington et al., 2004) corpora. OntoNotes differs from these two corpora with respect to corpus size and the inclusion of a few more genres. Benchmark datasets have of course also been created for other languages, e.g. the Prague Dependency Treebank (Hajič et al., 2018) for Czech, the ANCORA newspaper corpora of Spanish and Catalan (Martí et al., 2007) or TübA-D/Z (Naumann and Möller, 2006) as a newspaper corpus for German.

Despite the fact that OntoNotes contains multiple genres, it is unsuited as a data basis for other domains with very different properties. One example for such a domain is the biomedical domain, for which Gasperin and Briscoe (2008) have shown that the text differs considerably from other text genres such as news or dialogue, and that the complex nature of the texts is for example reflected in the heavy use of abstract entities, such as results or variables. As a result, a lot of corpora have been annotated (Castaño et al. (2002), Cohen et al. (2010), Gasperin et al. (2007), Batista-Navarro and Ananiadou (2011), a.o.) for this domain. It has been shown that coreference resolution for the biomedical domain benefits a lot from in-domain training data (Rösiger and Teufel, 2014).

Literary texts also differ a lot from news texts or dialogue. It has been shown to comprise rather sophisticated language, with a rich vocabulary, direct and indirect speech and a larger set of syntactic constructions (van Cranenburgh and Bod, 2017). Krug et al. (2015) found that the average sentence length is larger in novels and the number of pronouns, as well as the percentage of direct speech is higher. They have also presented a German corpus in which they annotated the syntactic heads of all coreferent expressions referring to a character, and built a rule-based system to detect them automatically. In contrast to this, we decided to annotate general coreference as not to limit the use cases to DH tasks revolving around characters, but to also allow experimentation with other research questions. The German NoSta-D corpus (Dipper et al., 2013) contains a small fraction of Kafka's *Der Prozess* (about 7000 tokens). The ARRAU corpus (Poesio and Artstein, 2008; Uryupina et al., to appear) contains a number of spoken narratives as part of their PEAR domain. However, these texts consist of spontaneous speech and therefore have very different properties than the rather sophisticated literary texts that we aim to annotate in our project. The Phrase Detectives project (Poesio et al., 2013), a linguistic annotation game designed to collect an ever-growing amount of annotated data, also contains English narrative texts from Gutenberg, including a number of tales and more advanced narratives such as Sherlock Holmes and Alice in Wonderland. To the best of our knowledge, standard guidelines were applied to all the genres in this corpus, and no domain-specific considerations were taken into account for the annotation of the literary texts. We believe that the typically long and often non-standard texts pose a challenge for the annotation, which should be reflected in the annotation guidelines.

3   Literary-specific phenomena/considerations

This section gives an overview of the characteristics of literary texts which have to be taken into consideration for the annotation of coreference. We discuss phenomena that we encountered during the on-going annotation of a corpus of literary texts. It comprises thirteen literary texts which stem from different centuries and cover different literary forms. Johann Wolfgang von Goethe's *The Sorrows of Young Werther* (German title: Die Leiden des jungen Werther) is an epistolary novel from 1774. Our annotations are based on a revised version of 1787 and include the introductory words of the fictional editor as well as the first letters of Werther to his friend Wilhelm. Leo Perutz' novel *From nine to nine* (German title: Zwischen neun und neun, original title: Freiheit) was first published in 1918, the novels *Der Mond lacht*[1] and *Nur ein Druck auf den Knopf*[1] followed in 1930.

Moreover, we include the plays *Miss Sara Sampson* by Gotthold Ephraim Lessing and *The Robbers* (German title: Die Räuber) by Friedrich Schiller. As an example of shorter literary texts, we include six German fairytales by the Brothers Grimm: *Frog Prince* (German title: Der Frosckönig), *Hansel and Gretel* (German title: Hänsel und Grethel), *Cinderella* (German title: Aschenputtel), *The Town Musicians of Bremen* (German title: Die Bremer Stadtmusikanten), *Rumpelstiltskin* (German title: Rumpelstilzchen) and *Rapunzel*.

In addition to these German texts, our corpus contains one English text, *A Narrative of the Captivity and Restoration of Mrs. Mary Rowlandson*, from the 17th century which describes encounters between European explorers and settlers and the native peoples (US captivity narratives)[2].

Two narrative spheres.   Literary narrative texts differ from other text types in the fact that they exist in "two basic spheres: that of the narrator (and optionally, his narratee) and that of the narrated (individual narrative agents, events, and states of affairs)" (Margolin, 1991, p. 518). This division leads to two levels of texts: the textual actual world which is the intersubjective reality of the text and the subjective subdomain of the narrator and the narrative agents which include subjective views, beliefs and which leads to layers of alternative narrated worlds (Margolin, 1991). As a result, narrative texts pose a complex web of different levels of knowledge of the reader, the narrator and the characters of the fictional world. This difference in knowledge can give ground to a purposefully deployed play with given and new information which influences the information structure and thus the operating principle of coreference in a text.

Genericity.   While genericity is not specific to literary texts, the rate of switching between the generic and non-generic use of noun phrases is. The fact that readers readily and often unconsciously connect instances and classes makes the annotation rather challenging.

(1) DER WIRT. [...] Was liegt mir daran, ob ich es weiß, oder nicht, was Sie für eine Ursache hierher führt, und warum Sie bei mir im Verborgnen sein wollen? Ein Wirt nimmt sein Geld, und läßt seine Gäste machen, was ihnen gut dünkt. Waitwell hat mir zwar gesagt, [...]

EN translation: LANDLORD. [...] What is it to me, whether I know or not, what cause has brought you hither, and why you wish to live in seclusion in my house? A landlord takes his money and lets his guests do as they think best. Waitwell, it is true, has told me that [...].

In 1, "A landlord" is a generic expression that refers to the class of landlords. Given the context it is clear, however, that the landlord (who is uttering this sentence), *also* talks about himself.

(2) [Sie]₁ ließ [[ihren]₂ Regenschirm]₃ fallen. [Jeder junge Mann]₄ wird in einem solchen Fall blitzschnell nach [dem Schirm]₅ greifen und [ihn]₆ [der Dame]₇ überreichen. Und [die Dame]₈ bedankt sich vielmals. Aber diesmal geschah etwas Unerhörtes. [Stanislaus Demba]₉ ließ [den Schirm]₁₀ liegen.

[She dropped [[her]₂ umbrella]₃. [Every young man in such a situation]₄ would catch [the umbrella]₅ blazingly fast and hand [it]₆ on to [the lady]₇. And [the lady]₈ would thank [him]₈ a great many times. But this time, something outrageous happened. [Stanislaus Demba]₉ left [the umbrella]₁₀ on the ground.

A similar case is shown in 2, yet a bit more complex. Mentions 1 and 2 refer to a concrete individual, whose umbrella (mention 3) falls down. The following sentence switches to a generic reading (signified by mention 4). The definite noun phrase 5 also needs to be understood as generic, and thus starts a new coreference chain, similarly to the entity lady (7 and 8). The last sentence again switches to the individual level, and describes that a concrete individual (9) does not pick up the umbrella introduced in 3.

---

[1]Published in: Herr, erbarme dich meiner. Not translated into English.

[2]Made available under Creative Common licence by EEBO-TCP which is a partnership between the Universities of Michigan and Oxford and the publisher ProQuest to create accurately transcribed and encoded texts based on the image sets published by ProQuest via their Early English Books Online (EEBO) database (http://eebo.chadwyck.com).

Entity development. One of the key characteristics of narratives is that change takes place: The (fictional) world changes, and so do the characters that reside in it. This does not only include the name of marrying (mostly female) characters, but also promotions (e.g., in Goethe's Elective Affinities, Captain Otto is promoted to major after half the book, and henceforth only referred to as 'Major'). In such cases where the name of a character or his profession changes, one can argue that the referent probably stays the same. However, characters can also change more drastically, e.g. turning evil or good, where it is then questionable whether the referent remains the same. Another interesting issue is the appearance of dead or unreal characters: Are dreamed and fictional but real characters the same entity? Is the ghost of Hamlet's father the same entity as Hamlet's father?

A more frequent issue is the creation of groups, and plural references to such groups. In Act II, Scene 2 of Schiller's *The Robbers*, a group of six different characters argue. They decide on whether to become robbers but are divided. Various coalitions are formed, and their exact composition is unclear in many cases.

Text knowledge. Characters in narratives simulate individual entities and thus have varying states of knowledge. For plays, mix-ups are an important plot element for an entire genre with a tradition of over 2000 years (e.g., Electra unknowingly meets her brother in Sophocles' play, written about 400 BCE). A lot of the tension in these cases comes from the fact that the reader or audience indeed realizes the truth. Some crime novels also reveal the identity of the perpetrator early on. It is an important question whether the annotations reflect characters' or readers' knowledge, and how much text knowledge one can assume in readers. In our guidelines, we have decided to annotate from the reader's point of view. To deal with the fact that some of the novels have been read by the annotators, the text knowledge is fixed to the knowledge of the annotator after one read-through. Another stylistic device which is sometimes used in literary text is gender confusion. Gender is typically an important marker in pronouns which aids the resolution to the correct noun phrase. Hirst (1981, p. 10) cites an example from *Even Cowgirls get the blues* (Robbins, 1976), where a character called *The Countess* turns out to be male after a couple of pages by implicitly using the pronoun *he* for referencing him.

World knowledge. In historic literary texts, we have the problem that contemporary annotators do not have the same knowledge as the author or typical reader at the time of the works' publication. To overcome this, we try to approximate the world knowledge of a typical reader: wherever the annotator gets the feeling that something is assumed to be common knowledge, he/she is allowed to look up the missing facts to derive the right references.

(3) HERMANN. [...]Da [Karl] auf der Welt nichts mehr zu hoffen hatte, zog ihn der Hall von [Friederichs]₁ siegreicher Trommel nach Böhmen. Erlaubt mir, sagte er [zum großen Schwerin]₂, da ich den Tod sterbe auf dem Bette der Helden [...].

EN translation: For Karl had nothing to hope for in the world, he was drawn to Bohemia to the sound of [Friederich's]₁ triumphant drums. Allow me, he said to [the Great Schwerin]₂ that I might die on the beds of heroes ...

For example in 3, "zum großen Schwerin" refers to 'Kurt Christoph Graf von Schwerin', an important and popular general under Friedrich II. This is obvious for contemporaries, but not for today's readers. From discourse context alone, an annotator might annotate 1 and 2 as co-referent, which is not in line with the author's (presumed) intentions.

Lexical variation. One of the main properties of literary texts is the high amount of lexical variation and paraphrasing as a stylistic means. As a result, it is sometimes difficult to decide where coreference ends and bridging begins, such as in 4, where *Verbindung* refers to both the wedding (event) and marriage (state):

(4) MELLEFONT. Mit Unrecht tadelt sie die Verzgerung [einer Zeremonie] [...].
SARA. Neue Freunde sollen die Zeugen [unserer Verbindung] sein? Grausamer [...]

MELLEFONT. Aber überlegen Sie denn nicht, Miss, dass [unserer Verbindung] hier diejenige Feier fehlen würde, die wir ihr zu geben schuldig sind?

EN translation: MELLEFONT. Unjustly, she condemns the delay of [a ceremony].
SARA. New friends shall be the witnesses of [our union]?
MELLEFONT. But bear in mind, Miss, that [our bond] would be lacking the festivity, which we are responsible to give.

Text length. Whereas a discourse in a newspaper is typically rather short, a discourse in literary texts can span hundreds of pages, which poses a challenge for the annotators. For pronominal reference this is not problematic, as pronominal coreference is limited with respect to the attention span of the reader in every text, i.e. the author chooses a pronoun when he/she can be sure that the reader remembers the referent/antecedent. Cases of nominal coreference, however, might now span hundreds of pages. One example for a text which is broken up into different planes and surrounded by a frame story is the appearance of Scheherazade in *One Thousand and One Nights*, where we observe co-references across very long distances.

Obviously, annotators cannot remember every discourse entity that appeared in the first chapter while reading the last chapter. Depending on the importance of the entity for the narrative, co-reference might still be established with additional means by the authors (e.g., the gun that Werther uses for shooting himself is introduced early on). To allow annotation of long coreference chains, the annotators have access to all previously annotated entities and can for example additionally search the text for a certain headword (c.f. Section 4.2 for the annotation tool we developed).

Idiomatic expressions. Idiomatic expressions are arguably more frequent in literary texts than in newspaper text. While they are generally considered non-referring expressions, it is sometimes difficult to decide which of the expressions are idiomatic expressions and which are referring:

(5) 'mit verzerrtem Gesicht' (with a twisted face)

(6) 'Gott sei dank' (thank God)

In the context of (5), the face is mentioned regularly and an established discourse referent. The 'twisted face' is used an idiomatic expression, but can also be understood literally in this context. In (6) this distinction probably depends on the religious beliefs of the person.

Sub-token annotation. While it is typically assumed that pre-modifiers in compounds can only be picked up again in case they are proper nouns (cf. for example in the OntoNotes guidelines), this is not always true in literary texts, as in 7. Additionally, for German, we are faced with the problem that compounds are not multi-words, i.e. they are not separated by blanks. As a result, the word level is sometimes unsuited as an annotation level. Our new tool thus also allows the annotation of mentions within tokens.

(7) Eine schlechte Vorbereitung, eine [trost]suchende Betrübte zu empfangen. Warum sucht sie [ihn] auch bei mir?
A bad preparation for receiving one who seeks [comfort]. But why does she seek [it] from me?

True ambiguity A basic assumption made in many NLP tasks is that there is a ground truth, thus one label that is the correct label when annotating certain phenomena in data. In our corpus, however, we encounter a kind of disagreement between annotators that is not a mistake resulting from the incorrect application of the annotation guidelines but from diverging interpretations of the text. These ambiguities can be used intentionally as a stylistic device in literary texts. Such ambiguities should be preserved in the annotation since they are interesting for literature analysis. An example for how different readings can lead to such a disagreement in the annotation of coreference comes from *The Sorrows of Young Werther*. In (8), the chosen antecedent of the abstract anaphor *Das* (mention 3) was different in the two annotations: one annotator chose a non-nominal-antecedent (mention 1), whereas the other chose a shorter, nominal antecedent (mention 2). Another disagreement occurred in the resolution of *seiner selbst* (mention 6). One annotator assigned it to the chain with mention 5 (*the feeling heart*). This reflects a rather poetic interpretation where the feeling heart enjoys the beauty of the garden. Annotator 2 chose *the Count of M.* (mention 4) as the antecedent which enjoys the beauty of the garden. Note that in the English translation this ambiguity is not preserved.

(8) [[Die Stadt selbst ist unangenehm, dagegen rings umher [eine unaussprechliche Schönheit der Natur]$_1$]$_2$. [Das]$_3$ bewog [den verstorbenen Grafen von M.]$_4$ seinen Garten auf einem der Hügel anzulegen, die mit der schönsten Mannichfaltigkeit sich kreuzen, und die lieblichsten Thäler bilden. Der Garten ist einfach, und man fühlt gleich bei dem Eintritte, daß nicht ein wissenschaftlicher Gärtner, sondern [ein fühlendes Herz]$_5$ den Plan gezeichnet, das [seiner selbst]$_6$ hier genießen wollte.

[[The city itself is unpleasant, whereas round and round there is [an inexpressible beauty of nature]$_1$]$_2$. [This]$_3$ made [the late Count of M.]$_4$ to build his garden on one of the hills, which have cross-bred with the most beautiful diversity, and which make up lovely valleys. The garden is simple, and one can feel it instantly that the plans were not made by a scientific gardener, but [a feeling heart]$_5$, which wanted to enjoy [itself]$_6$.

4 Annotation

4.1 Guidelines

Our annotation guidelines are based on the NoSta-D guidelines.[3] In the following, we outline the differences and extensions between this template and our annotation guidelines. These differences are mainly motivated by factors explained in Section 3. The guidelines have been tested and clarified in an iterative process through parallel annotations. Cases in which differences in the double annotations appeared were discussed. When necessary, the guidelines were modified. In the following, we describe in which points we deviate from the NoSta-D guidelines.

Annotation of entity clusters instead of binary links. We do not annotate links between mentions, but rather assign mentions to entities. This entity-centric view will be explained in more detail in Section 4.2.

World and text knowledge. As explained above, the world and text knowledge poses a challenge for the annotation. To standardize the annotations, we set the text knowledge to the knowledge of the annotators after one thorough read-through. Temporally developing changes throughout the text are fixed to the knowledge at the end of a text. As for world knowledge, we allow annotators to look up relevant knowledge, which is presented in a way that we can assume that the expression refers to given information (see the example about *zum großen Schwerin*, above).

Genericity. In contrast to the NoSta-D guidelines, we do not annotate "bound" relations but introduce generic entity types instead. Generic chains can only contain generic entities and should not be mixed with non-generic entities.

No annotation of link type. As we assign mentions to entity clusters, we do not annotate the link type (e.g. anaphoric, coreferent, cataphoric).

No singletons. In NoSta-D, all mentions are marked, and at the end of the annotation process, singletons are filtered out. We do not initially mark all NPs as potential chain members but manually determine the candidates during the annotation process (and after the text has been read in its full length before the annotation).

---

[3]https://www.linguistik.hu-berlin.de/de/institut/professuren/korpuslinguistik/forschung/nosta-d/nosta-d-cor-1.1.

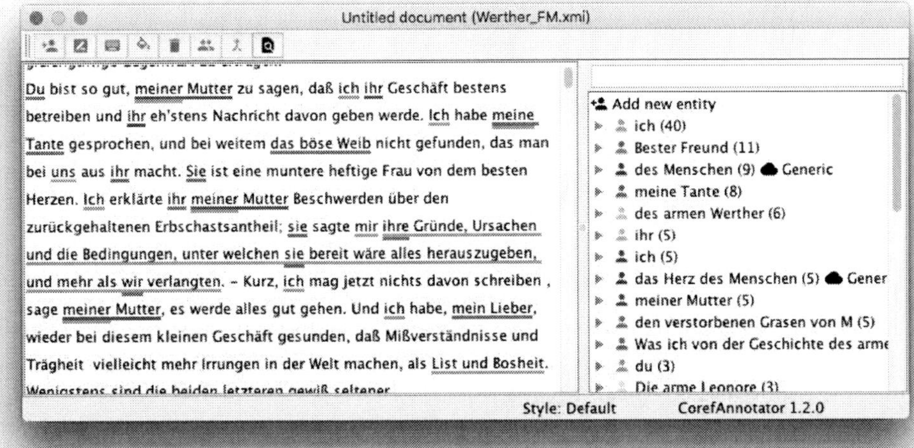

Figure 1: Screenshot of the annotation tool, showing the text left and the annotated entities on the right

Non-nominal antecedents. We allow non-nominal antecedents in the case of event references. This means that in addition to NPs, VPs, clauses as well as several sentences can be members of a chain in some cases.

(9) I love [baking cakes]. [It] is an activity I used to do with my mom.

Text/document length. We annotate chains that span the entirety of a book, instead of considering chapters or other sub-divisions as documents. This way, we can cover long dependencies that are e.g. spanning frame stories.

Groups/aggregated coreference. We annotate group relations if two members of a group appear apart from each other in a text and if they are subsequently referred to by a mass pronoun subsuming them as in the example below, where mention 3 refers to mention 1 and mention 2 (*John and Paul*).

(10) [John]$_1$ cut the tomatoes and [Paul]$_2$ the carrots. [They]$_3$ liked cooking together.

Idiomatic expressions. We do not annotate NPs in an idiomatic expression:

(11) [the ball] is in your court (not-annotated) vs. [the ball] bounced off the ground (annotated if coreferent with another mention)

Lexical variation. We distinguish cases of bridging from coreferent anaphora. Cases of bridging are not annotated. As mentioned above, the distinction can be tricky in literary texts, and the resolution of individual cases is left to the annotators.

4.2 Annotation tool

The annotations have been produced with a new annotation tool that we make available with an open source license (Apache 2.0).[4] The tool is optimized for fast annotations with a keyboard and departs from existing coreference annotation tools in a number of ways:

Coreference annotations are conceptualized as equivalence sets. All mentions that belong to one coreference chain form a set, and are treated equally. The tool does not support the annotation of relations between mentions (i.e., we cannot annotate a binary relation as cataphoric, for instance). Annotating a

---

[4]https://github.com/nilsreiter/CorefAnnotator.

mention into a chain adds it directly to the set. Each entity is represented by a color, and can optionally be named. All mentions that belong to the same entity are underlined with the same color in the text view, multiple annotations on the same span result in multiple underlines on different levels.

We also make no assumptions on related tasks. Arbitrary text spans can be annotated as mentions, including sub-token annotations (by default, however, partial token annotations are expanded to the full token). Internally, all annotations are represented as stand-off annotation, using the UIMA framework[5] for text and annotation representation. This allows flexible import and export in a variety of formats (e.g., CoNLL 2012 [given token and sentence boundaries], TEI/XML [as long as the result is valid XML]).

The general usage philosophy is to support keyboard based annotation. Text spans can be selected with the keyboard, and the appropriate entity can be searched for. In addition, selected text spans can be dragged onto the entity. Fast, large scale annotation can be performed via the search function. It supports regular expressions, and all or some found spans can be annotated as a new or existing entity with a single click or press. We are currently exploring ways to represent conflicting/diverging annotations.

If the texts contain appropriate annotation (e.g., stage directions or headings), they can be used to control the formatting (bigger headings and italic stage directions, for instance). This makes reading and annotating more accessible, in particular for long texts. The annotation tool is fully localized in English and German, and can be localized to more languages.

5 Conclusion and Future Work

We have presented an analysis of coreference-related phenomena that we encountered during an annotation study conducted on literary texts. Based on these observations, we propose a number of adaptations to the annotation guidelines. We show that a domain can have a considerable influence on linguistic phenomena and that this has to be reflected in the guidelines to adequately capture them in the annotation. To fully incorporate the peculiarities of this domain and the potential needs of scholars using coreference as an analysis step, deeper changes to the annotation workflow are required: Literary texts may contain references to discourse entities that are intentionally ambiguous. Making a majority-based decision is certainly possible, but does not do justice to the complexities of language use. This has already been observed for annotation in the area of narratology (Gius and Jacke, 2017), but we can showcase it also for 'classic' NLP annotation layers.

Therefore, it will be required to cope with annotated corpora that contain multiple, conflicting annotations, which has severe implications in several areas: a) A number of conceptual questions arise regarding representation in file formats. E.g., do we take annotators' decisions as a whole or do we break them apart into smaller units? b) How do we evaluate annotations properly? Measuring inter-annotator agreement quantitatively assumes that a single ground truth is achievable, which just might not be the case here. c) What does this entail for the way method development works in computational linguistics? How can we use such data sets for training/testing purposes?

As a next step, we will employ the annotation guidelines sketched above to create a corpus of a selection of German literary texts. This corpus can be made openly available and will contain texts written by Goethe, Perutz, as well as several folktales.

References

R.T. Batista-Navarro and S. Ananiadou. 2011. Building a coreference-annotated corpus from the domain of biochemistry. *ACL HLT 2011*, page 83.

José Castaño, Jason Zhang, and James Pustejovsky. 2002. Anaphora resolution in biomedical literature. In *Proceedings of the International Symposium on Reference Resolution for NLP*.

Kevin Clark and Christopher D. Manning. 2016. Deep reinforcement learning for mention-ranking coreference models. In *Empirical Methods on Natural Language Processing*.

---

[5]`htttp://uima.apache.org`

K. Bretonnel Cohen, Arrick Lanfranchi, William Corvey, William A. Baumgartner Jr., Christophe Roeder, Philip V. Ogrena, Martha Palmer, and Lawrence E. Hunter. 2010. Annotation of all coreference in biomedical text: Guideline selection and adaptation. In *Proceedings of the Second Workshop on Building and Evaluating Resources for Biomedical Text Mining (BioTxtM 2010), LREC 2010*.

Stefanie Dipper, Anke Lüdeling, and Marc Reznicek. 2013. NoSta-D: A corpus of German non-standard varieties. *Non-Standard Data Sources in Corpus-Based Research*, (5):69–76.

George R. Doddington, Alexis Mitchell, Mark A. Przybocki, Lance A. Ramshaw, Stephanie Strassel, and Ralph M. Weischedel. 2004. The Automatic Content Extraction (ACE) Program - Tasks, Data, and Evaluation. In *LREC*. European Language Resources Association.

Caroline Gasperin and Ted Briscoe. 2008. Statistical anaphora resolution in biomedical texts. In *Proceedings of the 22nd International Conference on Computational Linguistics-Volume 1*, pages 257–264. Association for Computational Linguistics.

Caroline Gasperin, Nikiforos Karamanis, and Ruth Seal. 2007. Annotation of anaphoric relations in biomedical full-text articles using a domain-relevant scheme. In *Proceedings of the 6th Discourse Anaphora and Anaphor Resolution Colloquium*.

Evelyn Gius and Janina Jacke. 2017. The hermeneutic profit of annotation: On preventing and fostering disagreement in literary analysis. *International Journal of Humanities and Arts Computing*, 11(2):233–254, October.

Jan Hajič, Eduard Bejček, Alevtina Bémová, Eva Buráňová, Eva Hajičová, Jiří Havelka, Petr Homola, Jiří Kárník, Václava Kettnerová, Natalia Klyueva, Veronika Kolářová, Lucie Kučová, Markéta Lopatková, Marie Mikulová, Jiří Mírovský, Anna Nedoluzhko, Petr Pajas, Jarmila Panevová, Lucie Poláková, Magdaléna Rysová, Petr Sgall, Johanka Spoustová, Pavel Straňák, Pavlína Synková, Magda Ševčíková, Jan Štěpánek, Zdeňka Urešová, Barbora Vidová Hladká, Daniel Zeman, Šárka Zikánová, and Zdeněk Žabokrtský. 2018. Prague dependency treebank 3.5. LINDAT/CLARIN digital library at the Institute of Formal and Applied Linguistics (ÚFAL), Faculty of Mathematics and Physics, Charles University.

Lynette Hirschman and Nancy Chinchor. 1998. Appendix F: MUC-7 Coreference Task Definition (version 3.0). In *MUC*.

G. Hirst. 1981. *Anaphora in Natural Language Understanding: A Survey*. Lecture Notes in Computer Science. Springer Berlin Heidelberg.

Markus Krug, Frank Puppe, Fotis Jannidis, Luisa Macharowsky, Isabella Reger, and Lukas Weimar. 2015. Rule-based coreference resolution in German historic novels. In *Proceedings of the Fourth Workshop on Computational Linguistics for Literature*, pages 98–104.

Uri Margolin. 1991. Reference, coreference, referring, and the dual structure of literary narrative. *Poetics Today*, 12(3):517–542.

M.A. Martí, M. Taulé, M. Bertran, and L. Márquez. 2007. AnCora: Multilingual and Multilevel Annotated Corpora.

Karin Naumann and V Möller. 2006. Manual for the annotation of in-document referential relations. *University of Tübingen*.

Vincent Ng. 2010. Supervised noun phrase coreference research: The first fifteen years. In *Proceedings of the 48th Annual Meeting of the Association for Computational Linguistics*, pages 1396–1411. Association for Computational Linguistics.

Massimo Poesio and Ron Artstein. 2008. Anaphoric Annotation in the ARRAU Corpus. In *International Conference on Language Resources and Evaluation (LREC)*, Marrakech, Morocco, May.

Massimo Poesio, Jon Chamberlain, Udo Kruschwitz, Livio Robaldo, and Luca Ducceschi. 2013. Phrase detectives: Utilizing collective intelligence for internet-scale language resource creation. *ACM Transactions on Interactive Intelligent Systems (TiiS)*, 3(1):3.

T. Robbins. 1976. *Even cowgirls get the blues*. Bantam Books: Novel. Bantam Books.

Ina Rösiger and Simone Teufel. 2014. Resolving coreferent and associative noun phrases in scientific text. In *Proceedings of EACL*.

Olga Uryupina, Ron Artstein, Antonella Bristot, Frederica Cavicchio, Francesca Delogu, Kepa Rodriguez, and Massimo Poesio. to appear. Annotating a broad range of anaphoric phenomena, in a variety of genres: the ARRAU Corpus. *Journal of Natural Language Engineering*.

Andreas van Cranenburgh and Rens Bod. 2017. A data-oriented model of literary language. In *Proceedings of EACL*.

Ralph Weischedel, Eduard Hovy, Mitchell Marcus, Martha Palmer, Robert Belvin, Sameer Pradhan, Lance Ramshaw, and Nianwen Xue. 2011. Ontonotes: A large training corpus for enhanced processing. pages 54–63.

An Evaluation of Lexicon-based Sentiment Analysis Techniques for the Plays of Gotthold Ephraim Lessing

Thomas Schmidt
Media Informatics Group
Regensburg University
93040 Regensburg, Germany
thomas.schmidt@ur.de

Manuel Burghardt
Computational Humanities Group
Leipzig University
04109 Leipzig, Germany
burghardt@informatik.uni-leipzig.de

Abstract

We present results from a project on sentiment analysis of drama texts, more concretely the plays of Gotthold Ephraim Lessing. We conducted an annotation study to create a gold standard for a systematic evaluation. The gold standard consists of 200 speeches of Lessing's plays and was manually annotated with sentiment information by five annotators. We use the gold standard data to evaluate the performance of different German sentiment lexicons and processing configurations like lemmatization, the extension of lexicons with historical linguistic variants, and stop words elimination, to explore the influence of these parameters and to find best practices for our domain of application. The best performing configuration accomplishes an accuracy of 70%. We discuss the problems and challenges for sentiment analysis in this area and describe our next steps toward further research.

1 Introduction

As drama provides a number of structural features, such as speakers, acts or stage directions, it can be considered a literary genre that is particularly convenient and accessible for computational approaches. Accordingly, we find a number of quantitative approaches for the analysis of drama in general (cf. Fucks and Lauter, 1965; Solomon, 1971; Ilsemann; 2008), but also with a focus on the analysis of emotion (Mohammad, 2011) and sentiment (Nalisnick and Baird, 2013). More concretely, Mohammad (2011) uses the *NRC Emotion Lexicon* (Mohammad and Turney, 2010) to analyze the distribution and the progression of eight basic emotions in a selection of Shakespeare's plays. Nalisnick and Baird (2013) focus on speaker relations to analyze sentiment in Shakespeare's plays.

The goal of our study is to extend these existing approaches to computational sentiment analysis by taking into account historic, German plays. Further, we address some of the limitations of the current research on sentiment analysis in drama (Mohammad, 2011; Nalisnick and Baird, 2013), e.g. the ad hoc usage of sentiment lexicons without any pre-processing steps or other adjustments (Mohammad, 2011; Nalisnick and Baird, 2013). Our main contribution to the field of sentiment analysis for drama is the systematic evaluation of lexicon-based sentiment analysis techniques for the works of the German playwright Gotthold Ephraim Lessing. The evaluation takes into account a number of existing sentiment lexicons for contemporary German language (Võ et al., 2009; Clematide and Klenner, 2010; Mohammad and Turney, 2010; Remus et al., 2010; Waltinger, 2010) and various related NLP techniques, such as German lemmatizers, stop words lists and spelling variant dictionaries. The various combinations of existing lexicons and NLP tools are evaluated against a human annotated subsample, which serves as a gold standard.

2 Related Work: Sentiment Analysis in Literary Studies

As literary scholars have been interested in the emotions and feelings expressed in narrative texts for quite some time (cf. Winko, 2003; Mellmann, 2015), it is not surprising that computational sentiment analysis techniques have found their way into the realm of literary studies, for instance with Alm and Sproat (2005) and Alm et al. (2005), who examined the sentiment annotation of sentences in fairy tales. Other examples include Kakkonen and Kakkonen (2011), who used lexicon-based sentiment analysis to

Proceedings of Workshop on Computational Linguistics for Cultural Heritage, Social Sciences, Humanities and Literature, pages 139–149
Santa Fe, New Mexico, USA, August 25, 2018.

visualize and compare the emotions of gothic novels in a graph-based structure. Ashok et al. (2013) found a connection between the distribution of sentiment bearing words and the success of novels. Elsner (2012) included sentiment analysis to examine the plot structure in novels. In the same area, Jockers (2015) authored several blog posts about the use of sentiment analysis for the interpretation and visualization of plot arcs in novels. Reagan et al. (2016) extended Jockers work and use supervised as well as unsupervised learning to identify six core emotional arcs in fiction stories. Jannidis et al. (2016) used the results of lexicon-based sentiment analysis as features to detect "happy endings" in German novels of the 19th century. Heuser et al. (2016) used crowdsourcing, close reading and lexicon-based sentiment analysis to connect sentiments with locations of London in 19th century novels and visualize the information on maps of historic London. Kim et al. (2017) used lexical emotion features as part of a bigger feature set to successfully predict the genre of fiction books via machine learning. Buechel et al. (2016) identified the historical language of past centuries as a major challenge for sentiment analysis and therefore constructed a sentiment lexicon for the use case of 18th and 19th century German to analyze emotional trends and distributions in different genres.

3   Evaluation Design

3.1   Corpus

In order to investigate the practicability of lexicon-based sentiment analysis techniques for historical German drama, we gathered an experimental corpus of twelve plays by Gotthold Ephraim Lessing, which comprises overall 8,224 speeches. The plays were written between 1747 and 1779. Eight of the dramas are attributed to the genre of comedy while three are tragedies and one is referred to as dramatic poem. The most famous plays of the corpus are *"Nathan der Weise"* and *"Emilia Galotti"*. The average length of the speeches of the entire corpus is 24.15 words; the median is 13 words, which shows that the corpus consists of many rather short speeches. The longest speech consists of 775 words. Also note that the plays have very different lengths, with the shortest consisting of 183 and the longest of 1,331 speeches. All texts in our corpus are available in XML format and come with structural and speaker-related information for the drama text[1].

3.2   Gold Standard Creation

To be able to assess the quality of results from our evaluation study of lexicon-based approaches to sentiment analysis in Lessing's plays, we created a human annotated gold standard for 200 speeches. It is important to note that we were primarily interested in the overall sentiment of a self-contained character speech, as speeches are typically the smallest meaningful unit of analysis in quantitative approaches to the study of drama (cf. Ilsemann, 2008; Wilhelm, Burghardt and Wolff, 2013; Nalisnick and Baird, 2013). To create a representative sample of the 200 speeches, several characteristics of the corpus were taken into consideration: First, we only selected speeches longer than 18 words, which represents -25% of the average word length of speeches of the corpus, as we wanted to eliminate very short speeches that may contain no information at all. In related work, very short text snippets have been reported to be problematic for sentiment annotation, due to the lack of context and content (Alm and Sproat, 2005; Liu, 2016, p. 10). From the remaining speeches, we randomly selected speeches so that the proportion of speeches per drama in our gold standard represents the proportion per drama of the entire corpus, i.e. there are proportionally more speeches for longer dramas. We reviewed all speeches manually and replaced some speeches that consisted of French and Latin words, since those speeches might be problematic for our German speaking annotators. The final gold standard corpus had an average length of 50.68 words per speech and a median of 38 with the longest speech being 306 words long.

Five annotators, all native speakers in German, annotated the 200 speeches. During the annotation process, every speech was presented to the annotators with the preceding and the subsequent speech as contextual information. For the annotation scheme, we used two different approaches, which are oriented toward similar annotation studies (Bosco et al., 2014; Saif et al., 2014; Momtazi, 2012, Takala et al., 2014). First, annotators had to assign each speech to one of six categories: very negative, negative, neutral, mixed, positive, very positive. We refer to this annotation as *differentiated polarity*. In a second step, participants had to choose a *binary polarity*: negative or positive. This means, if annotators chose

---

[1] All electronic texts were gathered from the *TextGrid Repository* (https://textgridrep.org/repository.html).

neutral or *mixed* in the first step, they had to choose a binary polarity based on the overall tendency. With the first annotation, we wanted to gather some basic insights into sentiment distributions. However, several studies have shown that the agreement is very low for differentiated schemes like this (Momtazi, 2012; Takala et al., 2014); therefore, we also presented the binary annotation. Figure 1 illustrates the annotation scheme.

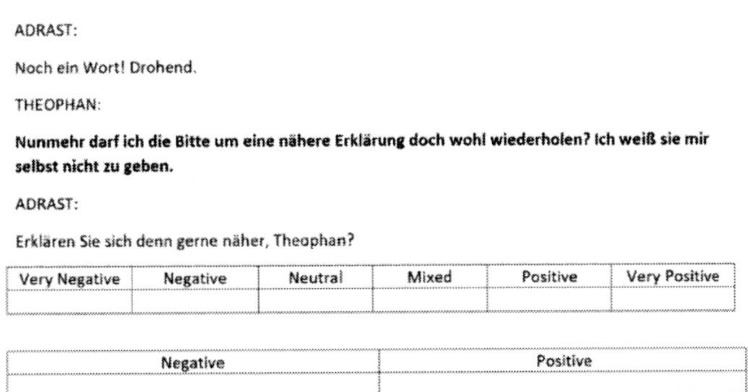

Figure 1. Example annotation

All five annotators had two weeks of time to conduct the entire annotation of 200 speeches, independently from each other. According to the annotators, the task took around five hours. An analysis of the differentiated annotations shows that the majority of annotations are *negative* or *very negative* (47%), while *positive* or *very positive* annotations are rather rare (16%). The results of the annotation also show that mixed (23%) and neutral (14%) annotations are a relevant annotation category as well. For the binary annotation, 67% of the annotations are negative and 33% are positive.

We analyzed the agreement of the annotations with *Krippendorff's* α (Krippendorff, 2011) and the average percentage of agreement of all annotator pairs (APA). Table 1 summarizes the results for the agreement of both annotation types.

	Krippendorff's α	APA
Differentiated polarity	0.22	40%
Binary polarity	0.47	77%

Table 1. Measures of agreement

Krippendorff's α and the average percentage of agreement of all annotator pairs point to a low agreement for the differentiated polarity. The degree of agreement is moderate for the binary polarity according to the interpretation of Landis and Koch (1971).

Since the degree of agreement is considerably higher for the binary polarity, we only regarded the binary polarity for the construction of our gold standard corpus. We selected the polarity chosen by the majority (>=3) of the annotators as the final value in our gold standard. This approach leads to 61 speeches being annotated as positive and 139 as negative. The entire gold standard corpus with all speeches, the final annotations and all other annotation data are publicly available[2].

3.3 Parameters of Evaluation

The results of automatic sentiment analysis approaches are influenced by a number of parameters. To find out which configuration of parameters yields the best results for historic plays in German language, we evaluated the following five variables:

---

[2] https://docs.google.com/spreadsheets/d/1f72hS2WDRBOrxzSY_tsM_igChG2bvxYTyMVZP6kOnuk/edit#gid=0

i) Sentiment lexicon

A sentiment lexicon is a list of words annotated with sentiment information. These words are also referred to as sentiment bearing words (*SBWs*). We identified five general purpose sentiment lexicons for German and evaluated their performance: *SentiWortschatz* (SentiWS, Remus et al., 2010), the *Berlin Affective Word List* (BAWL, Võ et al., 2009), *German Polarity Clues* (GPC; Waltinger, 2010), the German translation of the *NRC Emotion Lexicon* (NRC, Mohammad and Turney, 2010) and a sentiment lexicon by Clematide and Klenner (2010), further referred to as *CK*. Note, that all of the sentiment lexicons have different sizes and were created in different ways. They also differ in their overall composition: Some have simple binary polarity annotations, i.e. a word is either positive or negative. We refer to this kind of annotation as *dichotomous polarity*. Others have additional polarity strengths, which are values on a continuous scale e.g. ranging from -1 (very negative) to +1 (very positive) (SentiWS, CK, BAWL). Most of the lexicons consist of the base forms of words (lemmas), but some are manually appended with inflections of the words (SentiWS, GPC). Besides the lexicons, we also created and evaluated a combination of all five lexicons. To do this, we simplified the basic idea of sentiment lexicon combination by Emerson and Declerk (2014), i.e. we merged all words of all lexicons. If words were annotated ambiguously, we selected the polarity annotation that occurred in the majority of lexicons. For this process, we only regarded the dichotomous polarity of the lexicons.

ii) Extension with linguistic variants

The development of the aforementioned lexicons is based on modern online lexicons (Võ et al., 2009), corpora of product reviews (Remus et al., 2010), news articles (Clematide and Klenner, 2010) and the usage of crowdsourcing (Mohammad and Turney, 2010). Therefore, the lexicons were rather created to be used for contemporary language than for poetic German language of the 18th century. Some early studies in this area already identified the problem of historical language for contemporary sentiment lexicons (Alm and Sproat, 2005; Sprugnoli et al., 2016; Buechel et al., 2016). To examine this problem, we used a tool of the *Deutsches Textarchiv* (DTA) that produces historical linguistic variants of German words, e.g. different orthographical variants a word had throughout history (Jurish, 2012). The tool also provides historical inflected forms of the words. We used this tool to extend the sentiment lexicons as we gathered all historical linguistic variants for each word of every lexicon and added those words to the lexicon with the same polarity annotation of the base. This procedure increased the size of the lexicons to a large degree, since for every orthographic variant all inflections were added (example: size of BAWL before extension: 2,842; after extension: 75,436). However, one of the dangers of this approach is the possible addition of words that are not really sentiment bearing words, which may skew the polarity calculation. Further, the DTA tool has not yet been evaluated for this specific use case, so the quality of the produced variants is unclear. Hence, we evaluate the performance of the lexicons in their basic form (*noExtension*) as well as with the extension (*dtaExtended*).

iii) Stop words lists

We also analyzed the influence of stop words and frequently occurring words of the corpus on the sentiment calculation. Saif et al. (2014) showed that the elimination of these words can have a positive influence on performance of sentiment analysis in the machine learning context. Stop words and frequent words might skew sentiment calculation of lexicon-based methods as well, since some of the lexicons actually contain stop words. There are also some highly frequent words in our corpus that are listed in many of the lexicons as sentiment bearing words, but are actually overused because of the particular language style of the 18th century. We use different types of stop words lists to explore the influence of those types of words:

- a basic German stop word list of 462 words (upper and lower case*; standardList*),
- the same list extended by the remaining 100 most frequent words of the entire Lessing corpus (*extendedList*),
- and the same list manually filtered by words that are indeed very frequent, but are still sentiment bearing (e.g. Liebe/love; *filteredExtendedList*).

Besides, we also evaluate the condition to use no stop words list at all (*noStopWords*).

iv) Lemmatizers

We evaluate lemmatization by using and comparing two lemmatizers for German: the *treetagger* by Schmidt (1995) and the *pattern lemmatizer* by De Smedt and Daelemans (2012). Many of the lexicons only include base forms of SBWs, so lemmatization is a necessary step for those lexicons to identify inflections. However, due to the general problems of automatic lemmatization in German (Eger et al., 2016) and the special challenges historical and poetic language pose to automatic lemmatizers, mistakes and problems might occur that distort the detection of SBWs. Besides the general comparison between the two lemmatizers and no lemmatization at all, we also compared the automatic lemmatization with the manually added inflections some lexicons contain and the extension with inflections by the tool of the DTA.

v) Case-sensitivity

Related studies with lexicon-based methods typically lowercase all words for reasons of processing and normalization (Klinger et al., 2016). We wanted to explore if case affects the evaluation results (*caseSensitive* vs. *caseInSensitive*), as several words in German have a change in meaning depending on case, especially with regard to their sentiment.

3.4 Sentiment Calculation

To calculate the sentiment of a speech we employed a simple term counting method, often used with lexicon-based methods (Kennedy and Inkpen, 2006). The number of positive words according to the used configuration of parameters is subtracted by the number of negative words to get a general polarity score. If this score is negative, the speech is regarded as negative, otherwise as positive. If a sentiment lexicon contains polarity strengths for the SBWs, we additionally used these values in a similar way to calculate a sentiment score. Therefore, for these lexicons we calculated and compared two scores: one for dichotomous polarity and one for polarity strengths.

4   Results

In this chapter we present results from our evaluation of all possible combinations of the previously described parameters in comparison to the human annotated gold standard data. We used well-established metrics for sentiment analysis evaluation (Gonçalves et al., 2013). Our main metric is *accuracy*, which is the proportion of the correctly predicted speeches of all speeches. To get a more holistic view of the results, we also looked at *recall, precision* and *F-measures*. We furthermore analyzed the metrics for positive and negative speeches separately. Since our gold standard has an overrepresentation of negative speeches, misbehaviors of configurations like a general prediction of negative speeches would otherwise go undetected. We use the random baseline, the majority baseline and agreement measures as benchmarks. Because of the unequal distribution, the random baseline is set to 0.525 and the majority baseline is set to 0.695 for the accuracy. Mozetic et al. (2016) propose the average percentage of agreement of all annotator pairs (APA, 77%) as baseline for sentiment analysis evaluations. We also take this baseline into account when assessing the performance.

As we analyzed more than 400 different configurations, we are not able present all evaluation results in detail in this paper. However, an evaluation table of the best configurations ordered by accuracy is available online[3]. Note that we removed configurations from the table that tend to predict almost all speeches as negative and therefore accomplish accuracies close to the majority baseline, but are actually flawed. Figure 2 shows a snippet of the top part of the table.

---

[3] https://docs.google.com/spreadsheets/d/1yOv0U99SDI0dFUkctJcGmTXHSxcRByRJihnqRhEIkNY/edit#gid=0

	Metric	DTAExtension	Lemmatizer	Stopwords	CaseSensitivity	accuracy	F-MeasurePositi	F-MeasureNega
1	Metric	DTAExtension	Lemmatizer	Stopwords	CaseSensitivity	accuracy	F-MeasurePositi	F-MeasureNega
2	polaritySentiWS	dtaExtended	treetagger	noStopwordList	caseInSensitive	0,705	0,4587155963	0,7972508591
3	polaritySentiWS	dtaExtended	treetagger	noStopwordList	caseSensitive	0,695	0,4299065421	0,7918088737
4	polarityCombined	dtaExtended	treetagger	noStopwordList	caseInSensitive	0,675	0,4444444444	0,7703180212
5	polarityCombined	dtaExtended	pattern	noStopwordList	caseInSensitive	0,675	0,4247787611	0,7735191638
6	polarityCombined	dtaExtended	pattern	noStopwordList	caseSensitive	0,675	0,4247787611	0,7735191638
7	polaritySentiWS	dtaExtended	pattern	noStopwordList	caseInSensitive	0,675	0,3925233645	0,7781569966
8	polarityCombined	dtaExtended	noLemmatization	noStopwordList	caseInSensitive	0,67	0,4677419355	0,7608695652
9	polaritySentiWS	dtaExtended	noLemmatization	noStopwordList	caseInSensitive	0,67	0,4107142857	0,7708333333
10	polaritySentiWS	dtaExtended	pattern	noStopwordList	caseSensitive	0,67	0,3653846154	0,777027027
11	polarityCombined	dtaExtended	noLemmatization	noStopwordList	caseSensitive	0,665	0,4462809917	0,7598566308
12	polarityCK	dtaExtended	treetagger	enhancedFiltered	caseSensitive	0,605	0,5536723164	0,6457399103
13	polarityGpc	dtaExtended	pattern	enhancedFiltered	caseSensitive	0,605	0,7213114754	0,4150943396
14	polarityCK	dtaExtended	treetagger	enhancedFiltered	caseInSensitive	0,6	0,5505617978	0,6396396396
15	polarityGpc	dtaExtended	pattern	enhancedFiltered	caseInSensitive	0,6	0,7213114754	0,4112149533
16	polarityCK	dtaExtended	pattern	enhancedList	caseInSensitive	0,595	0,5149700599	0,652360515
17	polarityCK	dtaExtended	treetagger	enhancedList	caseInSensitive	0,59	0,4383561644	0,6771653543
18	polarityCK	dtaExtended	treetagger	enhancedList	caseSensitive	0,59	0,4383561644	0,6771653543
19	polarityGpc	dtaExtended	noLemmatization	enhancedFiltered	caseInSensitive	0,59	0,6885245902	0,4
20	polarityGpc	dtaExtended	noLemmatization	enhancedFiltered	caseSensitive	0,59	0,6885245902	0,4
21	polarityGpc	dtaExtended	pattern	enhancedList	caseInSensitive	0,59	0,6393442623	0,3939393939
22	polarityCKDichotom	dtaExtended	treetagger	enhancedList	caseSensitive	0,53	0,3896103896	0,6178861789
23	polarityCKDichotom	dtaExtended	treetagger	enhancedList	caseInSensitive	0,525	0,3870967742	0,612244898
24	polarityNrc	dtaExtended	treetagger	noStopwordList	caseInSensitive	0,525	0,4378698225	0,5887445887
25	polarityCKDichotom	dtaExtended	treetagger	enhancedFiltered	caseSensitive	0,52	0,4838709677	0,5514018692
26	polarityCKDichotom	dtaExtended	treetagger	enhancedFiltered	caseInSensitive	0,515	0,4812834225	0,544600939

Figure 2. Table snippet of the results of the evaluation of all configurations

Table 2 reduces the results to the best configurations of every single sentiment lexicon and shows the corresponding accuracies as well as F-measures for both polarity classes (positive/negative).

lexicon	extension	lemmatization	stop words	case	accuracy	F-Positive	F-Negative
SentiWS (Polarity Strengths)	dtaExtended	treetagger	noStopWords	caseInSensitive	0.7	0.46	0.79
Combined Lexicon	dtaExtended	treetagger	noStopWords	caseInSensitive	0.68	0.44	0.77
CK (Polarity Strengths)	dtaExtended	treetagger	enhancedFilteredList	caseSensitive	0.6	0.55	0.65
GPC	dtaExtended	pattern	enhancedFilteredList	caseSensitive	0.6	0.72	0.42
NRC	dtaExtended	treetagger	noStopWords	caseInSensitive	0.53	0.44	0.59
BAWL	dtaExtended	treetagger	noStopWords	caseInSensitive	0.49	0.50	0.46

Table 2. Best configurations per sentiment lexicon

In the following we summarize the main findings of our evaluation study:
- The overall best performance is delivered by the SentiWS lexicon and the combined lexicon if the remaining parameters are the same

- When a lexicon has polarity strengths, calculation with those always outperform calculations with the dichotomous polarity of the lexicon. Apart from BAWL, the general rule is that lexicons with polarity strengths (SentiWS, CK) in general outperform all other lexicons with only dichotomous polarities (GPC, NRC)

- The extension with historical linguistic variants consistently yields the strongest performance boost for all lexicons. The extension with historical inflections is better than just automatic lemmatization.

- Stop words lists have differentiated influences. Some lexicons (e.g. GPC) tend to excessive prediction of one polarity class, because of stop words and frequent words. However, this does not always lead to worse accuracies but in-depth word analysis shows incorrect sentiment assignments to words. We therefore recommend the usage of stop word lists when lexicons contain stop words or when stop words are generated by means of additional NLP processes. The best rated lexicons (e.g. SentiWS) are not influenced by stop words at all.

- Both lemmatizers perform almost equally good. A detailed analysis of the results shows that both lemmatizers have problems with the historical language of the speeches. However, for lexicons that consist only of base forms, lemmatization leads to a better overall performance. The results for lexicons with manually added inflections show that those inflections work better than the automatic lemmatization. For many lexicons, a combination of both yields better results.

- Case-sensitivity does not have an effect on the overall quality of sentiment evaluations in our test corpus.

The best overall performance is accomplished with the polarity strengths of the SentiWS lexicon extended with historical linguistic variants, lemmatization via *treetagger*, no stop words lists and ignoring case-sensitivity. The accuracy for this performance is 0.705 with 141 speeches correctly predicted. This result is over the benchmark of the random and majority baseline but below the average percentage of agreement of the annotator pairs (77%).

5   Discussion and Outlook

We made several contributions to the research area of sentiment analysis in historical drama texts, one being the creation of an annotated corpus of drama speeches. However, there are some limitations concerning the annotation study: We identified low to mediocre levels of agreement among the annotators for the polarity annotation. The low level of agreement for annotation schemes with multiple categories is also found in several other research areas (Momtazi, 2012; Takala et al., 2014). The mediocre levels of agreement for the binary annotation are in line with similar research in the field of literary texts (Alm and Sproat, 2005; Alm et al., 2005) and texts with historical language (Sprugnoli et al., 2016). However, compared to other types of text, the agreement for the binary polarity is rather low (e.g. Thet et al., 2010; Prabowo and Thelwall, 2009). Sentiment annotation of literary texts seems to be a rather subjective and challenging task. Our annotators also reported difficulties due to the lack of context and general problems in understanding the poetic and historical language of Lessing. Note that many of the challenges very likely occurred because the annotators were non-experts concerning the drama texts. Some feedback of the annotators also points to the possibility that the used annotation schemes were not sufficient or representative for the application area of sentiment in historical plays. Another limitation is the small size of the corpus: 200 speeches amount to 2% of the speeches of our original Lessing corpus. While such small sample sizes are not uncommon for sentiment annotation of literary texts (Alm and Sproat, 2005), they certainly lessen the significance of the results. To address some of the mentioned limitations, we are planning to conduct larger annotation studies with trained experts in the field of Lessing, more speeches and a more sophisticated annotation scheme.

Our major contribution is the systematic evaluation of different configurations of lexicon-based sentiment analysis techniques. Many of our findings are important not only for sentiment analysis of German drama texts, but for sentiment analysis of corpora with historical and poetic language in general. We identified SentiWS (Remus et al., 2010) as the best performing lexicon for our corpus. The accuracy of the combined lexicon is overall slightly lower than the top rated SentiWS-configuration. The reason for this might be the extension of SentiWS by many problematic and distorting sentiment bearing words that can be regarded as noise. Furthermore, the transfer of some problems of other lexicons, like the missing of manually added inflections, may be responsible for the decreased performance of the combined lexicon as compared to SentiWS alone.

We highly recommend the usage of sentiment lexicons with polarity strengths, since they consistently outperform dichotomous polarity calculations. This proves that for calculation purposes, sentiment bearing words are better represented on a continuous scale. The calculation with polarity strengths seems to better represent human sentiment annotation than the usage of dichotomous values (+1 / -1), as many sentiment bearing words indeed have different intensities that are perceived differently by human annotators and therefore should also be weighted differently for the automatic sentiment calculation.

The noticeable and consistent performance boost from the extension of lexicons by historical linguistic variants highlights the linguistic differences between the contemporary language of the lexicons and the historical language of the 18th century. The creation of sentiment lexicons, especially for the historical language of past centuries, is a beneficial next step and possibilities for historical German are already examined (Buechel et al., 2016). Considering stop words, we highly recommend checking sentiment lexicons for highly frequent words of the corpus, especially for historical and poetic language. The meaning concerning the sentiment of words can differ throughout history (Hamilton et al., 2016) and is also dependent on the linguistic style of a specific author. Therefore, stop words and other highly frequent words might have different sentiment connotations in contemporary and historic German language. It also shows that historic language poses challenges for automatic lemmatization, as it is not as effective as the extension by historical inflections.

Overall, we were able to achieve acceptable levels of accuracy with our best performing configuration (70%), considering the basic methods used, the linguistic challenges the corpus poses and the mediocre levels of agreement of the annotators. Furthermore, we did not consider sentiment classes like *neutral* or *mixed*, although the annotation study showed that many speeches of the corpus are actually not strictly *positive* or *negative*. However, accuracy results in other application areas of sentiment analysis like product reviews or social media are generally higher, e.g. around 90% (Vinodhini and Chandrasekaran, 2012). Besides the historical and poetic language difficulties, common problems of lexicon-based methods like the handling of irony and negations are certainly additional reasons for the mediocre accuracies. Based on our results, we consider the usage of general purpose lexicons alone as not sufficient to achieve acceptable accuracy scores. Using the results of the planned large-scale annotation studies, we will try to create corpora for evaluation and the development of more sophisticated methods of sentiment analysis, such as machine learning and hybrid techniques in order to improve accuracy and integrate other polarity classes as well.

We are also aware that more complex emotional categories like anger, trust or surprise are also of interest for sentiment analysis in literary texts (Alm and Sproat, 2005; Mohammad, 2011). While at the moment resources and best practices to include emotional categories in sentiment analysis are rare (Mohammad and Turney, 2010), we are expecting substantial progress from an ongoing shared task on implicit emotion recognition to gather more insights into this area[4].

Another limitation of the presented results is that we only regarded speeches for sentiment analysis. However to further explore the possibilities and use cases for sentiment analysis on drama texts, we developed a web tool[5] for the exploration of sentiment in Lessing's plays. The tool visualizes the results of the best performing configuration of our evaluation study. Literary scholars can explore sentiment polarity distributions and progressions on several levels, i.e. for the whole play, for single acts, scenes and speeches, but also for individual speakers or for the relationship between two speakers. Further, we also integrated the results of sentiment calculation with the NRC Emotion Lexicon (Mohammad and Turney, 2010), so besides polarity, more complex emotion categories like anger and surprise can be explored as well.

As an example, Figure 3 illustrates the polarity progression for Lessing's "Emilia Galotti" throughout the five acts of the play. On the x-axis, every act is represented by a bar. On the y-axis the polarity of the entire act is represented as an absolute value. The tool also enables the analysis of normalized values, e.g. by the length of the text unit. The tool shows that based on our polarity calculation the play starts with a rather positive polarity in the first act, but becomes more and more negative as the play progresses.

---

[4] More information about this shared task: http://implicitemotions.wassa2018.com/
[5] http://lauchblatt.github.io/QuantitativeDramenanalyseDH2015/FrontEnd/sa_selection.html

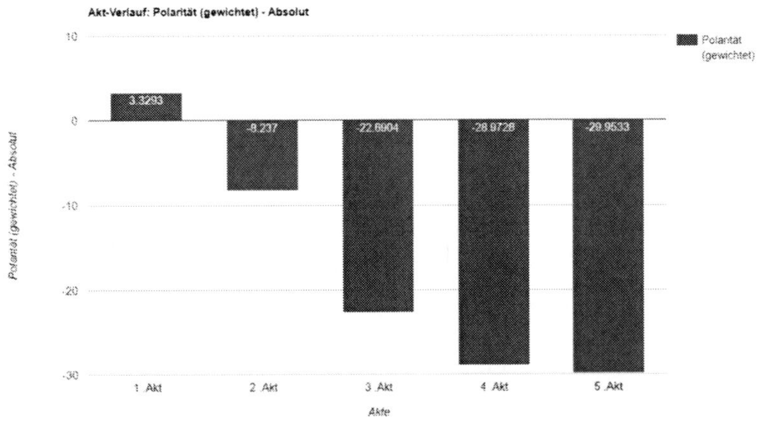

Figure 3. Polarity progression for Emilia Galotti per Act

This tool only represents a first prototype. Meanwhile, we are working close with literary scholars to gather more insights into needs and requirements for the literary analysis of emotion and sentiment in drama texts. By extending our corpus to other authors and eras, we also plan to explore sentiment analysis on drama texts beyond Lessing's plays.

Reference

Alm, C. O., Roth, D., & Sproat, R. (2005). Emotions from text: machine learning for text-based emotion prediction. In *Proceedings of the conference on human language technology and empirical methods in natural language processing* (pp. 579-586). Association for Computational Linguistics

Alm, C. O. & Sproat, R. (2005). Emotional sequencing and development in fairy tales. In *International Conference on Affective Computing and Intelligent Interaction* (pp. 668-674). Springer Berlin Heidelberg.

Ashok, V. G., Feng, S., & Choi, Y. (2013). Success with style: Using writing style to predict the success of novels. In *Proceedings of the 2013 conference on empirical methods in natural language processing* (pp. 1753-1764).

Bosco, C., Allisio, L., Mussa, V., Patti, V., Ruffo, G., Sanguinetti, M., & Sulis, E. (2014). Detecting happiness in Italian tweets: Towards an evaluation dataset for sentiment analysis in Felicitta. In *Proc. of the 5th International Workshop on Emotion, Social Signals, Sentiment and Linked Opena Data, ESSSLOD* (pp. 56-63).

Buechel, S., Hellrich, J., & Hahn, U. (2016). Feelings from the Past – Adapting Affective Lexicons for Historical Emotion Analysis. In *Proceedings of the Workshop on Language Technology Resources and Tools for Digital Humanities (LT4DH)* (pp. 54-61).

Clematide, S. & Klenner, M. (2010). Evaluation and extension of a polarity lexicon for German. *In Proceedings of the First Workshop on Computational Approaches to Subjectivity and Sentiment Analysis* (pp. 7-13).

De Smedt, T. & Daelemans, W. (2012). *Pattern for Python. Journal of Machine Learning Research*, 13, 2031–2035.

Eger, S., Gleim, R., & Mehler, A. (2016). Lemmatization and Morphological Tagging in German and Latin: A Comparison and a Survey of the State-of-the-art. In *LREC*.

Elsner, M. (2012). Character-based kernels for novelistic plot structure. In *Proceedings of the 13th Conference of the European Chapter of the Association for Computational Linguistics* (pp. 634-644). Association for Computational Linguistics.

Emerson, G. & Declerck, T. (2014). SentiMerge: Combining sentiment lexicons in a Bayesian framework. In *Proceedings of the Workshop on Lexical and Grammatical Re-sources for Language Processing* (pp. 30-38).

Fucks, W. & Lauter, J. (1965). Mathematische Analyse des literarischen Stils. In Kreuzer, H. & Gunzenhäuser, F. (Hrsg.), *Mathematik und Dichtung*, (pp. 107-122). München: Nymphenburger Verlagshandlung

Gonçalves, P., Araújo, M., Benevenuto, F., & Cha, M. (2013). Comparing and combining sentiment analysis methods. In *Proceedings of the first ACM conference on Online social networks* (pp. 27-38). ACM.

Hamilton, W. L., Clark, K., Leskovec, J., & Jurafsky, D. (2016). Inducing domain-specific sentiment lexicons from unlabeled corpora. In *Proceedings of the Conference on Empirical Methods in Natural Language Processing. Conference on Empirical Methods in Natural Language Processing* (Vol. 2016, p. 595). NIH Public Access.

Heuser, R., Moretti, F., & Steiner, E. (2016). *The emotions of London.* Retrieved from https://litlab.stanford.edu/LiteraryLabPamphlet13.pdf

Ilsemann, H. (2008). More statistical observations on speech lengths in Shakespeare's plays. *Literary and Linguistic Computing*, 23(4), 397-407.

Jannidis, F., Reger, I., Zehe, A., Becker, M., Hettinger, L. & Hotho, A. (2016). *Analyzing Features for the Detection of Happy Endings in German Novels.* arXiv preprint arXiv:1611.09028.

Jockers, M. L. (2015). *Revealing sentiment and plot arcs with the syuzhet package.* Retrieved from http://www.matthewjockers.net/2015/02/02/syuzhet/

Jurish, B. (2012). *Finite-state Canonicalization Techniques for Historical German.* PhD thesis, Universität Potsdam (defended 2011). URN urn:nbn:de:kobv:517-opus-55789.

Kakkonen, T. & Kakkonen, G. G. (2011). SentiProfiler: creating comparable visual profiles of sentimental content in texts. In *Proceedings of Language Technologies for Digital Humanities and Cultural Heritage* (pp. 62-69).

Kennedy, A., & Inkpen, D. (2006). Sentiment classification of movie reviews using contextual valence shifters. *Computational intelligence*, 22(2), 110-125.

Kim, E., Padó, S., & Klinger, R. (2017). Prototypical Emotion Developments in Literary Genres. In *Proceedings of the Joint SIGHUM Workshop on Computational Linguistics for Cultural Heritage, Social Sciences, Humanities and Literature* (pp. 17–26).

Klinger, R., Suliya, S. S., & Reiter, N. (2016). Automatic Emotion Detection for Quantitative Literary Studies. In *Digital Humanities Book of Abstracts 2016.*

Krippendorff, K. (2011). *Computing Krippendorff's Alpha-Reliability.* Retrieved from http://repository.upenn.edu/asc_papers/43

Landis, J. R., & Koch, G. G. (1977). The measurement of observer agreement for categorical data. *Biometrics*, 33(1), 159-174.

Liu, B. (2016). *Sentiment Analysis. Mining Opinions, Sentiments and Emotions.* New York: Cambridge University Press.

Mellmann, K. (2015). Literaturwissenschaftliche Emotionsforschung. In: Rüdiger Zymner (Hg.): *Handbuch Literarische Rhetorik.* Berlin/Boston, 173-192.

Mohammad, S. (2011). From once upon a time to happily ever after: Tracking emotions in novels and fairy tales. In *Proceedings of the 5th ACL-HLT Workshop on Language Technology for Cultural Heritage, Social Sciences, and Humanities* (pp. 105-114). Association for Computational Linguistics.

Mohammad, S. M., & Turney, P. D. (2010). Emotions evoked by common words and phrases: Using Mechanical Turk to create an emotion lexicon. In *Proceedings of the NAACL HLT 2010 workshop on computational approaches to analysis and generation of emotion in text* (pp. 26-34). Association for Computational Linguistics.

Momtazi, S. (2012). Fine-grained German Sentiment Analysis on Social Media. In *LREC* (pp. 1215-1220).

Mozetič, I., Grčar, M., & Smailović, J. (2016). Multilingual Twitter sentiment classification: The role of human annotators. *PloS one*, 11(5), e0155036.

Nalisnick, E. T. & Baird, H. S. (2013). Character-to-character sentiment analysis in shakespeare's plays. In *Proceedings of the 51st Annual Meeting of the Association for Computational Linguistics* (pp. 479–483).

Prabowo, R., & Thelwall, M. (2009). Sentiment analysis: A combined approach. *Journal of Informetrics*, 3(2), 143-157.

Reagan, A. J., Mitchell, L., Kiley, D., Danforth, C. M., & Dodds, P. S. (2016). The emotional arcs of stories are dominated by six basic shapes. *EPJ Data Science*, 5(1), 31.

Remus, R., Quasthoff, U. & Heyer, G. (2010). SentiWS-A Publicly Available German-language Resource for Sentiment Analysis. In *LREC* (pp. 1168-1171).

Saif, H., Fernandez, M., He, Y., Alani, H. (2014). On Stopwords, Filtering and Data Sparsity for Sentiment Analysis of Twitter. In: *Proc. 9th Language Resources and Evaluation Conference (LREC)* (pp. 810-817).

Schmid, H. (1995). Improvements in Part-of-Speech Tagging with an Application to German. In *Proceedings of the ACL SIGDAT-Workshop*.

Solomon, M. (1971). Ein mathematisch-linguistisches Dramenmodell. *Zeitschrift für Literaturwissenschaft und Linguistik*, 1(1), 139-152.

Sprugnoli, R., Tonelli, S., Marchetti, A., & Moretti, G. (2016). Towards sentiment analysis for historical texts. *Digital Scholarship in the Humanities*, 31(4), 762-772.

Takala, P., Malo, P., Sinha, A., & Ahlgren, O. (2014). Gold-standard for Topic-specific Sentiment Analysis of Economic Texts. In *LREC* (Vol. 2014, pp. 2152-2157).

Thet, T. T., Na, J. C., & Khoo, C. S. (2010). Aspect-based sentiment analysis of movie reviews on discussion boards. *Journal of information science*, 36(6), 823-848.

Vinodhini, G., & Chandrasekaran, R. M. (2012). Sentiment analysis and opinion mining: a survey. *International Journal of Advanced Research in Computer Science and Software Engineering*, 2(6), 282-292.

Võ, M. L., Conrad, M., Kuchinke, L., Urton, K., Hofmann, M. J., & Jacobs, A. M. (2009). The Berlin affective word list reloaded (BAWL-R). *Behavior research methods*, 41(2), 534-538.

Waltinger, U. (2010). Sentiment Analysis Reloaded: A Comparative Study On Sentiment Polarity Identification Combining Machine Learning And Subjectivity Features. In *Proceedings of the 6th International Conference on Web Information Systems and Technologies (WEBIST '10)*

Wilhelm, T., Burghardt, M., & Wolff, C. (2013). "To See or Not to See" - An Interactive Tool for the Visualization and Analysis of Shakespeare Plays. In R. Franken-Wendelstorf, E. Lindinger, & J. Sieck (Eds.), *Kultur und Informatik: Visual Worlds & Interactive Spaces* (pp. 175–185). Glückstadt: Verlag Werner Hülsbusch.

Winko, S. (2003). Über Regeln emotionaler Bedeutung in und von literarischen Texten. In: Fotis Jannidis & Gerhard Lauer & Matias Martinez & SW (eds.): *Regeln der Bedeutung. Zur Theorie der Bedeutung literarischer Texte*. Berlin, New York: de Gruyter, 329-348.

Automatic identification of unknown names with specific roles

Samia Touileb
Language Technology Group
Department of Informatics
University of Oslo
samiat@ifi.uio.no

Truls Pedersen
Department of Information
Science and Media Studies
University of Bergen
truls.pedersen@uib.no

Helle Sjøvaag
Department of Media
and Social Sciences
University of Stavanger
helle.sjovaag@uis.no

Abstract

Automatically identifying persons in a particular role within a large corpus can be a difficult task, especially if you don't know who you are actually looking for. Resources compiling names of persons can be available, but no exhaustive lists exist. However, such lists usually contain known names that are "visible" in the national public sphere, and tend to ignore the marginal and international ones. In this article we propose a method for automatically generating suggestions of names found in a corpus of Norwegian news articles, and which "naturally" belong to a given initial list of members, and that were not known (compiled in a list) beforehand. The approach is based, in part, on the assumption that surface level syntactic features reveal parts of the underlying semantic content and can help uncover the structure of the language.

1 Introduction

One important factor in media coverage of news is the use of diverse sources. Both prominent and marginal voices should be able to express their opinions and views, and be taken into consideration by media outlets. While prominent voices are easily identified and might already be compiled in existing lists (e.g. top level politicians or judges), the marginal ones remain unknown for most readers, and are often not included in precompiled lists. Marginal voices are not necessarily unknown by the public, but they are voices that are not that prominent in a given media coverage. In order to be able to actually quantify to what extent marginal voices are reflected in the media, it is important to be able to identify them.

Automated approaches can be used to identify the voices present in a large corpus of texts. Advances in Natural Language Processing (NLP) approaches allow the automatic identification of the named entities present in a corpus. While these advances have yielded good results for English, they are still at a basic stage for Norwegian. To the best of our knowledge, no approaches can identify the type of an entity (if it is a person name, an organization, ...) for Norwegian texts. However, there are some efforts made towards it, and we are able to identify entities from texts without being able to identify their types (Johansen, 2015). For Norwegian, it is still necessary to add a second step of analysis, usually a manual one, to be able to identify the type of each entity. Even when or if this approach succeeds, there is still a need for additional tools that classify a particular individual within a class of entities.

Linguistic theories show that words having the same context tend to share the same meaning (Harris, 1954), where context here is identified as the words appearing before and after a given word. We believe that this applies to named entities as well. We therefore argue that given a list of known person names, we can identify new unknown persons having similar roles, by analyzing the context in which their names co-occur.

In this work we focus on prominent Norwegian politicians that are mentioned in news, predefined in existing lists, and try to identify the marginal ones, which are not in these lists. The marginal politicians do not need to be unknown, they just have to not be part of a predefined list of politicians. The marginal politicians can be mayors, political representatives, or foreign politicians. Since very few or no resources

Proceedings of Workshop on Computational Linguistics for Cultural Heritage, Social Sciences, Humanities and Literature, pages 150–158
Santa Fe, New Mexico, USA, August 25, 2018.

exist for Norwegian, we rely on an unsupervised approach to automatically identify these unknown politicians.

In what follows, we start in Section 2 by giving an overview of the literature on which we build our work. Then, in Section 3 we give an overview of the corpus used during this investigation, along with the seed list of politicians. In Section 4 we define the methodological steps we followed, and present in Section 5 the results of this study. A discussion of our main contributions, findings, and future avenues are summarized in Section 6.

2 Literature review

Named entity recognition (NER) approaches allow us to automatically identify entities in a text, as well as which type of entities these are, ranging from person names, to organizations and places. NER systems automatically identify entities and their types in texts. These methods have been extensively developed for English, but no off-the shelf approaches currently exist for Norwegian. Some work has been made in this direction, so called Named Entity Chunking (NEC) (Johansen, 2015), that only focuses on the identification of the entities, without specifying their types. It is therefore still necessary, for Norwegian texts, to use pre-compiled lists of entities to be able to identify which types a NEC has located in a text. Challenges emerge, however, if we want to identify specific types of persons in texts, without actually knowing these persons' names.

Our motivations are based on the identification of marginal voices present in news articles. The marginal voices are those who are not precompiled in known lists, but who still express opinions in the news. When looking for indicators of source diversity in the news, the aim is to ascertain the extent to which a range of voices gain access to the sphere of public debate. Based on principles of representation in democratic deliberation procedures (Bennett, 1990; Brown et al., 1987; McQuail, 1992), a pluralistic media landscape reflects the ability of media systems to curtail imbalances in the distribution of social, political and economic power in society (Jeffres et al., 2000). As the news media is the primary arena where actors can exchange ideas and opinions (Skogerbø and Krumsvik, 2015), access to this space should ideally be equal for all (Baker, 2006).

Research shows, however, that marginal voices are often excluded from this arena (e.g. (Kleemans et al., 2017; Ross et al., 2013)). This is partly because the agenda setting function of the media (McCombs, 2005), and the critical and competitive nature of journalistic professionalism (Cook, 1998; Sparrow, 1999), tend to exclude marginal voices - especially voices that do not easily fall within the established narrative frames of political journalism (Wolfsfeld and Sheafer, 2006). The exclusion of marginal voices is especially prevalent in political journalism (Alexseev and Bennett, 1995; Baumgartner and Chaqués Bonafont, 2015; Figenschou and Beyer, 2014; Shehata, 2010). By and large, these findings reflect the fact that most of this research is conducted on elite media, while in fact, local media tend to include a broader range of voices (Berkowitz and Beach, 1993; Allern, 1996; Ross, 2007). In cases where media regulation aims to preserve the type of media outlets that do, in fact, contribute to increase the diversity of voices in the news (cf., (Kulturdepartementet, 2017)), we therefore need measures to empirically establish what those outlets are. Because automatic classifiers, topic modelling and conventional content analysis methods tend to negate marginal classification, improvements to these methods are sorely needed.

Research in linguistics has shown that it is possible, by only analyzing the surface form of the language, to identify structures yielding important information (Harris, 1954). Especially in the sublanguages of specialized domain languages (Harris, 1988). Information structures are linguistic structures representing the distributional structure of the language. Aligning sentences can uncover which words are typically used with selected words in specialized languages, and words that share the same context tend to have the same meaning. We believe that the journalistic language used to discuss politicians is specialized and stylized, which makes it subject to the repeated use of some linguistic patterns.

One of the first attempts to automate the identification of information structures is the work of Lamb (1961). He developed an approach to identify in a corpus of texts the different grouping of words into fixed parts of sentences, and interchangeable parts. His method would for example identify from these sentences "John bought a car", "John bought a bike", "John bought a house", "Norah bought a car", "Norah bought a bike" and "Norah bought a house", the following fixed part "bought a", and the interchangeable parts (John, Norah) and (car, bike, house). The fixed parts represent a grouping of sequences of horizontal elements/words (H-groups), and the interchangeable parts represent a set of vertical elements/words (V-groups). These information structures shed light on how words are being used similarly or differently in the same context next to given words.

Some of the work in the field of grammar inference are built on the insights of Harris (1954) and the work of Lamb (1961). Grammar induction approaches rely on the structural aspect of the language to extract information from textual data. These methods are usually used to induce complete grammars for a given language or text. However, some work has shown that methods developed in grammar induction can be used to automatically induce information structures that can identify what is being said about given issues, how it is being said, and can reflect some of the most important and distinctive content of a corpus (Salway et al., 2014; Touileb and Salway, 2014; Salway and Touileb, 2014).

An unsupervised grammar induction algorithm (first presented in (Solan et al., 2005)), that discovers hierarchical structures in sequential data, has been modified by Salway and Touileb (2014) into a text mining approach – henceforth referred to as SIMMS (Structure Induction for Mining Meaningful Snippets). The latter automatically, and in an unsupervised way, induces information structures from unannotated corpora. This algorithm is able to identify some of the most significant patterns (horizontal sequences of words) and equivalence classes (vertical groups of words) within the context of patterns, using statistical information, and running over a predetermined set of iterations. The patterns and equivalence classes respectively resemble the H-groups and V-groups presented by Lamb (1961). The method focuses on text snippets around key terms of interest rather than processing entire sentences. Instances of the most frequent induced patterns, representing information structures, are then replaced with unique identifiers in the input to make patterning around them more explicit in subsequent iterations. The induced structures are in the form of regular expressions, where elements of patterns are separated by whitespace, and the elements of the equivalence classes are separated by "|" representing "or". Considering the previous example of John and Norah, this approach will induce structures of the form "`(John|Norah) bought a (car|bike|house)`" which can be read as John *or* Norah bought a car *or* bike *or* house. We will in what follows refer to information structures and patterns interchangeably.

Based on this method and the linguistic theories on which it is built, we believe that given a sufficiently large corpus and a seed list containing a set of voices (both often described in specialized language and sufficiently homogeneous), we may isolate a set of new names (not contained in the seed list) which naturally extend the seed list. In our case, given a set of politicians' names, we may automatically find a disjoint set of names which will contain a relatively high portion of politicians. We therefore propose a method for expanding a list of known names to include previously undiscovered names occurring in similar contexts. In the following, we outline the steps in the implementation of an approach to enlarge a list of Norwegian politicians' names to include politicians which do not appear in the preexisting list (which we refer to as the seed list), from a corpus of news texts.

3 Data

We use two data sets: a large corpus of newspaper articles and a list of Norwegian politicians. The corpus of Norwegian news articles was scraped hourly from 125 online newspapers, between October and December 2015 and 2016. These newspapers reflect diversity in ownership (state (one outlet, the Norwegian Broadcasting Corporation), corporate, foundation, or independent), and distribution (local (92 outlets), metropolitan (25 outlets) or national (8 outlets)). This resulted in more than 600,000 articles. We show in Table 1 the newspapers, and their distribution category.

The list of politicians contained 368 Norwegian politicians in parliament and government, as well as mayors and their deputies. The names of politicians from the parliament and government were collected from the open data of the Norwegian Parliament[1]. The names of mayors and their deputies were manually

---

[1]https://data.stortinget.no/no/dokumentasjon-og-hjelp/dagens-representanter/

<table>
<tr><td>National:</td><td>Aftenposten, Dag og Tid, Dagbladet, Dagen, Dagens Næringsliv, Dagsavisen, Dinside.no, Fiskeribladet Fiskaren, Klassekampen, Morgenbladet, Nationen, NRK, TV2, Vårt Land</td></tr>
<tr><td>Metropolitan:</td><td>Adresseavisa, Agderposten, Avisa Nordland, Bergensavisen, Bergens Tidende, Budstikka, Drammens Tidende, Fædrelandsvennen, Glåmdalen, Gudbrandsdølen Dagn, Haugesuns Avisa, Harstad Tidende, iTromsø, Moss Avis, Nordlys, Oppland Arbeiderblad, Rogalands Avis, Romerikes Blad, Romsdals Budstikke, Sandefjords Blad, Sarpsborg Arbeiderblad, Stavanger Aftenblad, Sunnmørsposten, Telemarkavisa, Tønsbergs Blad, Varden, Østlands-Posten</td></tr>
<tr><td>Local:</td><td>Altaposten, Akershus Amststidende, Arbeidets rett, Arendals Tidende, Askøyværingen, Aura Avis, Aust-Agder Blad, Avisa Nordhordland, Bladet Vesterålen, Brønnøysunds Avis, Bygdanytt, Bygdebladet Randaberg, Bømlonytt, Demokraten, Driva, Eidsvol Ullensaker Blad, Dølen, Eikerbladet, Enebakk Avis, Fanaposten, Firda, Firdaposten, Fjordenes Tidende, Fjordingen, Framtid i Nord, Fremover, Gjesdalbuen, Gjengangeren, Groruddalen, Halder Arbeiderblad, Hadeland, Helgelendingen, Hallingdølen, Hardanger Folkeblad, Helgelands Blad, Hitra-Frøya, Hålogalands Avis, iFinnmark, Indre Akershus Blad, Innherred Folkeblad, Jarlsberg Avis, Jærbladet, Kanalen, Kragerø Blad, Kvinneheringen, Kyst og Fjord, Laagendaksposten, Lierposten, Lillesandsposten, Lindesnes Avis, Lofotposten, Lygdals Avis, Lokalavisa Nordsalten, Møre-Nytt, Namdalsaisa, Norddalen, Nordre, Nye Troms, Porsgrunns Dagblad, Rakkestad Avis, Rana Blad, Ringerikes Blad, Ringesaker Blad, Røyken og Hurun Avis, Saltenposten, Sande Avis, Sandnesposten, Smaalenes Avis, Sogn Avis, Solabladet, Stjørdalens Blad, Sunnhordland, Sunnmøringen, Svalbardposten, Svelvikposten, Telen, Tidens Krav, Troms Folkeblad, Trønderbladet, Tvedestransposten, Tysnes, Tysvær Bygdeblad, Valdres, Vennesla Tidende, Vestby Avis, Vestnesavisa, Vestnytt, Vikebladet Vestposten, Østlandets Blad, Øyene, Åndalsnes Avis, Ås Avis, Åsane Tidende</td></tr>
</table>

Table 1: Overview of the newspapers in the corpus.

gathered from various online sources. The list comprises 298 names representing county mayors, county deputy mayors, sate secretaries, municipal councils, city councils, local chairmans, county councils, city council representatives, and local councils.

4 Approach

We start with the assumption that texts featuring politicians have certain common context-dependent characteristics across the corpus. This should therefore allow for the identification of language use patterns around the politicians' names and allow us to identify politicians that were not included in the seed list.

Given a corpus (C), we produce a list of all names occurring in it and isolate those that appear on the seed list of politicians. We select all sentences from C in which some politician is mentioned and apply SIMMS to these sentences. This yields a set of patterns, from which we may isolate a sub-corpus (D) of sentences (not full texts) which match these patterns. Names will occur in a number of sentences matching a number of patterns. We take the sum of these frequencies to denote the names' score. Names which score well, are presented to a human expert for validation.

In more details, the process starts by running a Norwegian NEC analysis (Johansen, 2015) on the news corpus. The list of identified entities was manually analyzed, with some algorithmic assistance (looking up names), to only select entities referring to persons. Then, using the list of Norwegian politicians, all sentences from all news articles containing the politicians' names from the seed list were identified and extracted. These names were then substituted with the placeholder-string "POL" in the sentences. This was done to create an abstract concept of politician and create more patterning in the input texts. It yields a set of sentences where known names have been removed, but permits our approach to distinguish between entities occurring in our target list (i.e. having roles similar to politicians) from other names. In the same sentences, we substituted each appearance of a person name (non-politician) entity, as identified by NEC and not present in the politician seed list, with the placeholder-codes "PER" for persons, and "ENT" for the remaining entities. The placeholders "POL", "PER", and "ENT" do not otherwise occur in the text.

Once the sentences containing known politician names are extracted, SIMMS (Salway et al., 2014) is applied in order to automatically induce salient patterns of language use around the coded politicians' names (i.e. the string "POL"). We start by creating snippets around POL as explained in (Salway et al., 2014). These snippets are of various sizes and contain between 0-12 words on either side of the string. These are used in the various iteration phases of the algorithm. The snippets are of increasingly large sizes which allows the algorithm, in each of its running iterations, to build more patterning around the already identified patterns. These patterns are information structures of word sequences, resembling information extraction templates (Salway et al., 2014).

153

ID.Pattern	Freq
P_0.((justisminister|arbeidsminister|kommunalminister|helseminister| utenriksminister|finansminister|stortingsrepresentant|ENT|næringsminister |partikollega|fiskeriminister|styreleder|ENT-ordfører|ordfører |ordførerkandidat|statsminister|statsråd|samferdselsminister| statssekretær) POL) *((justice minister|labor minister|minister of local government|health minister|minister of foreign affairs|finance minister|member of parliament|ENT|industry minister|party colleague|minister of fisheries|Chairman|ENT-mayor|mayor|mayor candidate|prime minister|council of state|minister of transport|state secretary) POL)*	13912
P_14.(klima- og (miljødepartementet|miljøminister|miljøministeren| miljøvernminister|miljøvernministeren)) *(climate and (environment ministry|environment minister|the environment minister|minister of the environment|the minister of the environment))*	440
P_44.(ENT (kommunalpolitiske|justispolitiske|likestillingspolitiske| helsepolitiske|innvandringspolitiske|mediepolitisk|mediepolitiske| finanspolitiske|landbrukspolitiske|fiskeripolitiske) talsperson) *((municipality's political|justice's political|equality's political|health's political|immigration's political|media political|media's political|finance's political|agriculture's political|fisheries' political) spokesperson)*	151
P_61.((påtroppende|kommende) byrådsleder) *((incoming|forthcoming) governing mayor)*	99
P_102.(ENT (utdanningspolitiske|helsepolitiske|finanspolitiske| fiskeripolitiske) talskvinne) *(ENT (education's political|health's political|fiscals' political|fisheries' political) spokeswoman)*	41
P_192.(sier helsepolitisk (talskvinne|talsmann)) *(says health's political (spokeswoman|spokesman))*	17

Table 2: A selection of induced structures.

A small sample of induced structures is shown in Table 2. The structures are shown in Norwegian, with English translations in italics. Structure P_0 is the most frequent of all induced structures, and seems to discuss politicians in different positions. Structure P_14 focuses on politicians related to climate and environment. Structures P_44, P_102, and P_192 discuss spokeswoman and spokesman in various political roles, while structure P_61 seem to discuss local politicians.

We automatically filtered the induced structures to keep only those that included the string "POL", or had the string in the exterior of the patterns within the matched sentences. We disregarded all structures that only included the strings "PER" or "ENT" without "POL" in their surroundings within their matched sentences. However, structures including "PER" or "ENT" and not including "POL" but having the string in the matched sentences were kept. This was done to focus our analysis on structures and sentences containing names of politicians indicated by the presence of the string "POL", and in order to identify which of the strings within "PER" are actually politicians. This process resulted in 108 patterns.

After we had discovered the patterns which seemed to identify politicians, we subsequently isolated the sentences which manifested these patterns into a sentence sub-corpus, D. We re-ran the NEC (Johansen, 2015) on this corpus to identify candidate names, which were thereafter compared to the seed list of politicians. The politicians that were present in the seed list were removed keeping only the list of new names that we believed were likely to be unknown politicians (i.e. not in the seed list). This list of unknown names was afterwards presented to human judges for manual analysis. The results of this were rather promising, as we show in the next section.

5   Results

We compute for each of the newly identified names a score representing its frequencies in the induced structures. The score is computed as the sum of all frequencies of the name in the various structures in which it appears. In Figure 1 we show the distribution of names and their frequencies. The figure on the right shows an excerpt of the most interesting range of the full range shown in the figure on the left. Most of the newly identified names have frequencies between 2 and 51, with some recurring spikes between frequency 51 and frequency 150. The frequency distribution flattens out after frequency 150 and there is only one name per frequency between frequency values 150 and 521.

Top 20 of the most frequent names and their frequencies, excluding the ones present in the seed list,

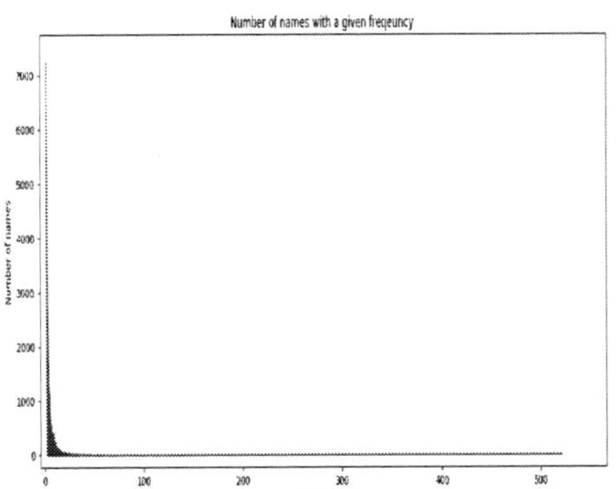 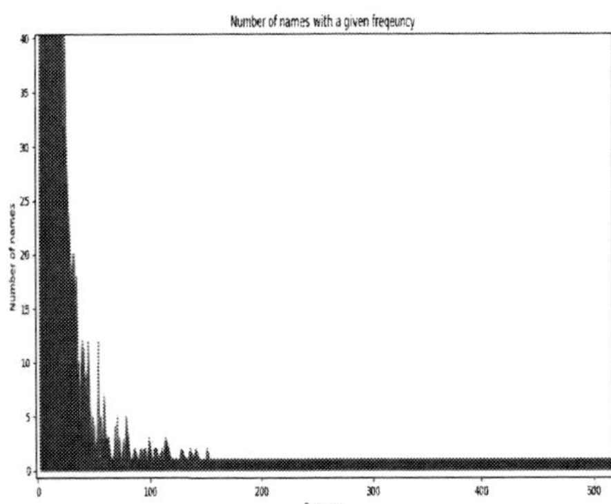

Figure 1: Number of names per frequency.

Name	Freq.	Cat.	Name	Freq.	Cat.
1. David Cameron	521	1	11. Ketil Solvik-olsen	280	1
2. Hege Storhaug	468	0	12. Monica Mæland	239	1
3. Henrik Kristoffersen	423	0	13. Kristoffer Ajer	227	0
4. Svein Aaser	410	0	14. Thorhild Widvey	218	1
5. Mads Stokkelien	375	0	15. Charles Michel	217	1
6. Benjamin Netanyahu	331	1	16. Manuel Valls	192	1
7. Ahmet Davutoglu	327	1	17. Knut Storberget	191	1
8. Angela Merkel	324	1	18. Bent Høie	180	1
9. Stefan Löfven	306	1	19. Alexander Kristoff	177	0
10. John Kerry	283	1	20. Kristoffer Barmen	172	0

Table 3: Top 20 of the most frequent names as identified by our approach, and their manually assigned categories (1: politician, 0: not politician).

are presented in Table 3. We also show which names are politicians using boolean values: 1 for politician and 0 for not politician. This decision was based on the manual analysis of the human judges.

We investigated two top-scoring intervals: a set of the best scoring names, and a subsequent set of best scoring names. The set of the best scoring names are all names that have a frequency equal or greater than 90% of the frequency of the most frequent name. The second top-scoring interval represents names with frequencies between 50 and 32. They yielded respectively 156/264 (60%) and 97/231 (42%) politicians including known politicians from the seed list. We argue that this already corroborates our assumptions about specialized language, that persons sharing the same role are discussed and talked about similarly.

Disregarding known politicians, the first set of best scoring names resulted in a sample of 167 unknown names, with frequencies spanning from 521 at maximum to minimum 51. We manually analyzed this sample of names and identified which ones were actually politicians. From these 167 names, we were not able to classify 6 names either because they were incomplete, or ambiguous. From the 161 names remaining, 33% were manually classified as politicians (53 names out of 161). The remaining 67% mostly represented athletes. The second best scoring interval of names resulted in a set of 170 unknown names, from which 8 were unclassified. From the remaining 162 we were able to classify 28 names as politicians, representing 17.28%. As in the previous interval, most of the remaining names referred to athletes. That is, had we presented the unrecognized top-scoring names, a human expert would verify every third name as a politician which we could correctly add to our seed list of politicians. Table 4 summarizes our findings on unknown politician names.

A total of 67% of the newly identified politicians, in the first set of best scoring names, represented Norwegian politician names (local and national), and 33% were international politicians (Canada, UK,

Results	Set of best scoring names	Subsequent set of best scoring names
#unknown names	167	170
#incomplete/ambiguous names	6	8
#politicians	53 (33%)	28 (17.28%)
#Norwegian politicians	36 (67%)	23 (82.15%)
#international politicians	17 (33%)	5 (17.85%)

Table 4: Number of politicians (Norwegian and international) identified by our method, in both investigated top-scoring intervals.

Germany, USA, Sweden, France, Spain, Russia, Palestine, Poland, Croatia, Italy, Israel, Turkey, Denmark, Belgium). In the remaining names of the first set of best scoring names, 59% referred to football players, football coaches, general managers of football clubs, or football commentators. About 9% referred to athletes in other sports like cycling, and handball. A total of 12% were person names known in winter sports like skiing, ice hockey players, and alpinists. The remaining 20% were political activists, journalists, police, jurists, lawyers, celebrities, union leaders, musicians, and company leaders.

In the second set of best scoring names, a total of 82.15% of the newly identified politician names were Norwegian politicians, and 17.85% were international ones (from Canada, Germany, and UK). The person names that were not politicians were mostly related to sports. These were football players/coaches, other sports like handball, ski or ice hockey athletes and represent 50.31% of the 161 identified names. The remaining 16.69% were political activists, journalists, celebrities, union leaders, musicians, and company leaders.

6 Conclusion and future work

In this paper, we have addressed the problem of automatically identifying person names sharing similar political roles from a corpus of news articles. We have used a text mining approach able to automatically induce patterns of language use around known politician names from a predefined seed list. This approach is able to group together words appearing in similar contexts, and hence person names sharing similar roles.

Automatically identifying and extracting names is a difficult task, especially in Norwegian, as no off-the shelf named entity recognition (NER) approaches exists. In this work, we have used a named entity chunker (NEC) (Johansen, 2015) that is able to identify entities, but not their types. In order to be able to differentiate person names from other types of entities, we in part relied on computer assisted manual analysis. We have shown that our approach is able to identify new names that naturally extend the seed list, as these new names have similar roles.

There are many parameters that may influence this approach. If our seed list is actually complete, there would be no names to add and our approach would only present names not belonging to it. If our seed list is heterogeneous, or contains names belonging to a group which is generally not discussed by a specialized language, we may expect the human expert to be presented with many names which do not naturally extend our list.

Although we have only tested our approach on a list of politicians' names, we feel there is good reason to believe that many other natural sets of names satisfy the conditions our approach relies on. It suffices that the entities named in the seed list share some attributes or characteristics which makes it likely that they will be discussed in similar ways in some specialized language.

Most of the names identified were not politicians, but a relatively high proportion were. We removed all known politicians before compiling the results presented in this article. This justifies the fact that 33% is regarded as good results for a first step. We believe that this might be due to the nature of the corpus. The corpus was a collection of news articles covering all newsworthy issues from sport to politics. Based on the induced structures, it seems that the way politicians are talked about, the words used to describe them or discuss issues around them, resembles the way athletes and sports related events are talked about.

We plan to improve our approach by first running a topic modeling approach on the corpus, to filter out the news articles not covering political issues, and then re-run the presented approach. This will give, we believe, a more focused corpus as input, and we might be able to solely identify new names of politicians. We also think that it would be interesting to use word embeddings, and investigate if politicians' names are nearer in the vector space model as opposed to non-politicians.

References

Mikhail A. Alexseev and W. Lance Bennett. 1995. For whom the gates open: News reporting and government source patterns in the united states, great britain, and russia. *Political communication*, 12(4):395–412.

Sigurd Allern. 1996. *Kildenes makt: Ytringsfrihetens politiske økonomi*. Pax.

C. Edwin Baker. 2006. *Media concentration and democracy: Why ownership matters*. Cambridge University Press.

Frank R. Baumgartner and Laura Chaqués Bonafont. 2015. All news is bad news: Newspaper coverage of political parties in spain. *Political Communication*, 32(2):268–291.

W. Lance Bennett. 1990. Toward a theory of press-state relations in the united states. *Journal of communication*, 40(2):103–127.

Dan Berkowitz and Douglas W. Beach. 1993. News sources and news context: The effect of routine news, conflict and proximity. *Journalism Quarterly*, 70(1):4–12.

Jane Delano Brown, Carl R. Bybee, Stanley T. Wearden, and Dulcie Murdock Straughan. 1987. Invisible power: Newspaper news sources and the limits of diversity. *Journalism Quarterly*, 64(1):45–54.

Timothy E. Cook. 1998. *Governing with the news: The news media as a political institution*. University of Chicago Press.

Tine Ustad Figenschou and Audun Beyer. 2014. Elites, minorities and the media-primary definers in the norwegian immigration debate. *Tidsskrift for Samfunnsforskning*, 55(1):23–51.

Zellig S. Harris. 1954. Distributional structure. *Word*, 10(2-3):146–162.

Zellig S. Harris. 1988. *Language and information*. Columbia University Press.

Leo W. Jeffres, Connie Cutietta, Leslie Sekerka, and Jae-won Lee. 2000. Newspapers, pluralism, and diversity in an urban context. *Mass Communication & Society*, 3(2-3):157–184.

Bjarte Johansen. 2015. Named-entity chunking for norwegian text using support vector machines. In *Norsk Informatikkonferanse (NIK)*, Ålesund, Norway.

Mariska Kleemans, Gabi Schaap, and Liesbeth Hermans. 2017. Citizen sources in the news: Above and beyond the vox pop? *Journalism*, 18(4):464–481.

Oslo: Kulturdepartementet. 2017. Det norske mediemangfoldet – en styrket mediepolitikk for borgerne. In *Norwegian media diversity: A strengthened media policy for citizens*.

Sydney M. Lamb. 1961. On the mechanization of syntactic analysis. *Conference on Machine Translation of Languages and Applied Language Analysis II*, pages 674–685.

Maxwell McCombs. 2005. A look at agenda-setting: Past, present and future. *Journalism studies*, 6(4):543–557.

Denis McQuail. 1992. *Media performance: Mass communication and the public interest*. Sage.

Karen Ross, Elizabeth Evans, Lisa Harrison, Mary Shears, and Khursheed Wadia. 2013. The gender of news and news of gender: a study of sex, politics, and press coverage of the 2010 british general election. *The International Journal of Press/Politics*, 18(1):3–20.

Karen Ross. 2007. The journalist, the housewife, the citizen and the press: Women and men as sources in local news narratives. *Journalism*, 8(4):449–473.

Andrew Salway and Samia Touileb. 2014. Applying grammar induction to text mining. In *Proceedings of the 52nd Annual Meeting of the Association for Computational Linguistics*, volume 2, pages 712–717, Baltimore, USA.

Andrew Salway, Samia Touileb, and Endre Tvinnereim. 2014. Inducing information structures for data-driven text analysis. In *Proceedings of the ACL 2014 Workshop on Language Technologies and Computational Social Science*, pages 28–32, Baltimore, USA.

Adam Shehata. 2010. Marking journalistic independence: Official dominance and the rule of product substitution in swedish press coverage. *European Journal of Communication*, 25(2):123–137.

Eli Skogerbø and Arne H. Krumsvik. 2015. Newspapers, facebook and twitter: Intermedial agenda setting in local election campaigns. *Journalism Practice*, 9(3):350–366.

Zach Solan, David Horn, Eytan Ruppin, and Shimon Edelman. 2005. Unsupervised learning of natural languages. *Proceedings of the National Academy of Sciences of the United States of America*, 102(33):11629–11634.

Bartholomew H. Sparrow. 1999. *Uncertain guardians: The news media as a political institution*. JHU Press.

Samia Touileb and Andrew Salway. 2014. Constructions: a new unit of analysis for corpus-based discourse analysis. In *Proceedings of the 28th Pacific Asia Conference on Language, Information and Computing*, pages 634–643, Phuket, Thailand.

Gadi Wolfsfeld and Tamir Sheafer. 2006. Competing actors and the construction of political news: The contest over waves in israel. *Political Communication*, 23(3):333–354.

Induction of a Large-Scale Knowledge Graph from the *Regesta Imperii*

Juri Opitz   **Leo Born**   **Vivi Nastase**
Institute for Computational Linguistics
Heidelberg University
69120 Heidelberg
`{opitz,born,nastase}@cl.uni-heidelberg.de`

Abstract

We induce and visualize a Knowledge Graph over the Regesta Imperii (RI), an important large-scale resource for medieval history research. The RI comprise more than 150,000 digitized abstracts of medieval charters issued by the Roman-German kings and popes distributed over many European locations and a time span of more than 700 years. Our goal is to provide a resource for historians to visualize and query the RI, possibly aiding medieval history research. The resulting medieval graph and visualization tools are shared publicly.

1 Introduction

We describe here the process of inducing and visualizing a Knowledge Graph (KG) that structures information from the Regesta Imperii (RI), an important large-scale resource for medieval history research. Having important information from the RI in a structured format makes it easier to visualize, and possibly aid medieval history research.

The *Regesta Imperii* (RI) comprises documents, *regests*, that can be seen as abstracts of charters issued by Roman-German emperors and popes, starting from the Carolingian dynasty to Maximilan I. The project was initiated in 1829 by a German librarian, *Johann Friedrich Böhmer*, who started to collect and summarize the charters. Today, more than 175,000 regests have been converted to Unicode and are stored in a publicly available and continuously increasing online database[1] due to the efforts of various research projects.[2]

We extract relations and entities from the regest texts and meta information, and build a large-scale knowledge graph that covers approximately 83% of the documents (Sections 2-3). Information about the entity types and about the events themselves reveal interesting observations about the behaviour of emperors and popes with respect to their subjects. The graph can be explored through a web-based visualization tool (Section 4).

2 Constructing the RI Knowledge Graph

The RI corpus. With regard to the referenced charters, the RI are unevenly distributed over a large time span (Figure 1). Many regests reference charters from the later medieval times issued by the emperors Karl IV (1316-1378, 15,595 regests), Friedrich III (1415-1493, 21,477 regests) and Maximilian I (1459-1519, 22,153 regests) and very often consist of one, often complicated sentence, describing an action performed by the issuer (usually an emperor or pope) towards one or several of his subjects, as can be seen

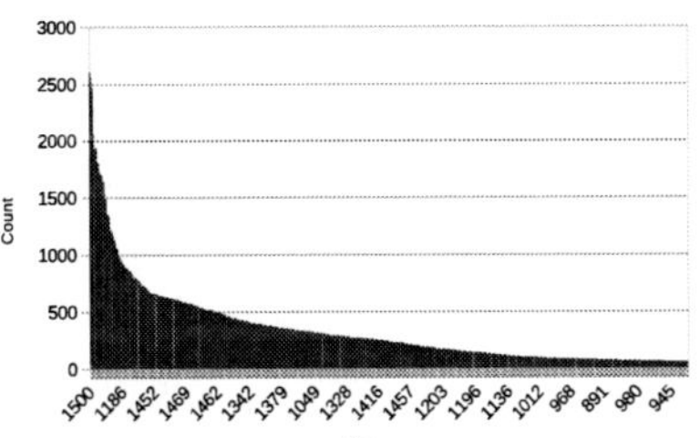

Figure 1: Distribution of regests over time with respect to year of charter creation.

[1] `http://www.regesta-imperii.de/en/home.html`

[2] Under the umbrella of the *German commission for the handling of the Regesta Imperii e. V. (Deutsche Kommission für die Bearbeitung der Regesta Imperii e. V.)*.

Proceedings of Workshop on Computational Linguistics for Cultural Heritage, Social Sciences, Humanities and Literature, pages 159–168
Santa Fe, New Mexico, USA, August 25, 2018.

[rel verspricht] dem Kurfürsten [oa_rel Ludwig von der Pfalz] für dessen allenfallsige Wahlstimme ihm alle seine [oa_oc Privilegien Reichspfandschaften] (Oppenheim, Gauodernheim, Ober- u. Nieder-Ingelheim, Winterheim, Dexheim, Nierstein, Schwabsburg, Kaiserslautern, Barr, Ortenberg, Offenburg, Gengenbach, Zell, Sels) u. s. w. zu [oc bestätigen]. Mitsiegler Burggraf Friedrich VI v. Nürnberg.

[rel promises] the Elector Palatine [oa_rel Ludwig of the Palatinate] that if he gets his vote, that he [oc confirms] all the Palatine Elector's [oa_oc privileges earnests] (Oppenheim, Gauodernheim, Ober- u. Nieder-Ingelheim, Winterheim, Dexheim, Nierstein, Schwabsburg, Kaiserslautern, Barr, Ortenberg, Offenburg, Gengenbach, Zell, Sels) etc. Also sealed by castle-count Friedrich VI of Nuremberg.

Figure 2: Regest summarizing a charter issued by emperor Sigmund in 1410 and (our) translation. *rel* is the main relation, *oa* (accusative object) indicates *whom* the emperor is promising something, *oc* (object clause) indicates *what* the emperor is promising. Green/orange indicate named entity persons/locations found by the automatic tool, which are all accurate in the example.

Kg. Ruprecht gibt seinem kuchenschriber Hermann von Mülin und dessen erben für seine treuen dienste sein haus und den stall daran zu eigen, "daz gelegen ist in unßer Stad Heidelberg by unsem marstalle off ein syte an der apoteken und off die andern syten an Zengels des smyts (...)"

King Ruprecht gives to his kitchen-bills-accountant Hermann von Mülin and his heirs for his faithful services his house and barn into his possession "which lies in our city of Heidelberg at the Marstall on one side the pharmacy and at the other side the blacksmith (...)"

Figure 3: German text and (our) English translation of a regest summarizing a charter issued by king *Ruprecht* in 1404. Code is switched to an older German variant in the middle of the text.

in the regest[3] in Figure 2. While this regest is syntactically quite complex, it contains only conventional German, where *conventional* means that syntax and spelling conform with contemporary German. Other regests, having been created earlier or by different authors, contain words with non-conventional spelling or nouns in lowercase, which is highly unconventional in contemporary German. An example is displayed in Figure 3.[4] *erben* (heirs) and *dienste* (services) are nouns currently written with an uppercase starting letter; *kuchenschriber* (kitchen bills accountant) is a (very rare) noun, spelled *Küchenschreiber* in contemporary German. In the middle of the text the code switches and we find a much older variant of German, a quotation from the original charter of 1404, where spelling and syntactic constructions differ significantly, e.g. *Stadt* (city) is written *Stad* and *Seite* (side) is spelled *syte*.

Corpus statistics are summarized in Table 1.[5] We find more than 16 million tokens and almost 2 million named entity mentions in the RI. Because the RI stem from different authors and times, the spelling of words can be very variable. For example, there are many spelling variants of the Austrian city *Innsbruck* (*Ynnsbrug, Ynsbrug, Innsbruck, Insprugk*, etc.). Code-switching is ubiquitous not only from author to author but

element	sum	types	μ	$\tilde{\mu}$	σ
regests	179,320	-	-	-	-
issuers	179,320	419	-	-	-
locations	179,320	13,656	-	-	-
tokens	16,525,042	488,619	92.2	56	150.7
NPs	4,097,632	903,383	22.9	14	34.7
NEs	1,977,866	363,162	11.0	7	15.7

Table 1: Corpus statistics.

also inside a regest, where the text often contains quotes in Latin and medieval German, taken from the original charter. Named entities in the RI can be rather complex, for example *Adelheid, tochter weiland Ulrichs von Minzenberg* (English: "Adelheid, daughter of former Ulrich of Minzenberg") includes a sub-named entity (*Ulrich von Minzenberg*). *tochter*, as a noun, should start with an uppercase letter and *weiland* is an outdated and uncommon German adverb, used in the sense of "formerly".

---

[3] URI: http://www.regesta-imperii.de/id/1410-08-05_4_0_11_1_0_4_4.

[4] URI: http://www.regesta-imperii.de/id/1404-06-26_1_0_10_0_0_3588_3584.

[5] Linguistic annotation was performed with spacy's German model v2.0.0: https://spacy.io/models/de.

160

Preprocessing. We use a state-of-the-art German preprocessing pipeline. The preprocessing model was trained on contemporary German texts, so it naturally makes more errors on the RI. We manually examine the outputs for 100 randomly chosen regests, and find that, particularly on the first sentence, all steps yield reasonably good results on named entity recognition, and the syntactic dependency parse is often correct in detecting the finite main verb and its object, or parts of it.[6]

Some errors are caused by non-conventional spelling (e.g. lowercased nouns tagged as verbs). We will address this type of errors in future work, mainly because countless rare nouns and a high rate of spelling variations make classical normalization techniques very challenging. Applying such techniques, e.g. techniques based on lexical lookups and minimum edit distance computations (Ristad and Yianilos, 1998; Yujian and Bo, 2007), may even introduce many new errors and manipulate the historic data in unwanted and difficult-to-detect ways.

We find, however, a specific type of error which is due to an eager sentence splitting model: e.g. a sentence split often is performed on title prefixes. In the RI a title – abbreviated with a period – often prefixes a named entity: e.g. *Gf. – Graf* (count), *Bf. – Bischof* (bishop), *Eb. – Erzbischof* (archbishop).

We introduce three processing steps to minimize this type of error: (1) iterate through 15,000 randomly sampled regests and aggregate the tokens occurring directly in front of named entities; (2) compute their frequencies; (3) filter instances starting with an uppercase letter, ending with a period, having a minimum frequency of 5 and a maximum length of 5 characters. Taking into account only the prefixes starting with an uppercase letter has the advantage of increased precision (verbs are not counted). Recall can be increased afterwards by taking into account the prefixes' lowercase variants as well (sometimes bishop was abbreviated *bf.* and at other times *Bf.*). After obtaining the possible abbreviations a historian helped us in manually filtering out 250 common abbreviations in the RI (false positives such as Roman numerals – e.g. *XI.* – were discarded in this step). After applying these steps, we obtain an interesting vocabulary of historic German abbreviations (Table 2). The amount of erroneous sentence splits was reduced by 10%.

abbreviation	title/function	freq.
Kgin.	queen	7
Kg., Ks.	king, emperor	1,125
Hz., Hrz., Hzg.	duke	369
Hzn., Hzin.	duchess	8
Mgf., Pfgf., Ldgf., Pfgr., Mgff., Bggf.	*various counts*	252
Eb., EB., Bf., BF., Erzb.	(arch-)bishop	121

Table 2: Some of the automatically collected medieval title abbreviations and their frequency in a random sample of 15,000 regests.

Edges and vertices. Based on the assumption that the first (and often only) sentence contains the relevant relation information, we process only this sentence. We rely on the fact that the main relation (edge) between a ruler and its subject entities (the vertices) very frequently occur in a subject-verb-object format with respect to the first finite verb. As arguments of the relation we consider the first occurring named entity and the named entity which acts as the accusative or dative object of the first finite verb. Named entities in a comma-separated list or appearing in *and*-conjunctions of which at least one has an object dependency relation to the main verb, are all added to the graph separately.

The source is the issuer or emperor, which we assume to be the subject of the first finite verb and which we extract from the metadata as it is often omitted in the regest text (cf. Figure 2). The KG will thus contain two types of vertices: (i) the issuers (emperor or pope) and (ii) named entities found by the NLP tool.

Edges are weighted: if a named entity is mentioned first after the finite verb *or* has an object dependency to it, the weight of the edge is increased by 0.5; if a named entity is mentioned first after the main verb *and* lies in

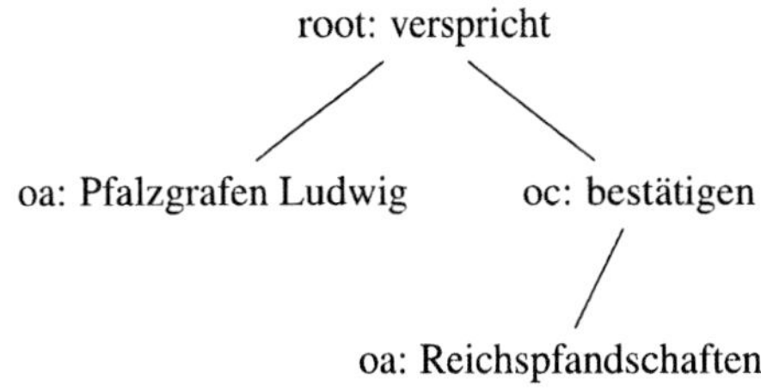

Figure 4: Dependency parse for Figure 2.

---

[6]The first two authors are German native speakers.

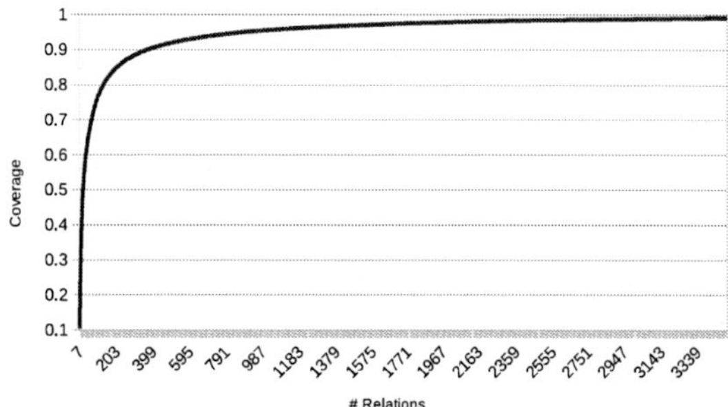

relation	translation	count	coverage
bestätigt	confirms	15,811	0.11
befiehlt	commands	8,408	0.06
verleiht	bestows	5,796	0.04
schreibt	writes	5,427	0.04
schenkt	donates	2,652	0.02
fordert	demands	1,619	0.01
gewährt	permits	1,425	0.01
bittet	asks	1,004	0.01

Figure 5: 400 out of 4,948 relations cover over 90% of the relations induced into our KG.

Table 3: The most frequent relations in our KG, with (our) English translations.

the object dependency of it, the weight is incremented by 1.0. For example, from Figure 2 (dependency tree: Figure 4) we retrieve the tuple *(Sigmund, promises, Ludwig of the Palatinate)*, and insert the subject and object into the graph (if not already contained). If the relation *promises* already exists between these entities in the KG, we increment the edge weight by 1.0, since, as can be seen in the example, *Ludwig of the Palatinate* was detected both as object of *promises* (+0.5) and as the first named entity (+0.5).

The more *promise*-events are instantiated between these two entities, the higher the weight of the edge. This implies that an edge or relation r with weight w between an emperor and one of its subjects means that in the data there were $1 \leq n \leq w$ instantiations of r detected between these entities and thus the edge weight can be interpreted both as a reliability measure of the relation and an indicator for how many times the relation was instantiated.

While we induced 4,948 distinct relations in the KG, the 400 most common relations cover 90% of the relations induced in the KG (Table 3 and Figure 5). Edge quality will be analyzed in the next section. Regests that do not contain verbs in the first sentence are discarded, e.g. *Geburt Karls, des jüngsten Sohnes Kaiser Ludwigs (d. Fr.) und seiner zweiten Gemahlin Judith* (English: "Birth of Karl, the youngest son of emperor Ludwig (the Pious) and his second wife Judith").[7] Applying these steps, more than 149,203 regests yield a relation, thus 83% of the RI have found their way into our KG.

Edge attributes. Each edge (relation) in the KG can be seen as representing one or more event(s) between an emperor and one of his subjects. We can associate an attribute list to each edge: date, time and location of creation of the event are taken from respective fields in the XML of the regests. We are also interested in key phrases associated with each event. For example, at one time king Sigmund may have promised *bestowal of land* to duke Ludwig and at another time he might have promised him *privileges* or *financial help*. To find associated key phrases, we formulate a text classification task, where we predict the main relation of a regest (i.e. the finite verb of the first sentence) using a bag of all contained phrases represented as a binary vector. We consider all phrases tagged as noun chunks or verbs (except the finite verb) as features. We only consider relations that occur more than 25 times, leaving us with 397 classes plus one catch-all class for the less frequent relations. Having fitted a logistic regression model to the task in a one-vs.-rest setting, we can rank the phrases describing an instantiation of a relation according to the learned weights for this relation. For example, given that the relation extracted from the example regest *Sigmund→promises→Ludwig of the Palatinate* was instantiated only one time, a list associated with this edge contains the description of one specific event. The event took place in 1410 at the location *Ofen* and, after having queried the model's coefficients for the relation *promise*, we see that highly associated key phrases of the event are the noun chunks *Privilegien* (priviliges) and *Reichspfandschaften* (earnests). If there was another regest with a *promise*-relation between those same entities, we add another event description to the edge attribute list and increment the weight of the edge accordingly. The key phrase ranking relation-prediction approach is evaluated and examined more closely in the next section.

---

[7]URI: `http://www.regesta-imperii.de/id/0823-06-13_1_0_1_2_1_1_1`.

Kg. Ruprecht$_{NOUN \to PROPN}$ gibt seinem kuchenschriber$_{ADJ \to NOUN}$ Hermann$_{NOUN \to PROPN}$ von Mülin und dessen erben$_{VERB \to NOUN}$ für seine treuen dienste$_{ADJ \to NOUN}$ sein haus und den stall$_{X \to NOUN}$ daran zu eigen.
[Kg.]$_{PERSON}$ [Ruprecht]$_{ORG}$ gibt seinem kuchenschriber [Hermann von Mülin]$_{PERSON}$ und dessen erben für seine treuen dienste sein haus und den stall daran zu eigen.

Figure 6: Part-of-speech (top) and NER annotations (bottom). Severe errors are marked in red. An arrow indicates the correct tag.

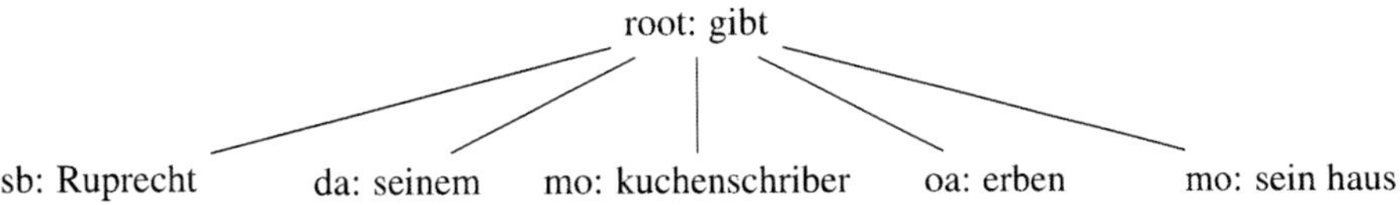

Figure 7: The erroneous dependency parse for Figure 3. *kuchenschriber* (kitchen bills accountant) is mislabeled as the relation modifier (mo) and *erben* (heirs) is mislabeled as accusative object (oa) – *sein haus* (his house) would have been the correct accusative object.

3 Problem Analysis

Despite syntactic parse errors due to the text complexity, we find that many named entities are being captured and the syntactic parse is often partially correct with respect to detecting the direct object of the finite verb, as can be seen in Figure 4. In some cases, however, we obtain very erroneous parse trees.

The regest in Figure 3 gets an erroneous dependency tree (Figure 7). The main reasons for this seem to be errors from preceding pipeline steps (Figure 6): even when disregarding the quote in the older variant of German, the text is annotated with false part-of-speech tags, propagating errors through the rest of the pipeline and into the dependency parse. Nevertheless, the relation is correctly induced with a weight of 0.5 because *Hermann von Mülin* is correctly detected as the first named entity after the verb. On the other hand, the regest in Figure 2, mostly written in today's conventional German, is correctly parsed with respect to the main relation, its accusative object and even the distant object clause.

For future work we want to experiment with fine-tuning the preprocessing models for the RI data. This is a non-trivial task because manual annotation would require domain experts. Other means such as bootstrapping the NER-pipeline by filtering and crawling part-of-speech patterns may introduce new errors, possibly even worsening the overall performance of the system, which is difficult to assess without manually labeled data. For further graph refinement one could consider disambiguating the named entities and merging their nodes. The KG could also be improved by identifying the (minority of) cases where the regest is not an event description of the emperor unidirectionally interacting with other entities but vice-versa (e.g. an entity gives a present to the emperor).

Inspection and Evaluation of the Relation Prediction Model. To investigate the performance of the model on unseen data, we divide the RI into a training set of 100,000 instances and 79,320 test instances, and use key phrases, issuers, locations and dates as binary features to predict one of the 398 relations (397 most common with KG-induction frequency of > 25 and one rest-class). This classification task is difficult because the many classes are also unevenly distributed, varying in frequency from 44,303 to 26, with an average of 450.5 and a median of 76 instances per class. The results are shown in Table 4. The relation classifier achieves an accuracy of 0.487 and macro f1 of 0.141, significantly higher than the baselines (majority baseline: 0.003 f1). Both baselines, majority voter and random baseline (drawing classes according to estimated class probabilities in the training data), lag behind not only the full-feature model but also a logistic regression model which uses only location or issuer features. We conclude that certain issuers and locations are more associated with specific relations than others. Our model's learnt coefficients can also be used to investigate these associations. For example, we find that the coefficients for emperor Friedrich III. have the highest value for the relations *quittirt* (signs), *legitimirt* (legitimates),

feature type	#features	acc.	macro f1
all	447,028	**0.487**	**0.141**
key phrase	436,508	0.461	0.113
issuer	401	0.267	0.007
year	821	0.258	0.005
location	9,298	0.267	0.007
maj. baseline	-	0.247	0.001
ran. baseline	-	0.008	0.003

Table 4: Evaluation of the 398-class relation prediction task.

scenario	micro error	macro error
all	0.083	0.934
confident (@397)	0.052	0.174
@1	0.0	0.0
@5	0.0	0.0
@25	0.0	0.0
@125	0.03	0.104

Table 5: (Pessimistic) estimates of weighted (micro) and unweighted error (macro) of induced relations due to false part-of-speech tags.@n: considering the n relations in the KG which were induced most often.

gibt (gives), *gebietet* (dictates), *befiehlt* (commands), *erlaubt* (permits), while for emperor Maximilian I., there is a different picture and we find many financial relations such as *schuldet* (owes), *verbucht* (books) and *bezahlt* (pays). Maximilian I. was well known for his debts he accumulated due to many wars and a rather extravagant lifestyle and we can see that this is also statistically reflected in the RI.

Inspecting the fitted model's coefficients for the relation *verhängt* (imposes), we see that among highly associated phrases are *die Reichsacht, die Acht, die Aberacht, Klage, den Bann, die Reichsaberacht, das Anathem*, which are mostly outdated German words for banning (excommunicating) somebody (*Acht, Aberacht, Bann*) and also anathema (*Anathem*). Highly weighted terms for the relation describing *verleiht* (bestow) are *das Pallium* (a religous clothing), *Regalien* (regalian rights), *ein Wapen*[8] (a crest), *Lehens- und Landesrecht* (land rights), *Gerichtsstandsprivileg* (court-right), *Doktorwürde* (doctorate) and *Halsgericht* or *Blutbann*, both old German terms in the context of the relation *bestows* referring to the right to speak the death sentence (a right which was granted only to selected cities). We conclude that our binary, bag-of-phrases representation for relation classification is a robust and straightforward way not only to rank key phrases describing medieval events but also to gain deeper insights into the RI.

Quality of Graph Edges We evaluate the quality of graph edges (first detected finite verb in a regest): (i) to assess the overall quality of edges and (ii) from the point of view of a user or historian, who might be interested in the quality of high-confidence edges, e.g. he choses to consider only relations with weight $> w$. The relation extraction experiments indicate that a falsely induced relation is due to false positive verb errors from POS tagging. We manually checked the 397 most commonly induced relations and found 69 to be incorrectly POS tagged. Examples of errors include *wittwe* (widow) and *archidiacon* (archdeacon). Everything that was erroneously tagged as a verb was labeled an error – an exception were deverbal nouns.[9] We assume a pessimistic scenario of all relations with count equal to or less than 25 having been misclassified with false POS tags. This scenario is very pessimistic because we not only find many rare and generally uncommon German verbs with varied spellings in this subset (e.g. *vidimiert, vidimirt* – a very rare word meaning "he witnesses") but also deverbal nouns which can be useful. Thus, given n distinct relations $i = 1, ..., n$ and f_i returns the total number of times this relation was induced in the KG, and g_i returns 1 if the relation was likely falsely inserted and 0 if it likely was correctly inserted (regarding POS annotation), we estimate the weighted micro error:

$$\frac{\sum_{i=1}^n f_i \cdot g_i}{\sum_{i=1}^n f_i}. \tag{1}$$

For the unweighted macro error, $f_i = 1 \forall i$. The results are shown in Table 5. The macro error, i.e. when all relations have the same significance, is estimated at 0.17 for scenario (ii), when the manually annotated relation subset of the most frequent 397 relations was used. When taking into account as errors

[8]*Wapen* is not a mistake – the word is spelled *Wappen* in contemporary German but we find both forms in the RI.

[9]Specifically, those nouns were *belagerung* (siege), *Eintreffen* (arrival) and *belehnung* (mortgage).

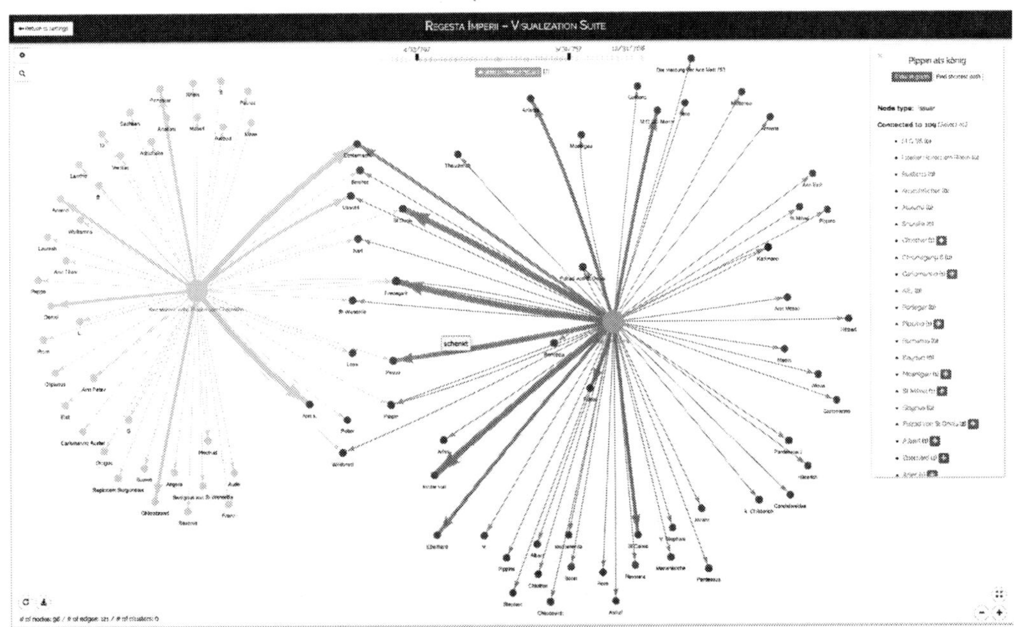

Figure 8: Example graph of the two issuers king *Pippin* (selected) and *Karl Martell* (father of Pippin) between 4/13/707 and 3/31/757 (96/148 nodes, 121/196 edges). Highlighted is an edge for the relation *schenkt* (endow). Edge thickness indicates edge weight and nodes are scaled by degree centrality. The figure is best seen in color.

all the other, less frequent relations, the macro error is < 0.93, which of course is a very pessimistic estimate. However, in most cases, assessing the weighted micro-error would be of much more interest – some relations cover a much larger proportion of induced relations. For example, a historian who is interested in the most frequent 125 relations (@125 in Table 5) would expect a weighted error of 0.03 and pessimistically an unweighted error of at most 0.104. When choosing the most common 25 relations (e.g. @25 in Table 5), the error is zero for both micro and macro calculations with regard to falsely induced relations due to POS tag errors.

4 Visualization: Diving into European Medieval Times

Visualization of textual (meta)-data is crucial both to make sense of the data itself and also to distribute the information in a more accessible way. Figure 9 displays our induced graph, where modularity clusters are colored differently. Inspecting the main clusters shows that some clusters roughly represent the universes of single emperors (violet: Friedrich III. (14.3% of all nodes), blue: Sigmund (9.54%), black: Karl IV. (6.14%)), while other clusters encapsulate multiple emperors (pink: the Palatine emperors Ruprecht I., Ruprecht II., and Ruprecht III. (7.45%)) and additionally there appear to be clusters which subsume the universes of less prevalent and especially earlier emperors (orange: Otto III., Otto I., Karl the Great, etc. (7.14%)).

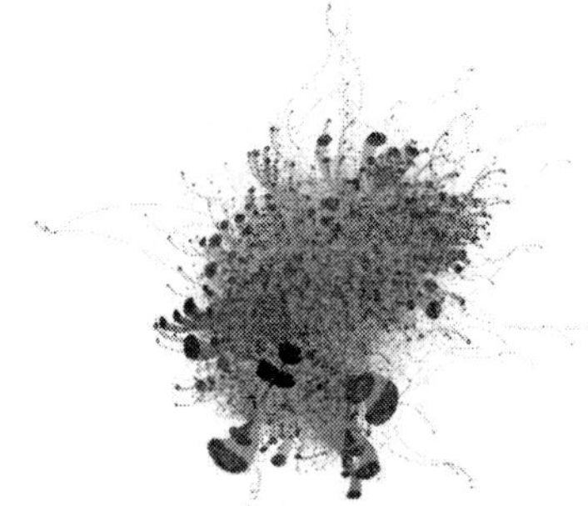

Figure 9: RI-graph with colored modularity clusters (Brandes et al., 2008) after application of ForceAtlas2 (Jacomy et al., 2014) in Gephi (Bastian et al., 2009).

Interactive visualization is a methodological tool to assist researchers in exploring the data, allowing for non-destructive data manipulation and filtering. For the Regesta Imperii we aim to provide an easy-to-use exploration tool of the extracted knowledge graph for historians. We built a web application to visualize the data. The application is JavaScript-based and uses AngularJS 1 as the frontend framework. Visualization is done using *vis.js*,[10] an open-source tool aimed at network and timeline visualizations.

Our KG contains 68,726 nodes and 154,797 edges. The average outdegree of nodes is 380 and average indegree is 2.65, showing that the KG is highly uni-directional with few central nodes (i.e. issuers) and most peripheral nodes having few incoming and almost no outgoing edges. Structurally speaking, the knowledge graph is weakly connected, consisting of 14 components with one large component containing 68,692 and the remaining ones containing < 5 nodes. In the largest component, of the 25 nodes with highest betweenness centrality, 7 are issuers and 18 are persons. This indicates that in terms of shortest paths between all node pairs, persons are especially important in establishing the connectivity of the graph. However, when looking at the 70 cut vertices of the component that are named entities,[11] we see that 55 are persons, but 11 denote place or region names (e.g. *Frankreich* or *Reutlingen*), indicating that certain regions also play a critical role in connecting multiple sub-networks.[12]

An example network is shown in Figure 8. Although the sheer size of the KG prohibits it from being visualized in its entirety, we use optimizations and ad-hoc querying to visualize sub-networks of the KG. With these, we were able to create interactive visualizations for networks of up to 12,000 nodes in practice. On the settings page, a user can choose one or more issuers. Based on the selected issuers, a network with all other nodes with which they interacted gets created. Furthermore, there are a number of additional settings, which can be divided into **limiting constraints** and **network enhancements**.

Limiting constraints. These limit the resulting network on an ad-hoc basis. Specifically, we allow to set a threshold X ($\leq X; = X; \geq X$) for the number of connections to display for a named entity and the number of relation instances. With these settings, specific requirements can be made, e.g. "show the network of Friedrich III. with relations that appear at least 40 times". A combination of constraints is also possible but per default, we set all constraints ≥ 1 so that the full graph will be rendered.

Network enhancements. These apply to the way the network gets rendered and can be interacted with. The first option visualizes the intensity of edges by their associated edge weights. The second option visualizes the importance of persons by means of a selected node centrality measure. Currently, we support degree, eigenvector, and betweenness centrality. The last option enables the *time slider* that allows for filtering the network by event dates. Per default, all three options are disabled.

To further reduce rendering speed, we implemented a decay factor to the number of iterations of the underlying physics solver used to calculate the graph layout. Starting with a network containing more than 150 nodes or 250 edges, the default number of iterations (1,000) is reduced by a factor of 0.1 for every additional 150 nodes or 250 edges.[13] We set the lower-bound to 100 iterations to give the solver some time to calculate the layout. Using this decay factor and the above-mentioned constraints drastically reduces the load times for very large networks. For example, the network of Karl IV. containing 7,359 nodes and 13,760 edges takes a couple of minutes to render. With the decay factor and the constraint that named entities have exactly 2 edges, the graph is reduced to 785 nodes and 1,568 edges, and is rendered in 80 seconds with 576 iterations.[14] Furthermore, we allow to save graphs as JSON files that can later be re-uploaded, further reducing load times. These are promising results as in a later production stage, the application can be supplemented by a database containing pre-calculated network layouts.

5   Related Work

Historical Text Processing. Piotrowski (2012) gives an overview of the many challenges arising when applying NLP to historical documents. The idea of normalization is often explored, yet we encountered the same problem as the author who reports that the effectiveness of normalization to a large degree depends on text type and language – most satisfying results are achieved only on more recent texts. For

---

[10] `visjs.org`.

[11] We exclude issuers from this analysis as cutting them almost always increases the number of components because of their central role.

[12] The remaining four are generic entities such as Roman numerals.

[13] Furthermore, if the node-edge difference is > 900, we consider the edge number to be determining the decay factor.

[14] 40 seconds of that are needed to process the data from our KG file, the remaining time is the rendering time.

this reason, we applied little and careful normalization to the regests. We concur that "the highly variable spelling found in many historical texts has remained one of the most troublesome issues for NLP" (p. 83), a fact that may be especially true with regard to the RI. Due to these issues, the research conducted in processing of (German) historical texts has been diverse and very task-specific, see i.a. (Massad et al., 2013; Meroño-Peñuela et al., 2015; Seemann et al., 2017; Hench, 2017; Schulz and Keller, 2016).

Regesta Imperii. Not much NLP research has been conducted on the RI. Kuczera (2015), in an example experiment, projects attributes and relations between entities from the times of Friedrich III. (i.e. a subset of the RI) into a graph database. He applies no NLP in these steps, but relies on the manually created person registers for the universe of Friedrich III. While currently only the registers for Friedrich III. are available, we think that they may be used in future work to fine tune the NER system to achieve better performance not only on the sub-corpus of Friedrich III. but also on the whole RI. A caveat is that the regests of the other emperors differ significantly not only in named entities but also in linguistic variety and thus such a system may fail to generalize. Opitz and Frank (2016) manually labeled 500 randomly sampled regests with 12 medieval themes and players of interest (e.g. *nobles*, *spiritual institutions*, *war and peace* or *justice*) and trained binary classifiers to in the end label all regests and compute statistics about the importance of the medieval themes and players with regard to time.

Relation Extraction For relation extraction from the Regesta Imperii we work in an "extreme" environment – no annotated data; few language resources (particularly because of the German language variations used in the corpus); no tools like named entity taggers or chunkers that would help in identifying relations and relation arguments; and low or no redundancy in relation instances (for computing extraction reliability scores). Because of this, the inspiration for the applied methods comes from open information extraction (Open IE), particularly work where relations are described through POS and grammatical patterns (Banko et al., 2007), and using the assumption that binary relations often appear in a subject-verb-object format. Wu and Weld (2010) extend a previous distantly supervised system that learns using Wikipedia infobox relations, and describe relations (through POS and dependency patterns) as phrases consisting of at least one verb and/or a preposition. To counter noisy extractions (often phrases that are too long and too specific to constitute a relation), Fader et al. (2011) introduce ReVerb, where lexical and syntactic constraints on relation expressions serve to produce cleaner extractions, with less uninformative or incoherent expressions. To increase recall, Mausam et al. (2012) expand the patterns by allowing relational nouns (e.g. Bill Gates, *co-founder* of Microsoft ...). Patterns are gathered and generalized (e.g., from words to parts-of-speech), which boosts recall. All these relation extraction methods rely on redundancy in the data to verify the relation patterns and the extracted candidates through various reliability scores. This cannot be applied to the RI corpus. We rely instead on the relatively simple structure of the regest texts and the grammatical information obtained from a parser.

6 Conclusions

We induced a Knowledge Graph from the medieval Regesta Imperii corpus. Nodes represent medieval named entities, the (weighted) edges indicate relations between those entities, which may have occurred at multiple times in history. High linguistic variation and code switching within single regests pose challenges for modern-day NLP systems, despite their seemingly simple structure. We added preprocessing heuristics to prevent erroneous sentence splitting, and in the process acquired a list of nobility titles. We explored relation classification as multi-class classification based on a binary bag-of-phrases representation of the regests. This not only gives us an option to inject further useful information into the KG describing the encapsulated events more closely, but also allows us to explore phrases highly associated with specific relations. The resulting Knowledge Graph was embedded in an isolated web application, enabling the visualization and querying of the data. The data and application are shared publicly.[15]

For future work we are planning to further refine the Knowledge Graph, introduce more structure using nobility titles and entity types and develop and evaluate it together with historians to adjust visualization and querying methods to their needs.

---

[15]`https://gitlab.cl.uni-heidelberg.de/born/ri-visualization.`

References

Michele Banko, Michael Cafarella, Stephen Sonderland, Matt Broadhead, and Oren Etzioni. 2007. Open information extraction from the Web. In *Proceedings of the 22nd Conference on the Advancement of Artificial Intelligence,* Vancouver, B.C., Canada, 22-26 July 2007, pages 2670–2676.

Mathieu Bastian, Sebastien Heymann, and Mathieu Jacomy. 2009. Gephi: An Open Source Software for Exploring and Manipulating Networks.

Ulrik Brandes, Daniel Delling, Marco Gaertler, Robert Gorke, Martin Hoefer, Zoran Nikoloski, and Dorothea Wagner. 2008. On Modularity Clustering. *IEEE Trans. on Knowl. and Data Eng.*, 20(2):172–188, February.

Anthony Fader, Stephen Soderland, and Oren Etzioni. 2011. Identifying relations for open information extraction. In *Proceedings of the 2011 Conference on Empirical Methods in Natural Language Processing,* Edinburgh, UK, 26-29 July 2011, pages 1535–1545.

Christopher Hench. 2017. Phonological Soundscapes in Medieval Poetry. In *Proceedings of the Joint SIGHUM Workshop on Computational Linguistics for Cultural Heritage, Social Sciences, Humanities and Literature,* pages 46–56, Vancouver, Canada, August. Association for Computational Linguistics.

Mathieu Jacomy, Tommaso Venturini, Sebastien Heymann, and Mathieu Bastian. 2014. ForceAtlas2, a continuous graph layout algorithm for handy network visualization designed for the Gephi software. *PloS one*, 9(6):e98679.

Andreas Kuczera. 2015. Graphdatenbanken für Historiker. Netzwerke in den Registern der Regesten Kaiser Friedrichs III. mit neo4j und Gephi. *Mittelalter. Interdisziplinäre Forschung und Rezeptionsgeschichte.*

D Massad, E Omodei, C Strohecker, Y Xu, J Garland, M Zhang, and LF Seoane. 2013. Unfolding History: Classification and analysis of written history as a complex system.

Mausam, Michael Schmitz, Robert Bart, Stephen Soderland, and Oren Etzioni. 2012. Open language learning for information extraction. In *Proceedings of the 2012 Conference on Empirical Methods in Natural Language Processing,* Jeju Island, Korea, 12-14 July 2012, pages 523–534.

Albert Meroño-Peñuela, Ashkan Ashkpour, Marieke van Erp, Kees Mandemakers, Leen Breure, Andrea Scharnhorst, Stefan Schlobach, and Frank van Harmelen. 2015. Semantic technologies for historical research: A survey. *Semantic Web*, 6(6):539–564.

Juri Opitz and Anette Frank. 2016. Deriving Players & Themes in the Regesta Imperii using SVMs and Neural Networks. In *Proceedings of the 10th SIGHUM Workshop on Language Technology for Cultural Heritage, Social Sciences, and Humanities*, pages 74–83. Association for Computational Linguistics.

Michael Piotrowski. 2012. *Natural Language Processing for Historical Texts.* Synthesis Lectures on Human Language Technologies. Morgan & Claypool Publishers.

Eric Sven Ristad and Peter N. Yianilos. 1998. Learning String-Edit Distance. *IEEE Trans. Pattern Anal. Mach. Intell.*, 20(5):522–532, May.

Sarah Schulz and Mareike Keller. 2016. Code-Switching Ubique Est - Language Identification and Part-of-Speech Tagging for Historical Mixed Text. In *Proceedings of the 10th SIGHUM Workshop on Language Technology for Cultural Heritage, Social Sciences, and Humanities*, pages 43–51, Berlin, Germany, August. Association for Computational Linguistics.

Nina Seemann, Marie-Luis Merten, Michaela Geierhos, Doris Tophinke, and Eyke Hüllermeier. 2017. Annotation Challenges for Reconstructing the Structural Elaboration of Middle Low German. In *Proceedings of the Joint SIGHUM Workshop on Computational Linguistics for Cultural Heritage, Social Sciences, Humanities and Literature*, pages 40–45, Vancouver, Canada, August. Association for Computational Linguistics.

Fei Wu and Daniel S. Weld. 2010. Open information extraction using Wikipedia. In *Proceedings of the 48th Annual Meeting of the Association for Computational Linguistics,* Uppsala, Sweden, 11-16 July 2010, pages 118–127.

Li Yujian and Liu Bo. 2007. A Normalized Levenshtein Distance Metric. *IEEE Trans. Pattern Anal. Mach. Intell.*, 29(6):1091–1095, June.

Author Index

Association for Computational Linguistics
209 N. Eighth Street
Stroudsburg, Pennsylvania 18360

ISBN 978-1-5108-6910-3

9 781510 869103